ALEC WAUGH

# *In Praise of Wine*

## *and Certain Noble Spirits*

WILLIAM MORROW & COMPANY, INC.

*Fourth Printing, May 1971*

*TO those many men and women*
*who feel as I do that a*
*meal without wine is a*
*day without sunlight*
*I dedicate*
*this tribute to the God of Wine*

🎺

# Bordeaux Wines

MÉDOC
Gironde R.
BLAYE-BOURG
FRONSAC
POMEROL
SAINT-EMILION

Chateau Lafite
Ch. Léoville-Lascases
Chateau Margaux

Ch. Brane-Cantenac
Chateau Giscours
Chateau Cantemerle
Ch. Le Tertre
Chateau La Lagune
BORDEAUX
Ch. Haut-Brion
Chateau Haut-Bailly

BAS MÉDOC

ENTRE-DEUX-MERS
Isle R.
Dordogne R.
Garonne R.
STE FOY

GRAVES
Cérons
Myrat
Loupiac
St. Croix du Mont
SAUTERNES
Chateau D'Yquem

ANJOU
COTEAUX DU TOUR
MUSCADETS
COTEAUX DU LAYON
Nantes
Charente
Cognac
Charente R.
F R
Gironde R.
Pauillac
St. Julien
Margaux
Cantenac
Bordeaux
Monbazi
Bergerac
Dord
Gail
Adour R.
Jurancon
Pau
Garonne
Tou
Rives

Rioja
Ebro River

Port
Douro R.
Freixo

S P A I N

Tagus River
Madrid

Guadiana River

Viña de Mesa

Guadalquivir River

P O R T U G A L

Sevilla
Jerez
Sherry
Cadiz

## ACKNOWLEDGMENTS

A number of friends have helped me with this book. In the course of it I have thanked them personally. I have quoted from Duff Cooper's *Old Men Forget* (published by Rupert Hart-Davis Ltd.) and Evelyn Waugh's *Brideshead Revisited* (published by Little, Brown & Co.). I am very grateful for having been given permission to do so.

Much of this book was written at the MacDowell Colony in Peterborough, New Hampshire. I am once again deeply indebted to the governors of that excellent association for their hospitality.

# CONTENTS

# In Praise of Wine

## And Certain Noble Spirits

**A**T THE END of the second war, I was one of the few Englishmen with access to a reasonable cellar. In the summer of 1934, a novel of mine made a fleeting appearance in the best-seller list and I found myself with an unbudgeted credit balance of three hundred pounds. I invested it in wine, mostly in vintage port—Croft's 1912, Graham's 1920, Oftley's Boa Vista 1923 (rarely met but excellent, if slightly over-sweet, and now, I should imagine, unobtainable), Dow's 1924 and Cockburn's 1927. At that time you could buy the '27 vintage for three pounds a dozen, and I acquired quite a quantity of wine with my surplus pennies.

My wife owns a house called Edrington, on the Hampshire-Berkshire borders between Basingstoke and Reading, and I sent it there. I had barely finished the Boa Vista when war broke out, scattering my family, as so many others. I went, as an Intelligence Officer, to the Middle East; my wife, an Australian, took our children to Melbourne; the Government requisitioned Edrington. I, if not she, and I think in the last analysis she too, was lucky in her tenants. If a service mess had taken it, before many guest nights had passed, the locks on the cellar door would have been torn apart, but Edrington was occupied by evacuated infants, and though children up to the age of five can, and in this case did, inflict a great deal of damage up to a height of four-foot-six, they do not pillage cellars. I had laid down a treasure below the earth which moth and dust could not corrupt nor thieves break in upon and steal.

When the Home Office took over Edrington, a scrupulous inventory was taken of its contents. I asked to be sent the details of the cellar. I carried the typed list in my wallet, next to the snapshots of my family. I do not know at which I looked more often.

I had many occasions to look at that list wistfully. Paiforce—the Persia and Iraq command, where I spent the last three years of the war—was a wineless area. The city of the caliphs was no longer the pleasure dome of Haroun al Rashid. The elaborate system of irrigation that had made it the center of a rich and prosperous country had been destroyed in the fifteenth century. Its population had dwindled from twenty to five millions. Date palms grew along the Tigris and the Euphrates, but all else was desert.

Baghdad was the least considered villayet in the Ottoman Empire. The Turkish administration was over-bureaucratic, over-centralized; a minor official would describe himself as occupying not a post but a seat in the Government and he would perch himself for hours at a desk filling out in exquisite Arabic script reams of often meaningless instructions. During the First World War, for months after Basra had fallen into British hands, clerks in Baghdad indited shipping orders to offices that were non-existent. Baghdad today, through its oil royalties, is restoring Iraq to the position which it held in the Middle Ages, but in 1942 the country was still handicapped by centuries of neglect. It exported dates. It had recently begun to develop its oil wells in Kirkuk, where Shadrach, Meshach and Abednego had walked "through a burning fiery furnace," but it had to import all its necessities, and being a Moslem country it did not regard alcohol as a necessity.

Today it has a brewery, but it had not then. It produced in very small quantities a thick sweet unpleasant wine called Habdah, and it distilled from dates an arrack, that smelled like turpentine and at a first sip tasted as one would expect turpentine to do. I got to like it in the end, but only because of the effect that it produced and the circumstances under which I drank it. It was not sold in restaurants that were in bounds to troops, but as an Intelligence Officer I was allowed to wear civilian clothes and on summer evenings a brother officer and I would sit in a garden by the river, capping quotations and sipping arrack, at peace with an embattled world.

Ninety-nine per cent of the personnel of Paiforce had to depend upon imported alcohol; transport was short and Baghdad was in the center of the desert. We were rationed to one bottle of Scotch whisky a month and two bottles of beer a week. How much beer meant to us during those long parched summers when the thermometer never fell below 110 degrees and went up to 124 degrees, can be gauged from the following experience. Early one November, our mess received with its rations twenty-four unexpected tins of Schlitz's beer. We presumed them to be a Christmas present, and decided to open them before lunch on Christmas day. We talked about that beer frequently. It was the first time that we had had American beer: we usually received quart bottles from Canada or Australia.

We played football on Christmas morning. Keats, I reminded my brother officers, used to pepper his tongue to heighten the flavor of claret. Football would fulfill that function. We arrived in the mess at noon, in an appropriate temper of anticipation. The cans were brought from the icebox. The glasses were set out. The steward produced the opener. He drove its sharp point into the top. I passed the tip of my tongue round my mouth. He made the second puncture, and reversed the can over a glass. But to our dismay, the pale frothing amber liquid that we had expected did not appear. Instead, we saw a dribble of a thick slimy substance. There was a grim, gloomy silence. Slowly we realized what had happened. In a period of universal shortage, a consignment of empty beer tins had been filled with marmalade. "And our wives in England," the colonel said, "would be delighted to find marmalade where they expected beer."

I only drink beer when I am thirsty. But "beer night" in Baghdad was the high point of my week. Fine beer it was, too, specially fortified for travel in the tropics. It was cold and strong and stung the palate. There are other flavors that I recall less gratefully. Many strange bottles crossed the desert or were landed at the Shatt el Arab. There was vodka from Persia; Keo gin from Cyprus; Palestinian wines with pretentious labels and Palestinian liqueurs that in point of fact did taste in terms of their appearance; there was South African brandy and Corio, an Australian whisky. When Hollywood stages the Arabian nights, Baghdad is presented in terms of wine and dancing girls. But except when I dined at the British Embassy, I did not drink a single good glass of wine during my three years there and I only had two meals alone in feminine society. I had many occasions to study the list of wines that were ripening in Edrington for my return.

For the last eight months of the first war, I was a prisoner in Germany; for the first weeks of my captivity I was very hungry. We were issued with two loaves of brown bread a week. I would mark out on the crust the limit of each day's ration. But it was difficult to keep within those limits. On the last evening I would find myself with a single crust. If I ate it now, I should have nothing next morning with my *ersatz* coffee. I knew the emotions of the pauper with a shilling in his pocket who has to decide between the claims of supper and of breakfast. As I lay, hungry, in bed, I would think of the good food I had enjoyed on my last leave and I devised the menus that I would order when the war was over. In novels, I gloated over the descriptions of meals. I read a great deal of Dickens. I was a teetotaler then and did not pine for port.

In the second war my position was reversed. Though I was technically at liberty, Baghdad, with the desert stretching on every side of it, was a kind of prison; one day followed another with little difference of routine. There was nowhere to go for a weekend, and though I was eating far better than my friends in England, I was denied what was for me the decisive pleasure of the table. During the intervening quarter of a century, a meal without wine had become for me a day without sunlight. In England and America I had known no such days. Between 1934 and 1939, I had drunk as much good wine as anyone. It was a domestic period for me. My travels were confined to crossings of the Atlantic. Prohibition was over and there was as much fine wine in New York as in London. During my Baghdad siestas I would remember the succession of excellent wines by which my lunches and dinners had been regaled. I used to attend the meetings of the Wine and Food Society. I was on the wine committee of the Savile Club. As a member of the Saintsbury Club I was entertained in Paris by the Club des Cents. Many of my friends were amateurs of wine. I had much to remember, gratefully and nostalgically. In the same way that in the prison camp at Mainz I had re-read every description of a banquet, I now lingered over the poetry and prose of wine, relishing in my imagination the delights that were denied me.

I wished I had some of the books that were stored in a depository in Reading out of reach of the marauding fingers of evacuated urchins—Constable's *Wine Library*, Saintsbury's *Notes on a Cellar-book*, André Simon's *Bottlescrew Days*, one or two of the privately printed opuscula of the Odd Volumes, Maurice Healy's *Irish Wine* (he always maintained that Haut-Brion was a French corruption of O'Brien), Vaux Huggett's *Rhenish*. Theodore Maynard had collected an anthology of drinking songs called "A Tankard of Ale." I wondered if there was an anthology in prose and verse of the various tributes that had been paid to wine. If there was not, there should be and I wished that there was in Baghdad an equivalent for the London Library, so that I could spend my leisure on its compilation.

There was one book in particular that I should have liked to read, a book that described what had been drunk at different periods and in different countries. The cult of wine could serve as windows opening onto history. My knowledge of the subject was fragmentary and intermittent. I knew how fashions in wine had changed in England during the last hundred years. I know how much the social life of London had been altered by the introduction of tea, coffee and cocoa. I knew that the popularity of port in England was the direct result of a treaty with Portugal designed to spite the French, and that Gladstone, a century and a half later, in

order to help French economy, had reduced the duty on
French table wines and brought claret within the reach of
the middle classes, thereby ruining the South African wine
trade for seventy-five years. I knew a little, but how much
I did not know! Chancellors of the Exchequer had frequently altered the drinking habits of a nation with their
excise duties. Was there any single book that described these
changes?

I wrote to the London Library to inquire. No, I was
told, there was not. In that case, I thought, I had better fill
the gap. One is wise to aim at writing the kind of book that
one would like to read oneself. It was in 1944 that I made
that resolution; I seem to have taken a long time getting
around to it.

And now that I have got down to it, I am writing this
opening chapter with grave misgiving. How much, I wonder,
will I be hindered by my lack of scholarship? I am not even
quarter-educated. I never went to a university. In 1915, I
was in the army at the age of seventeen. When the war
ended, I was launched as a novelist. There was in England
no equivalent of the G.I. Bill of Rights. I was claimed by the
demands of livelihood.

The gaps in my information are vast and deep. An
educated man is somebody who knows something about everything and everything about something. I am someone who
knows enough about some half-dozen subjects—of which
wine is one—to know that I am barely on the brink of an
acquaintanceship. I wondered whether I would not be wise
to find a well-informed collaborator, who was experienced
in the technique of research. I addressed myself to Vyvyan
Holland.

He shook his head. "You are," he said, "one of my
oldest and dearest friends. When we were young, and bache-
lors in London, we found ourselves now and then in competi-

tion, in matters of the heart. Our friendship survived that, but I doubt if, at our age, it would survive a collaboration. I will do this, however. I will try to answer any questions that you put; if I cannot answer them I will tell you where you can find the answers, and I will read your proofs to protect you against grosser errors; on this condition, that whenever you have a series of questions to set to me, you will invite me to lunch or dinner. I will choose the restaurant and I will arrange the menu and select the wines."

That seemed to me not only an equitable offer but a pleasant one, since it would ensure that during the writing of the book—and this is the kind of book that is worked on intermittently, unlike a novel that must be taken in one's stride on a single wave of mounting emotion (I estimated that it would take two years) I should be seeing Vyvyan Holland regularly.

I have already taken abundant advantage of his offer, and by the time the book is finished I shall have made much further use of it. But here, at the beginning, I should like to express how great is my gratitude to him. I could not have had more help if he had been my collaborator. I should have been very lost without him, and I am greatly enjoying our lunches.

# THE MOSLEM VETO

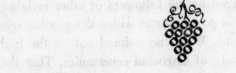

**T**HE FIRST SERIES of problems that I brought to Vyvyan Holland concerned Baghdad, where the idea for this book had come to me. Its civilization is one of the oldest in the Western world, but its entire texture was changed by Mahommed in the seventh century A.D. In terms of the pleasures of the table, how did they live at Nineveh and why did Mahommed "set his canon against wine"? In the Old Testament there are frequent references to wine. How had it come about that the men of Paiforce in the twentieth century had to rely on imported spirits?

I wish I could quote in full the answer that he sent me, but I would prefer this book to be included in the catalogue of public libraries rather than indexed by secondhand booksellers under "curiosa," and I can scarcely print his amusingly embroidered theory that the prophet was anxious to protect his followers from the fate that befell Lot at the hands of his rapacious daughters. He did, however, seriously suggest that Mahommed was concerned in general to make Moslem rites and habits as different as possible from those that were practiced by the followers of other religions in the neighborhood, in particular to widen the gap between Christians and Moslems. Wine, he pointed out, is the high symbol in the most holy of Christian ceremonies. That theory seems defensible.

If one can trust Burton—and if one cannot trust Burton whom can one trust?—it was by slow degreees that Mahommed made up his mind about alcohol, and the Koranic law is by no means as stern as the mullahs have made it since. Wine and spirits may be used medicinally, and the word "medicinally" is infinitely elastic. I have been assured —though I have no proof of this—that if you enter a wine shop in a Moslem country needing what in England is called "a double," you ask for a "Mahommedan's glass," because the Mahommedan when assailed by thirst has to drink quickly before his co-religionists observe him.

There are not many references to wine in the *Arabian Nights* but those few are by no means hostile. There is the admonitory example of King Omar bin Al Nie'uman who plies a damsel with wine and then offers her hashish so that he may fulfil his "base purposes" while she is unconscious. And Ali Nur Al-din, when Miriam the girdle girl persuades him to take wine, spits it out, saying, "This is bitter." But most of the references are adulatory. "Wine breeds gladness, music merriment, and their offspring is joy." "Wine," sings the poet, "digesteth food and disperseth care and dispelleth flatulence and clarifieth the blood and cleareth the complexion and quickeneth the body and hearteneth the hen-hearted and fortifieth the sexual power in man, but to name all its vurtues would be tedious. In short, had not Allah forbidden it, there were not aught on the face of the earth to stand in its stead."

It is a question of climate, possibly, as so much is. I had many opportunities during my four years' service in the Middle East—and since the war I have spent several weeks in Arab countries—of appreciating the deep qualities of the Arab way of life, and I learned much during the month I spent in the Hauran in the summer of 1942. There was serious danger then of a wheat shortage in Syria and the Lebanon, and Major General Sir Edward Spears, the British Minister, organized the O.C.P. (Office des Ceréales Panifiables) to supervise the collection and distribution of the crop. I was stationed at Der'a, a hundred miles south of Damascus, the scene of one of T. E. Lawrence's more spectacular feats of arms. I was supplied with an interpreter and a chauffeur. Every day I drove out to one or other of the villages, or townships, to interview the moukhtar or mutaserif and discuss the contribution that each district could make to the central store.

The Hauran was one of the chief granaries of the Roman Empire. Its villages have been built on and over and out of the ruins of Roman houses. Everywhere you will see signs of Rome. Stones with Roman inscriptions support the flimsy fabric of a mud-built cottage. Columns rise unexpectedly out of a dingy side street. Sometimes the head of a column showing a few feet above the ground will demonstrate to what extent succeeding generations have superimposed layer after layer of mud and rubble onto the original site.

Sheltered by the mountains of the north, the Hauran is a long, broad, boulder-strewn, undulating plain that rises every so often into a protuberance on which a village stands.

For mile after mile the landscape is the same; field after
field of low-growing wheat and maize, the earth showing
red between the stubble where the crops have been cut or
the ground left fallow. Where the ground is barren an occasional group of Bedouins sit idle under their long low
tents. There are no trees, no gardens, there is nothing green.
Along the road are stone shelters like sentry boxes to protect
the guardians of the fields in winter. In summer there is the
animated noise of harvest. Camel trains laden with wheat,
led by small boys on ponies, go by with a jingling of bells;
four or five camels form a train, their long necks seeming to
move in and out of their loads. The villages are collections
of low gray-black one-storied buildings of mud and boul-
ders, peaked by the spire of a minaret, surrounded hedge-
wise by a succession of low brick walls. Inside these walls
the wheat is being threshed. A pony or a mule is driven
around in circles, drawing a broad, flat board on which
stands the driver—a child or an old man. A fine yellow
dust rises as the wheat is tossed into the air.

The villages are farmyards, little else. There is no
sanitation. There is a large central pond usually of Roman origin, where clothes are washed and cattle drink. The
houses are gaps in a mud wall. There will be a pen or two
for the hens and cattle; there will be a roofed-in pen or
two for the family. The village women do not wear veils.
They are shapeless bundles of old clothes, with blue tattoo-
ing on their chins and lower lips. The children roll about
happily in the dirt.

Yet in the house of the headman, the moukhtar, in
even the smallest village there is a sense of leisure, of culture, of inherited immemorial manners. His reception room,
though it is only a roofed-in cattle-pen, will be high and
cool. There will be carpets on the floor and stools and cush-
ions arranged against the wall. In the center there will be

the smoldering ashes of a fire, set with coffee pots. Old men will be puffing at narghiles, very old men who sit there day after day, doing nothing, rarely speaking, but whose age entitles them to be present when the moukhtar receives his guests.

Everywhere I was struck by the same characteristics of dignity, good manners and a refusal to be hurried. In the small as in the larger villages there would be the ceremonial serving of coffee: black, bitter coffee which one only sipped. One must never refuse the second cup, and after the third, one rotates the cup to show that one has had enough. There were long ceremonial speeches in which the chief would welcome me to his house. He would dilate on the honor that had been paid him. I would then take up the duet. As a schoolboy, I would say, I had read the *Arabian Nights*. I had prayed that one day a magic carpet would carry me to the proud city of the caliphs. I had read in my Bible of Abnar and Pharpar, the rivers of Damascus. I had prayed that one day I should sit beside their banks. But I had never dared to dream that one day I should be honored by the hospitality and friendship of one of the great chieftains of the desert. My host would then resume his role. He had all his life admired that great statesman, soldier and man of letters, Winston Churchill. There was no one greater in the world. He had never dared to dream that one day this great man should specially select a personal emissary to bear him greetings. He was honored to be able to honor the brave British captain whom Winston Churchill had chosen to represent him.

So it went on for an hour, two hours, three hours. To hurry would have been bad manners. The war, as regards the Middle East, was at that point in a critical condition. Rommel was threatening the Nile valley. The Arab states were uncertain which horse to back. A famine that winter would have been disastrous. I was anxious to finish my negotiations and move on to the next village. But I had to check my impatience. The ritual of oratorical exchange had to be continued. I spoke of the greatness of France; of the firm ties of friendship that bound the British to the Arab world. I listened to elaborate tributes to the courage and honesty of my fellow countrymen who had delivered the Arabs from the Turkish yoke. Throughout these speeches there was movement going on around us. The chief was holding his divan and the notables had the right of entry. They would move in silently and salute their leader. They would take their seats and coffee would be offered them. They would listen for half an hour, an hour, ninety minutes; then they would rise, salute, and take their leave; all the time outside there would be urchins looking through the door with an intent, curious stare. And the talks would go on and on till the meal was ready.

They were much the same, those meals. There would be high-piled dishes of rice and stews, of meat and vegetables. Sometimes there would be poultry; sometimes there would be an entire sheep. There would be flat round cakes of bread.

There would be first nearly always the ceremonial washing of the feet and hands and mouth. The food would be spread up on a carpet on the floor. We sat with our feet tucked under us. It is considered bad manners to point the toes. I have short legs and plump thighs and found this posture as difficult as it was uncomfortable. We ate with our right hands. The left hand is reserved for menial services. We did not have individual plates. We tore off pieces of bread and scooped up the stew. The host would select a particularly succulent morsel and feed his guest with it. The eye of a sheep is highly rated. Once a host honored me by popping one into my mouth. It was mercifully tasteless. The rice with which the sheep was stuffed was often rather hot and burned the tips of unroughened fingers, but the stews were usually tepid. They were stodgy and not highly flavored. There were no hot sauces. It was a diet designed for the desert where water is scarce.

Had liquid been served, I suspect that the food would have swollen uncomfortably inside me. We spoke little as we ate. After talking for three hours, Arabs settle down in silence to the serious business of consuming food. Within twenty minutes they are on their feet. They wash their hands, salute, exchange courtesies and take their leave. I had been told that it was good manners for a guest to show by belching that he has appreciated his host's hospitality. This information at first disturbed me because I cannot belch at will. But in point of fact I have never heard an Arab belch.

Normally I dislike a meal without beer or wine but I felt no need for alcohol during those long hot days when the sun beat down out of a cloudless sky and the glare of the parched earth dazzled me, but in the evenings, shortly before sunset when a breeze sprang up from the still snow-capped Hebron and the outline of the foothills was subdued, merging into a succession of level layers of rich soft colors dominated by a purplish-brown, and the camel trains moved in slow silhouette against the sunset and the dust of the chaff about the villages was flecked with orange; then as I drove back to Der'a, wearied by diplomacy, my eyes half-closed, savoring the peace of work completed, then I did indeed look forward to the long cool whisky and soda that awaited me.

How could I not? My whole organism had been conditioned to the need for alcohol at sunset. But an Arab's has not been. Certainly not a desert Arab's, and it was for the kinds of Arab with whom I had spent the day, not the sleek tycoons of Cairo, that Mahommed legislated. The qualities, the characteristics that I so admired, the dignity, the absence of haste, the courtesy might well have been imperiled in that climate by the use of alcohol. Alcohol creates thirst and thirst is to be avoided where water is scarce. Mahommed coupled together drinking and the casting of lots, that is to say, gambling. He was against them because he considered that the Arabs were too excitable for that kind of intoxication. The climate is in itself an intoxicant. The devout Arab genuinely believes that there is a demon in wine which enters the body of him who partakes of it and causes the lapses from good behavior that accompany excess. Alcohol might impair good manners and good manners are as much the essential framework of the Arab way of life as they are of the Japanese.

In addition, it must not be forgotten that the liquid which Mahommed prohibited was not the fermented juice of the grape but spirits, a distillation of dates and raisins.

The pleasures of the table are often stressed in the *Arabian Nights*. There are mouth-watering references to sherbets "compounded with sugar and lemon and perfumed with rose and willow water and the purest musk," but though there are references to the effects of wine there are none to its taste.

Léon Douarche, the author of an engaging book of memoirs, *Sidelights on the Third Republic*, who was for ten years between the wars director of the International Wine Office, has recounted how François I, when he wanted to conclude a pact with Suliman the Magnificent, sent as his ambassador to Turkey the owner of Château Carbonnieux, which produces a dry white full-bodied Graves. The ambassador brought two cases of it as a gift to the Sultan. Knowing that the Koran forbade the drinking of wine he described his gift as mineral water. "It is foolish to drink wine," said Suliman, "when they have such delicious mineral water as that of Carbonnieux."

Perhaps if Mahommed had received such an ambassador, he would have modified his strictures. Burton says that certain devout Moslems drink champagne and cognac, because they were unknown in Mahommed's day and therefore could not be included in his index. The strictly orthodox are invariably ingenious at re-interpreting holy script in their own interests. The Danish Mormons, on their arrival at Salt Lake City, were disconcerted to find that coffee was forbidden them. They took counsel together and decided that if Brother Joseph, a warm, human being who enjoyed dancing and singing, had known how necessary coffee was to the health and happiness of the Danes, he would have allowed them a dispensation. "Brother Joseph did not mean it for the Danes."

Though Tibet is its greatest stronghold, Buddhism appears to have its largest following in the lush countries of the tropics—Ceylon, Siam, China—under a climate of easy growth, and most Buddhists hold that the Buddha adjured them to practice temperance, not abstinence. Perhaps in a hundred years the theologians of Najaf and Mecca will decide that Mahommed would have permitted the enjoyment of wine, had he been introduced to it.

It was slowly that Mahommed came to his final judgment and in his framing of it, he expressed reluctance. "When they ask thee concerning wine and the casting of lots, say, 'In both are great sin and great advantage to mankind, but the sin of them both is greater than their advantage.'" It is a problem that has exercised mankind since Noah planted his first vineyard.

We all of us know men and women whose lives have been ruined by alcohol. We did not need psychiatry to teach us that heavy drinking is often a mental illness, a form of escape, of self-compensation. Jurgen spoke of "the charitable wine that cheats us into a favorable opinion of our-selves." The Shropshire Lad attests that

> *"Malt does more than Milton can*
> *To justify God's ways to man."*

There are many who for constitutional reasons should never touch wine or spirits. A single glass causes an internal revolution. But the essential question remains—are the majority, the very great majority, of us to be deprived of one of heaven's greatest gifts, because a few abuse it?

Remedies that may well prove beneficial to Asian people can be disastrous to Western. The American experiment in complete prohibition provides a salutary example.

I began to put down roots in New York in the late autumn of 1930, when I took a four months' lease of an apartment on Lexington and 36th. I cannot say that I led a typical New Yorker's life because I do not think there is any such thing as a typical New Yorker. I would prefer to say that I lived as a New Yorker, with my own servant, organizing my own household, playing squash for exercise, meeting my friends and making new ones, going to and giving parties. I like to think that during those four months I absorbed the New York way of life. Certainly I have felt at home there ever since.

During that period—with Prohibition still in force— New York was a wide-open town, and I learned how unmitigated an evil prohibition of that kind is and how deplorable are its effects upon its subjects. It was not that the whisky and the gin we drank were bad—at that period they were not—but that we drank a great deal too much and our lives centered around alcohol.

Drinking, because it was forbidden, became dramatic and romantic. A large proportion of our conversation was concerned with it. The British, limited by the Treasury since

the second war to holidays abroad on an allowance that
has varied between twenty-five and one hundred pounds,
spend a lamentably large part of those holidays discussing
with one another "how they manage." In the same spirit
New Yorkers in 1930 would cap each other's sagas of a
long night's drinking.

"First of all we had a couple of Martinis at that place
on 38th and Park, you know the one?"—"Yes, sure I know
it."—"A man there told us about a new place across the
way from Jack and Charlie's: we thought we'd case the
joint."—"What was that like?"—"Lousy. One Old-fashioned and we left."—"Where did you go then?"—"We went
over to Jack and Charlie's."—So it went on. "By that time
it was getting late. I said it was time to eat but Dolly'd
heard about a place uptown and Frank said he must call
his wife." On and on it went; and the extraordinary thing
about it was that we were all interested in those sagas, in-
terjected the appropriate comments and queries and waited
our turn patiently to contribute a similar Odyssey. To each
of these stories came the inevitable tailpiece, how we had
dealt with our inevitable hangover. I am a moderate
drinker, but during those four months I woke up at least
twice a week in no mood for work.

On my last evening there, Mrs. Wolcott Gibbs—she was
Elinor Sherwin then—said that she was glad I was going
away. I was surprised and hurt. I had hoped that she would
miss me; but a satisfactory explanation followed. If I
stayed longer, she said, I should get a stomach ulcer. In that
age of innocence, we believed that ulcers came from bootleg gin, not psychoneurosis. And very certainly the survivors
of that period are battle-scarred today. A large proportion
of them are members of Alcoholics Anonymous, and quite a
few are no longer capable of any active participation in
the world's affairs.

Wine may present a problem but for Westerners Prohibition is not its solution.

Most things have been said best by Shakespeare, and the issue is fairly put in all its implications in the scene in *Othello,* in which Iago makes Cassio drunk in order to involve him in a quarrel. But if I had to choose out of all literature a single passage that can be held to say the last word in wine, I should choose a paragraph that is slipped unobtrusively into Duff Cooper's memoirs, *Old Men Forget.*

"I should here acknowledge," he writes, "the consolation I have never failed to find in the fermented juice of the grape. Writing in my sixty-fourth year I can truthfully say that since I reached the age of discretion I have consistently drunk more than most people would say was good for me. Nor do I regeret it. Wine has been to me a firm friend and a wise counsellor. Often, as on the occasion just related, wine has shown me matters in their true perspective and has, as though by the touch of a magic wand, reduced great disasters to small inconveniences. Wine has lit up for me the pages of literature and revealed in life romance lurking in the common-place. Wine has made me bold but not foolish; has induced me to say silly things but not to do them. Under its influence words have often come too easily which had better not have been spoken and letters have been written which had better not have been sent. But if such small indiscretions standing in the debit column of wine's account were added up, they would amount to nothing in comparison with the vast accumulation on the credit side."

**I** LEARNED TWO LESSONS from the Prohibition era: first, the danger of heavy drinking; second, the necessity of accepting wine undramatically. In terms of those two lessons I was extremely anxious that my children should be educated into the habit of moderate drinking. I tried to teach them from the earliest age that wine is an integral part of civilized existence, to be taken as a matter of course like meat and fish and Coca-Cola. I taught them the ritual of wine.

When they were five and four, I took down my two elder children to the cellar every Saturday morning when I decanted port for our weekend guests. They enjoyed the machinery of the operation—the transference of the bottle from its bin to the wicker cradle, the silver funnel in the decanter,

the electric bulb under the bottle's neck; but their chief interest was in the drawing of the cork. I had a double-lever
corkscrew. They would hold down the bottle in its cradle
while I pressed the levers. "Oh, I do hope the cork won't
break," they chanted. But secretly they hoped it would. They
would await the result breathlessly. When the bottle had
been decanted, they would pour the dregs onto the stone
cellar floor and execute a war dance round it. I did not
know what was its significance, whether the dead dregs by
some process of association represented a foe slain in battle,
but I welcomed the display. It would imprint on their minds
that port went with ritual.

After lunch, when there were guests, they were brought
down to the drawing-room for coffee—those were the days
when one had nurses and not baby-sitters—and they were
allowed to scoop up the undissolved sugar crystals at the
bottom of the cups. On Saturdays and Sundays they were
granted, as a treat, a minute sip of port. "When you are
ten," I said, "you will have a quarter of a glass, when you
are fifteen half a glass, when you are eighteen a whole
glass." I hoped to show them that wine was something you
came to by stages; that just as you could lift a heavier
weight at twenty than you could at ten, so could a man
drink four times as much as a boy. I hoped to show them
that drinking too much was as reprehensible as gluttony.

My daughter sometimes took my instructions very literally. I had told her that she should roll port around her
mouth before swallowing it. One evening just after her
twelfth birthday when I went upstairs to say good night to
her, I noticed that her plastic toothbrush case contained a
pinkish liquid. "What on earth is that?" I asked. "My
port," she said. "I'm keeping it till tomorrow." She had held
her sip of port under her tongue for twenty minutes. I had
thought she was unusually silent.

My own education in wine was very different, but similar in ultimate effect. Wine was always on my father's table. He lived in a small new house in Hampstead, a quarter of a mile below the Bull and Bush. He was a hospitable, gregarious man, but he was subject to asthma and was deaf in one year. He did not like large parties, cigarette smoke irritated his throat and he was confused by a number of conversations going on simultaneously; he never gave formal parties, but he indulged in a great deal of casual entertaining. Friends who walked over Hampstead Heath to see him on a Saturday or Sunday afternoon would be persuaded to stay on to dinner. There was a phrase then—"take pot luck." And his guests were usually lucky.

My father kept a good table. But he did not keep a cellar. He was a man of habit, and he always drank the same red wine—an Australian Burgundy, Keystone, which came in flagons, with stoppers. If you ordered it by the dozen, you got an extra flagon. It was a ferruginous beverage of tonic qualities. My father emptied the flagon into an old ship's decanter, with a broad and slightly irregular base, so that if an unsteady hand replaced it on the table, it would right itself. He had a large glass goblet that had been his father's. He would fill it twice during a dinner. A flagon contained about a liter, and one flagon would last three meals.

Keystone Burgundy was the only wine served at my father's table till the 1920's when my brother and I, in our own interests, argued that it would be an economy for him to drink a light sound claret—such wines could be purchased then at thirty-six shillings a dozen. My father let himself be persuaded and our dinners at home became more enjoyable. After a month, however, he complained of eczema around his ankles. He attributed this to his change of wine. We assured him that it was one of the maladies inseparable from advancing years. He insisted, however, on returning to his Australian Burgundy. Within a week, to our relief for his sake, but dismay for our own, his eczema had vanished. Because of his asthma, he never took port, but at half-past nine a decanter of whisky and a siphon would be brought into the book-room and he would mix a very weak nightcap. When I lunched with him in London before going to a matinée, he took me to Gatti's Restaurant off the Strand, and he ordered himself a half-bottle of Beaune or Pommard.

In a sense I had no education in wine, but I absorbed in my father's house a valuable lesson. I assumed that an adult took wine with his meals. A roll of bread upon one's left side, a goblet of red wine upon one's right. I saw wine drunk in terms of enjoyment and moderation. My mother never took wine, but not on moral grounds. She did not like its taste. She never spoke against it; her restraint as much as my father's mild indulgence gave me the impression that wine was not an issue, that it was something to be accepted with enjoyment or declined without belligerence, that it was a part of life, in fact.

When I came back from France for my first leave in February, 1918, at the age of nineteen and a half, my father offered me wine at dinner. I shook my head. "Not yet," I said. Five weeks later I was taken prisoner by the Germans in the big retreat. When I returned in December, after the Armistice, my father again offered me wine on my first evening home. "Thank you very much," I said.

I drank my first bottle of wine on my twentieth birthday, in the citadel at Mainz. It was a hot and breathless afternoon. For two weeks I had been looking forward to the occasion. It would not be the first time I had tasted alcohol. At guest nights in England port had been passed to drink the King's health. I had felt it would be disloyal to refuse it. On passing-out day at the machine-gun school at Grantham, my squad stood themselves a dinner. I drank a great deal too much; so much too much that the other eleven decided I should be allowed to keep the bill, as a souvenir. I felt so ill next day that I was not tempted to repeat the experiment. Indeed I have only once since exceeded the limits to the same extent, then also under military auspices in 1944 in Khanaquin when I was entertained by a group of Russian officers who proposed perpetual toasts and laced my beer with brandy when I was not looking.

I kept the bill of that passing-out dinner in my wallet, and when I was taken prisoner it was the one document that the Germans did not confiscate.

My next experiment with alcohol came on the eve of the third battle of Ypres; my section commander suggested that I should take a tot of rum. "You'll need it before the night's through," he told me. I took it neat, in a single swallow. I felt I had put fire in my mouth. From then on the ration that I issued to the men was increased by my personal abstinence.

I had not until that afternoon in Mainz sat down in calm blood to a bottle of my own ordering. It was for my twentieth birthday, not only a celebration but an initiation. I wish I could remember now whom I invited to share that bottle with me. It might have been one of several. Gerard Hopkins was a fellow prisoner, so was Maurice Besley, the musician, so were Hugh Kingsmill, Milton Hayes, the author of *Green Eye of the Little Yellow God,* and John Holmes—a man of infinite promise who figured in William Gerhardi's *Memoirs of a Polyglot,* and died in his late thirties with nothing done. It might have been any of those five, but it might have been a room-mate of my own age who was my special friend there, whom I never saw after our ways divided at the repatriation center in Boulogne.

Across forty years I can recall the billiard room where the bar was set. It was on the second story of a barrack building. The gravel square lay below. Beyond the barbed wire, I could see the Rhine, flowing fast and cool toward the sea. The elm trees drooped in the heavy heat. It was siesta hour. The German sentry was adoze. There was complete silence except for the click of billiard balls. I can see it all except the companion who shared that first bottle with me.

A bottle of hock cost twenty marks, when a mark was worth a shilling and a subaltern was only allowed to draw five pounds a month. Wine was a luxury that could only be indulged in rarely. For two weeks I had looked forward to the day. I pictured what it would be like: the port on mess night, the succession of drinks gulped down in the excitement of "passing-out," the fiery rum at Ypres, gave me no indication as to what the calculated, leisurely appreciation of a bottle was to be. I pictured it in terms of literature: "Oh for a beaker full of the warm south." It would be cool and fragrant on the palate, it would flood my senses, leaving a warm glow behind. As a boy my favorite beverage had been Eiffel Tower lemonade. It came in a packet, as a powder. The powder was steeped in water which was boiled till the crystals dissolved. The result was an essence that was treated, when it had cooled, as Rose's lime juice is today. I found it delightful. It pleased my taste, it quenched my thirst and left me with the wish to take another glass. Its appearance on the lunch table in spring, in a spirally shaped decanter, was a herald of the warm days to come, and cricket. Wine would be like that, only richer, with a full taste and with the immense addition of the glow which it would send along my nerves, my present troubles would be dissolved and the future would spread before me an enchanted landscape as I sat sipping my wine through a long hot afternoon.

It was not a bit like that.

Hock was not, perhaps, the best initiator for a palate

trained on Eiffel Tower lemonade. It takes time to learn how to appreciate the greatest hocks; there are subtle after-flavors that the novice would fail to recognize. Moselle is an easier wine, a casual claret can be very pleasant, but an indifferent hock is often sour, and I do not suppose that the bottle I drank in the prison camp at Mainz was a particularly good one. Instead of adding a dimension to the delights of Eiffel Tower lemonade, it struck me as being a negligible improvement on the ipecacuanha that I had taken in the nursery for a cough; while the anticipated exhilaration was comparable with the relief from coughing that the medicine had brought. I felt at peace with the world when the bottle was finally finished, but it was the peace of achievement rather than enjoyment: it was the peace that follows a hard-fought game of football. The swallowing of each mouthful had been an effort.

"The first taste of the olive is bitter," Hugh Kingsmill reassured me, and I persisted in my attempts at self-education as far as a monthly allowance of five pounds permitted. But it was not till after the Armistice, when I could experiment with a wine list, that I drew any pleasure from the taste of wine.

The following three weeks were among the happiest I have ever known, as they were for so many, perhaps I should say too many, others. The war was over. We had won. Lord Curzon, announcing victory in Parliament, quoted from Shelley's "Hellas." "The world's great age begins anew, the golden years return." The crime of war would never again be committed. Europe had learned its lesson. The future stretched, infinite in possibility. The November skies were gray but my heart was high. The prison gates had been flung open. A revolution was in progress. The brigadier in charge of our camp had been dispossessed and the window cleaner put in charge. German troops were returning from the front; flags fluttered from every window. Germany was mercifully unaware of the troubles that lay in store for her. Mainz was light of heart, the banks let us cash five pounds a day instead of a month, and the ladies of the town were cordial to those who could offer them a bar of Sunlight soap.

I sat in a large airy café, listening to sentimental music, sipping a sweet sparkling wine, realizing how wine could not only wash away one's cares but heighten one's big moments. I returned to England by slow stages, pausing for five days in Nancy and three in Boulogne—townships that understand well the pleasures of the table. Remembering the flagons that my father had decanted, I ordered Burgundy at every meal and then at last I began to understand how deep and rich was the pleasure that good wine can give. I returned to civilian life, agreeing with Henri Murger that the first duty of a wine was to be red, adding my own corollary that its second duty was to be Burgundy.

In terms of wine—of a lot else for that matter—I have been self-taught and in 1919 there were not the aids to self-education that there are today. The Wine and Food Society did not exist; there were no ivory cards telling you which were the best years for which wines. Wine merchants did not publicize their wares instructionally, newspapers did not carry articles about wine, and the student will find that very few of the books about wine that are listed in bibliographies were published before 1920.

Between the autumn of 1919 and the spring of 1926, I was literary adviser to the publishing house of Chapman and Hall, of which my father was the Managing Director. In June, 1926 I resigned my post, went around the world and became a traveler, with the whole scope of my life altered. But during those six and a half years I was based

in London, as a Londoner, I had learned, by trial and error,
what kinds of wine I liked. Wine was not expensive then. I
did not smoke, I had not learned to like whisky, and I
only took short drinks when I was at a party. When I was
lunching, by myself, at the Savage or the Savile, I usually
drank cider. But I always drank half a bottle of wine at
dinner, preferably Burgundy, and normally I followed it
with a glass of port.

My choice of wine in those days was decided in large
part by my pocket. Hilaire Belloc said that in provincial
France he always drank the second cheapest claret on the
list because that was probably what the proprietor drank
himself. I usually aimed in restaurants about a third of
the way down the list. I asked my wine merchant to send me
a wine that was rich, full-bodied, smooth.

It is very hard to describe a flavor. To say that a wine
is velvety is inaccurate. How does velvet taste? You can say
that a wine caresses your palate in the same way that cash-
mere is caressing to your touch, and that was what I meant
when I asked for a velvety wine.

Tributes to wine usually concentrate on the effects that
it produces rather than its actual taste. The references to
taste are in terms of symbol; as a violet is to the eye, so is
a Moselle to the palate. Claret is like a queen, Burgundy
is like a king. Certain wines charm as a young girl charms,
others as a mature and gracious woman. The similes are
elegant, but they do not convey precise meanings. Geoffrey
Harrison in *Bristol Cream* quotes from a merchant's *avizo*
of the sixteenth century:

Of wines: it cannot be set down by pen or words the right knowledge of it for it is perceivable only by the taste and flavour. But the
best sorts of wines generally are, when they doe taste pleasant and
strong withall and when they drink cleane and quicke in the palate

of the mouth, and when they are clere and white hued if they be white wines, or of faire Orient red if they be red wines. But if they drink weake, rough, foule, flat, inclining to egernesse, or long, they are not good.

The distinction between "quick" and "long" wine is puzzling, but otherwise we have not in four hundred years got closer to describing the exact taste of wine.

Evelyn Waugh wrote in *Brideshead Revisited* of a Clos de Bèze 1904 that he drank in 1925:

How can I describe it? The pathetic fallacy resounds in all our praise of wine. For centuries every language has been strained to define its beauty and has produced only wild conceits or the stock epithets of the trade. This Burgundy seemed to me, then, serene and triumphant, a reminder that the world was an older and better place than Rex knew, that mankind in its long passion had learned another wisdom than his. By chance I met this same wine again, lunching with my wine merchant in St. James's Street, in the first autumn of the war; it had softened and faded in the intervening years, but it still spoke in the pure authentic accent of its prime and that day, as at Paillard's with Rex Mottram years before, it whispered faintly, but in the same lapidary phrase, the same words of hope.

It is equally difficult, equally impossible to explain why one wine is better than another, as difficult and impossible as to explain why one blank verse line is poetry and one is not. "What is the essential difference," the undiscerning will demand, "between 'Absent thee from felicity awhile' and 'Don't get too drunk, chaps, till I'm underground.' They both say the same thing, don't they, in ten syllables; and the second one seems more natural somehow." It is a question in wine as in poetry of training the natural instinctive taste with which nearly all of us are born.

In the early 1920's the men I knew did not talk knowledgeably of vintage years, except in regard to port. We were amateurs who liked drinking wine. It was not till later that I learned to discriminate between wines, tasting one year's and one Château's and in the case of Burgundy and champagne one shipper's produce against another's. It was in my middle thirties that wine became a hobby for me, as fascinating and as human a hobby as one can find. It appeals to the collector's, to the antiquarian's, to the historian's, to the student's instinct. It also appeals to a warmhearted human instinct to share the best things of life and in the fullest measure with our fellow men.

WINE IN CLASSIC
DAYS

ONE OF THE MOST FASCINATING ASPECTS of this, my late found hobby, is the extent to which I have been learning all the time.

In the early summer of 1957 Pelican Books issued in England L. W. Marrison's *Wines and Spirits*. It is the book for which wine-lovers have been waiting long. Mr. Marrison, an industrial research chemist, is also a man of letters, who, under the nom de plume of D. M. Dowley, has published several novels of distinction. He approaches the subject with knowledge and scholarship, with wit and warmth. He has studied the history of wine as a scholar. As a novelist he has written of the enjoyment of wine with wit and wisdom. As a chemist he has explained so simply that the layman can understand what happens between the vineyard and the vat and between the cask and the bottle and how the processes of fermentation are performed, including a few pages for the expert which the uninitiated like myself must be content to skip.

In one way the making of wine is very simple, and the essential method of doing so has not changed in a hundred centuries. Wine is the fermented juice of the grape, and the type from which wine can best be made—the *Vitis vinifera* —flourishes north of the equator, from Marakesh in the south to Bonn and California in the north. Below the equator there is a similar wine belt that includes Chile, South Africa, Australia and the Argentine. The grapes are gathered in the early autumn; they are pressed or trodden; the subsequent mush is left to ferment. You can ferment practically anything by adding yeast, but with grapes this addition is not needed. Innumerable yeast molds hover above the vineyards and settle upon the fruit. The sugar in the grape juice provides the alcohol. During fermentation the sugar is broken up into ethyl alcohol and carbon dioxide. The sweeter the grapes the greater the alcoholic content of the wine. When fermentation is complete, the wine is drawn off into casks, where it is racked and fined and left to mature. It is as simple as that.

Ford Madox Ford—a man of many theories—told me that he planned to write a history of the novel, starting with Henry James and ending with Petronius. "You should work from the known to the unknown," he wheezed. He never wrote that book, but his principle of working from the known to the unknown is a useful guide at this point. By comparing what we know today with what the ancients appear to have known we can guess at the kinds of wine they drank.

Science has taught us much of what happens during fermentation. Pasteur himself put his immense capacities to the subject. What the ancients learned by experiment and guesswork, we know as facts through scientific research and the future has no doubt more to reveal. We recognize now that the grapes bring to the vat two kinds of yeast—the wild yeasts and the wine yeasts. The wild yeasts begin the process of fermentation, but they are weak and cannot survive a concentration of over four per cent alcohol. The wine yeasts take over the half-finished job. They are able to raise the alcoholic content of the vat to as high a point as sixteen per cent of alcohol. But it is very unusual for there to be that much sugar. The average European percentage is ten per cent.

It is at this point that the wine must be taken from the vat. If it is not, the vinegar bacteria will attack the alcohol, convert it into acetic acid and turn the residue into vinegar. Finally the acetic acid will be attacked by the bacteria that have survived these many changes, and all that will remain except water will be ammonium salts.

The various stages overlap and the cellar master has to be on his guard lest the taste and durability of the wine is affected by harmful bacteria. The escaping carbon dioxide lifts to the surface a solid mass of skins and pips, and this mass has to be kept immersed as it assists the acetic acid bacteria. Men with staves press it down. In a few cellars a wine frame is set a little below the surface to prevent the mush from rising, but this device presents difficulties. It is not easy to keep it clean. The cellar master has also to maintain the proper temperature in the vats. If the temperature rises too high or sinks too low, the process of fermenting is bogged down. The problems are different in the cool climate of the Côte d'Or and the sub-tropic atmosphere of Algeria. There are several schools of thought as to the best temperature. A high temperature with a short fermentation means that the wine is less exposed to the air and the danger of the vinegar bacteria. A low temperature with a slow fermentation retains better the aroma of the wine. A hundred or so years ago it was found that sulphur dioxide killed off most of the minor bacteria that interfered with the work of the essential wine yeasts, but the use of sulphur in the hands of a careless *vigneron* is dangerous. The wine is ruined that has a taste of sulphur, and all wine-producing countries have legislated against oversulphuring. But they have been lenient in their strictures and many cheap European wines have an aftertaste of sulphur.

In very few countries today are grapes trodden by foot. The conservatives used to maintain that the human foot was superior to any machine because it did not crush the pips and pips give a bitter flavor to the wine, but it is generally conceded now that the modern *égrappoir* and press do their job efficiently.

There is a difference between the making of white wine and red. Though red wine cannot be made from white grapes, white wine can be made from red; much champagne is, for instance. It is by the skins, not the juice, that wine is colored, the coloring cells being concealed under the skin. When red grapes are used, the skins have to be removed before fermentation starts. When white grapes are fermented with their skins, the wine has a yellowish-green color.

When red wine is made the stalks are sometimes included in the fermentation; the Bordelais and the Californians maintain that the stalks give an unpleasant flavor, but the stalks contain tannin and tannin gives vitality and longevity. White wines are deficient in tannin, so tannin and tartaric acid are added. In cheap white wines the fermentation is checked before the sugar has been converted into alcohol.

*Rosé* wine is made in a number of ways. The best, such as Tavel, Rousillon and the Portuguese and Italian pink wines are made by removing the skins halfway through the fermentation. Sometimes red and white grapes are mixed in the vat, sometimes red grapes are very lightly pressed, sometimes red grapes are pressed without their skins and the wine is dyed with tasteless cochineal.

The wine that is drawn from the vat into casks is cloudy, and it is not till late November that it "falls bright." Much has happened in the meantime. In the first place the wine in the cask has diminished in volume, first through cooling and in the second place through evaporation, by the wine passing through the pores of the wood; even old casks take away one to two per cent of the volume and as alcohol passes through the wood more easily than water does, the wine gets weaker. The cask has to be refilled with wine either of the same or of a previous year.

All the time a sediment is forming in the bottom of the cask. There is now no carbon dioxide to raise this sediment to the surface so the wine can be racked, that is, drawn off through a pipe into another cask. Frequent rackings are necessary and finally the wine is fined with white of egg, fish glue or some of the modern patent powders which collect the various floating impurities and drag them to the bottom.

Most wines are drunk the year after they are made, and the amount of care that is devoted to wine depends upon its quality. Wines that are destined to be served in carafes with table d'hôte menus are not treated with the attention that is lavished on wines that are to be matured.

Mr. Marrison has, I think, said the last word in terms of the technique of wine production, but even he has not a great deal to tell us about the early history of wine.

The sources of information are scant. Noah is associated in popular legend nearly as much with his addiction to strong liquors as with his building of the Ark, but we do not know when he lived and we can only guess when Genesis was written. Archaeologists consider that grape wine was

made ten thousand years ago. Almost certainly honey was
fermented earlier, and palm wine and date wine probably
preceded grape wine. The first references to grape wine—I
quote L. W. Marrison—are found in Middle Eastern writ-
ings, about 2100 B.C. Sennacherib and Nebuchadnezzar
planted extensive vineyards; early Egyptian wall paintings
show that wine was made in the same way that it is today
and that harvest-time was a period of dance and song, to
say the least of it. Then as now the vines were arranged
on pergolas, though today the framework is lower so that the
grapes can receive by day the sun rays reflected by the earth
and by night the warm exhalations of the sun-soaked earth.
Possibly the grape vines were set higher from the soil in Egypt
because the heat was greater.

No vines exist now along the Nile or Tigris, and as
early as Herodotus's day—in the fifth century B.C.—Egypt
was importing its wine from Greece. The climate of Egypt
did not suit the vine, as the fate-favored Mediterranean's
did. Today Greek wine is not agreeable. It is flavored with
resin or pine-gum. "The taste for this can be acquired," is
Raymond Postgate's comment, "but there is no need to acquire it." Perhaps the wine Achilles loved was different.
The Greeks mixed it with water, and regarded as barbarians those who drank it neat. It was presumably a rougher
wine than ours, but the climate has to be considered. I traveled once in summer by a Messageries Maritimes mixed-
class liner from Marseilles to Tahiti. We were served a red
Côtes-du-Rhône as a table wine; for the first days it was
excellent, but after we had passed Tangier and were nearing
the Caribbean it seemed so heavy that I put ice in it.

We know about Greek wines from several sources. We
have Homer as a guide, and we have Plato's and Zenophon's
versions of the Symposium. We also have the coins that the
various States issued. The three exportable commodities of

the ancient world—the Mediterranean triad—were the corn of Demeter, the oil of Athene and the wine of Dionysius. The Greeks used their coins as propaganda to advertise their wares. We can picture an Athenian banquet. The Greeks appear to have eaten lightly and started to drink when their meal was finished. Girls were sent to the nearest well-house to fetch cold spring water. Wine was brought up from the cellar in rough amphorae and decanted into smaller, more elegant, amphorae; sometimes it was poured into vases packed with ice. Very often these vases were painted. They took the place of pictures. The Greeks had not yet thought of painting frescoes on inside walls.

Their vases were works of art, but they did not take the same pride in their wine vessels as did the Egyptians who used not only clay, but hard stone, alabaster, glass, ivory, bone porcelain, bronze, silver and gold.

The host would decide on the proportions in which the wine and water were mixed. Three of water to one of wine has been mentioned as a reasonable combination. The spring water of Greece was excellent, and it would seem at times that the water was rated more highly than the wine, though sometimes sea water was distilled to produce fresh water. If the Greeks knew this, it is surprising that they did not discover that brandy could be distilled from wine.

Symposium means "a drinking together" and Socrates' comment at the start of the evening might have been delivered yesterday.

"So far as drinking is concerned, gentlemen, you have my approval. Wine moistens the soul and lulls our grief to sleep while it also wakens kindly feelings. Yet I suspect that men's bodies react like those of growing plants. When a god gives plants too much water to drink they can't stand up straight and the winds flatten them, but when they drink exactly what they require they grow straight and tall and bear abundant fruit, and so it is with us."

The conviviality that followed is contemporary in its atmosphere and temper. At their ease, reclined on couches, men talked and there was a floor show. They left their womenfolk at home. It was rather like a Japanese geisha party. They quaffed rather than sipped their wine.

The late Charles Seltman recently published a book on the drinking habits of the ancients. He asserts that in Greece the grape mush was fermented for nine days, that sweet *hepsema* was added, that the wine was then poured into jars covered with lids that had been smeared with pine cones as a preservative. Every five weeks the jars were inspected and more pine flavor added. Light wines then as now were treated with resin as a preservative. In the spring the wine was bottled in amphorae.

The amphora was a standard measure for both the Greeks and Romans, the Attic containing nine gallons and the Roman six. Most of the important museums possess one. It stood about four feet; round the shoulders it had a circumference of about four feet; it had a thin, short neck and an opening three inches across; it had handles at each side. It tapered down, occasionally, into a foot but more often into a point that could be dug into the ground; sometimes a special stand was employed so that the amphora could keep its balance.

Seals were set on the handles and stoppers. Rhodes used the same seals as on its coins; there were oblong stamps bearing the name of the responsible official and the month when the wine was bottled. The jars from Thasos had a registration mark and bore the vintner's name.

It has always puzzled archaeologists that such a practical people should have favored such an unwieldy container. It has been suggested that while the amphora stood upright, the sediment in the wine could settle in its narrow point so that the clear wine could be ladled out, but that seems improbable since the opening at the top was so narrow that only a very curiously designed instrument could have reached the lower levels and no such instrument has been discovered. It has also been suggested—and this seems more possible—that amphorae were slung in a network from the beams in wineshops. The pointed end would fit in easily and safely, and the other end could be tipped up. Perhaps the straw-covered Chianti and Orvieto bottles of today are their lineal descendants. But it may be that the Greeks admired the proportions of the amphora, and for them beauty was more important that utility.

The wine that the Greeks exported was shipped in amphorae. Before the Second World War a cargo of seven hundred was found on the Italian Riviera, and later at Antheor amphorae of the first century B.C. have been discovered. The skill of modern divers will undoubtedly reveal many more. But when the Greeks traveled in small companies, they used presumably handier containers. In the days of Homer and Herodotus, wine skins were used not only to carry wine but to preserve it. The aperture was at the end of a leg that was tied up with strings. The skins were probably made watertight by a lining of pitch. The same form of preserving wine is much in use today. It is to this type of bottle that reference was made in the Biblical simile of new wine in old bottles. The wine was still effervescent and the old skin could not stretch to meet its liveliness. But the ancients also had leather bottles, so Joshua informs us, and there is a reference in Jeremiah to earthen bottles. In classic times wine was included in the equipment of a traveler, as the story of the Good Samaritan reminds us.

The Greeks recognized three colors of wine: red, straw-colored and amber. The Romans had an extra color: they divided red into black and blood-colored. Homer talked of the wine-dark sea. This epithet has puzzled some. Marrison calls it "one of the most mysterious of Homer's cliché epithets." But I have seen the Mediterranean assume every color between black and a glazed glassy white. Charles Seltman writes, "I have watched the sea between Zacynthus and the mainland of Elis from a ship on the way to Katakolo, the port of Pyrgos and Olympia, and have seen a heavy gray mercurial ocean suffused with the purple color of rich wine as the eastern sun worked its mysterious change."

It has been held that Greek wines were heavy and luscious; Henderson in his history of ancient and modern wines published in London a century and a half ago, says that Pramian was a port-type wine, the basis, as rum is, for mixed drinks. It was not unlike, perhaps, a kind of Tokay, with the grapes left on the vine, until there remained a bare drop of syrup, thick and sweet, a kind of attar. Seltman on the other hand argues that this view of Greek wine is due to our mistaken translation from the original Greek, that while *glukos* means sweet, *hidus* means agreeable to the palate, that is to say smooth.

Both the Greeks and the Romans compounded various herbs and flavors, almonds, cypress gums, pepper and honey with their wines to make them palatable. This is a practice that has been universally followed by the wine trade until recent years, when the wine-growing countries have drawn up strict legislation ensuring the purity of wine; there were no limits at which the wine merchants of the past were prepared to pause in their effort to conceal the deficiencies of their wines. Smollett complained that pigeon's dung was used as a sophistication, and in classic days when less was known about the technique of fermentation the final wine must very frequently have disappointed the *vigneron*.

There are many references in Homer to blended potions. When Hector bears the wounded Machaon to his tent, Hecamede mixes a potion of Pramian wine over which she sprinkles goats milk cheese and white barley meal, which is not unlike the addition of nutmeg and Angostura bitters to a rum punch.

Virgil's second Georgic contains an authoritative account of grape-growing in Roman days, and it shows that there was some knowledge then of the sequence of wines at table. They recognized, for instance, that the wines of certain areas were better suited to conclude a meal. It is a pity that the actual making of wine lay outside Virgil's province.

Some writers have assumed that the Greeks did not store their wine in cellars because there are references to their being in the same room as clothes and tapestries to which damp and darkness would have been injurious. The Romans kept their wine in *fumaria*, a kind of kiln. They sealed the mouth of the amphora, having protected the surface of the wine with a layer of olive oil and closed the pores of the amphora with plaster.

There are several references in Latin verse to this custom of the *fumarium*. Martial talks of "the smoky wines of Marseilles." Ovid writes, "He draws the wine which he had racked in his early years when stored in a smoky cask"; and Horace, "We'll pierce a glass with mellow juice replete, mellowed with smoke since Tully ruled the state."

Both the Greeks and the Romans aged their wines, or at least appreciated that there was a quality in ageing wines. Pindar in the ninth Olympian Ode, having had his poems scoffingly referred to by a senior and a rival as "new wine," says that he too had a reverence for old wine but preferred his wine to be fresh like flowers. Telemachus, when he sets out in search of his father, fills his ship with the oldest wines from the cellar. The Romans marked their amphorae with the dates and the name of the consul. Opimian wine, the product of the vintages when Opimius was consul—121 B.C. —was the highest prized. In the days of Augustus Caesar, Opimian was unobtainable in the open market and could only be found in private cellars. In the *Satyricon*, it is Opimian that Trimalchio, a vulgar *nouveau riche*, serves to his guests.

Presently came in two long-haired blacks, with small leather bottles, such as are used for the sprinkling of sand on the stage, and gave us wine to wash our hands in, but no one offered us water. . . . Thereupon large double-eared vessels of glass close plaistered over were brought up, with labels about their necks, upon which was this inscription OPIMIAN MUSCADINE OF AN HUNDRED YEARS OLD.

While we were reading the titles, Trimalchio clapped his hands. "Alas, alas," said he, "that wine should live longer than man! Wine is life and we'll try if it has held good since the consulship of Lucius Opimius or not: 'tis right Opimian and therefore make ready. I bought not so good yesterday, yet there were persons of better quality supped with me."

Falernian wine, so disappointing to us, which was then considered the best, was drunk in its tenth year.

The Romans in early days got their wines from Greece, and Virgil considered Greek wine superior to Italian.

> *"Nor our Italian wines produce the shape*
> *Or taste, or flavour of the Lesbian grape."*

The Greeks, carrying their culture with them, planted a vineyard wherever they founded a colony. The Romans did the same, except that in their planned economy they decided to make North Africa a grain- instead of a wine-producing country, and uprooted the vines of Carthage and later those of southern France. Italy, Spain and the Lebanon could supply the Empire's need of wine while Hungary could supply the legions along the Danube.

This policy set back viticulture along the south shores of the Mediterranean for many centuries. Under the domination of the Ottoman Empire wine was not needed, and it was not until the French occupation in the beginning of the nineteenth century that the vine was again tended. For that reason, Algerian wine has never received the regard it deserves. It is not referred to in classical literature and during the Second World War it acquired an unfortunate reputation from the bulk cargoes that were shipped back to England in empty convoy vessels. At such a time proper care could not be given to it. But good Algerian wine—Lung and Domaine de la Trappe—such as I have drunk since in Tangier and Nice is excellent. Smooth, full-bodied, rich-flavored, it seems to me a worthy substitute for Châteauneuf-du-Pape.

The Greeks colonized the southwestern seaboard of the Mediterranean; Marseilles was theirs and Málaga and Cadiz. They also, every good Burgundian claims, planted the Côte d'Or with vineyards. They reached the Caspian and founded the Crimean vineyards. The Romans flung their net still further. They reached as far north as rainsoaked Britain.

Before the Roman conquest, the diet of the bewoaded Britons was simple, according to Diodones. "Their food consisted chiefly of milk and venison. Their ordinary drink was water. Upon extraordinary occasions they drank a fermented liquor made of barley, honey or apples." They had, that is to say, beer and cider, with which all of us are familiar, and mead, which very few of us have drunk. I am one of the few who have. Margaret Lane (the Countess of Huntingdon) made a few bottles in 1944. The other day she opened one for me.

It tasted like audit ale, laced with a dark sherry. Its alcoholic content did not seem to me very high.

The Romans, who brought roads and architecture and central heating, introduced the Britons to the charms of wine; they also taught the Britons to make wine. The Normans indeed found so many vineyards in East Anglia that they called the Isle of Ely *L'île des Vignes*. The industry continued into the sixteenth century.

Messrs. Gilbey, to celebrate their firm's centenary in 1957, organized an excellent exhibition at the Café Royal of "Drinking through the Centuries," to which James Laver contributed a typically scholarly and charming brochure. "Are we to consider," he asked, "that the climate of these islands took a turn for the worse toward the end of the Middle Ages, or that with improved means of communication it became easier to import wines from abroad? It is tantalizing to know so little about British viticulture; tantalizing also to know that an experiment which lasted for centuries and which therefore cannot have been wholly unsuccessful, should have been abandoned. How pleasant it would be for the modern Englishman to sit down under his own vine and fig tree and quaff the product of his own holding. Was the wine the Romans produced here ever good or was it thin and acid? Alas, we shall never know."

Or should I add in emendation, "very few of us will ever know"? Sir Guy Salisbury-Jones, the Marshal of the British Diplomatic Corps, is reviving the English vine at Hambledon, the Bethlehem of cricket. The cost of labor makes prohibitive the production of wine at competitive prices but I am told that his is excellent and tastes like hock.

The GLORY of Rome passed. The East seceded from the West. The barbarians poured southward. The Moslem armies of the East swept the southern Mediterranean, occupied Tunisia, captured Gibraltar, reached the Pyrenees, struck north to Burgundy and Lyons, recoiled there in defeat, but made Spain their home. Darkness fell over Europe.

The might, majesty, dominion and power of the Caesars had become a legend, but something remained, much remained—not only the long straight roads down which the legions marched, the amphitheaters where they indulged their leisure, the columns that sustained their palaces, but certain qualities of spirit that survived the decay of ma-

sonry—a sense of justice and of order, of rectitude in conduct, of dignity in victory, of fortitude in defeat, a reverence for the household gods, a language from which our
own speech has been molded, a literature that has colored
the thought of all those who have been favored with a classical education. And finally there was the new-found faith
where monasteries and abbeys kept alight the torch of culture till it could, in the Middle Ages, illumine the new
princely Courts. It was in these pockets of resistance that
viticulture was maintained during the Dark Ages.

Each country became an island on its own, sometimes
an island that was divided into several islands; and in most
cases the drinking habits of each country over the years
stand as a window opening onto that country's history. Certainly that is true of England.

In terms of wine as in terms of so much else the Dark
Ages that followed the invasion of the Goths brought little
graciousness to England. The Saxons who followed the Romans were hard-drinking warriors. Ale, cider and mead
quenched their thirst and fired their blood and the Britons
followed their example. They enjoyed long drinks and their
immense drinking horns had no stands or legs. They had to
be emptied at a single draught. The upper-class Saxons
drank piment, which was wine flavored with honey and
spices. It was presumably wine of their own growing that
they drank, the cold and clammy climate demanding a
warm strong stimulant.

A thin wine during the ninth century was shipped from
La Rochelle. But in the middle of the twelfth century a great
piece of good fortune befell the country. Henry II married
Eleanor of Aquitaine, and her dowry included with all the
west of France the great wine-producing lands of the Médoc.
Englishmen could now drink the finest wines that nature can

produce—wines to which over the years can be paid Saintsbury's tribute to another area, "The Almighty might no doubt have caused a better wine to exist, but he never did."

The popularity of those noble wines was responsible for the birth of the English navy, Edward III issuing currency regulations that forced the Bordeaux merchants to establish their bases across the Channel and the English having to build a fleet to fetch their wine.

Another important event took place during the reign of Edward III. England forged its first links with Portugal, a treaty being arranged which allowed Portuguese ships to fish for cod off the English coast. During the days on shore, the Portuguese bartered for English manufactured goods the wine that they had brought in skins and casks. This link has never snapped. After the Reformation, when the country ceased to observe the Lenten fast and Ember days, the Devonshire and Cornish sailors could find no home sale for the dried Newfoundland cod that had been the staple fish-day's diet. They had to seek markets overseas, and Portugal, a Catholic country, was ready to accept "penitential cod" in return for wine. It was not, however, the port that we know today that the merchants of the period brought back in exchange for fish, but a table wine, not from the Douro district but from Minho, fifty miles further north.

There was another earlier link with Portugal. L. W. Marrison refers to the belief that the Crusaders sampled Portuguese wines on their way to the Holy Land, and that some of them decided to remain where the wine was so good and join Ferdinand I of Castile in his campaign against the Saracens. At any rate a colony of English merchants certainly settled fifty miles north of Oporto in Vianna do Castella.

The English were also drinking at this time a sweet Spanish wine called Bastard. The English have always needed strong dessert wines as an antidote to their damp climate. The butt of malmsey in which Clarence was drowned came from Cyprus. Though it is hard to see how the operation was performed, the only opening would have been the bung through which the wine was drawn till the cask was empty. In the film "Richard III," starring Laurence Olivier, Clarence was pitched into a cask that had been stood on its end, but it is inconceivable that this cask could have contained wine, for that would mean that it was the practice in the royal cellars to stand casks on their ends and ladle out the wine with buckets—an exposure to the air that would have speedily ruined the wine. Clarence must have been drowned in a butt that had once contained malmsey and had been filled with water. There is no reason to believe that mercy was shown to Clarence and that his end was made swifter and more pleasant by an engulfing, suffocating drunkenness.

An early fourteenth-century poem gives an extended list of the wines that were then in favor:

> *Ye shall have Rumney and Malmesyne*
> *Both Hippocras and Vernage wine,*
> *Mount Rose and wines of Greke*
> *Both Algrade and despice eke*
> *Antioche and Bastarde*
> *Pyment also and Garnarde:*
> *Wine of Greek and Muscadell,*
> *Both clare, pyment and Rochell.*

Hippocras, a very favorite medieval drink, was a mixture of wine and spices. The aristocracy compounded hippocras with ginger, cinnamon and sugar. Sugar was a rare and expensive commodity, and the proletariat, the "comyn pepull," had to be content with honey as a substitute for sugar and long pepper instead of cinnamon. At that period, tea, coffee and cocoa were unknown. The Sugar Islands of the Caribbean had not been discovered, and the Crusades had not revealed to Europe the riches of the Orient. It was from the Saracens that we recovered the lost art of glass-making.

There are many references to wine in the Canterbury Tales.

> *Now keep ye from the white and from the red*
> *And namely from the white wine of Lepe*
> *That is to sell in Fish Street as in Chepe.*
> *This wine of Spain creepith subtilly*
> *In other wines, growing fast by,*
> *Of which there rises such fumositee*
> *That when a man has drunken draughtes three,*
> *And wenith that he be at home in Chepe*
> *He is at home right in the town of Lepe*
> *Not at the Rochelle, nor at Bordeaux town.*

Lepe is held to be Niebla, a town between Seville and Moguci. Its wines now are white, dry and not particularly strong. In Chaucer's day its wines were sold under its own name, and had the characteristics of malmsey. Probably it was fortified at this time.

Over the fourteenth century hangs the shadow of the Black Death. The population of the country was halved, culture was delayed and it was not till the Elizabethan age that literature could again guide us to the drinking tastes of the English.

Wine-lovers all over the world are deeply in debt to André Simon, that great historian of wine. During the 1930's he was one of the most valued members of a small dining club "Ye Sette of Odde Volumes," which still exists in its eightieth year and which meets on the fourth Tuesday of the month five months a year. It consists of twenty-one members, known as Odd Volumes, this being the number of volumes in the Variorum edition of Shakespeare, but the membership is brought up to forty-two by the addition of twenty-one Supplementary Odd Volumes, the general biographical thesis being that human beings, like books, are odd volumes until they join a set.

The Club was founded in the 1870's by the bookseller Bernard Quaritch, who apparently having grown tired of paying for his friends' meals, decided that by forming a club, he could ensure that his intimates would be self-supporting. The constitution was drawn up in terms of what the 1880's considered humorous; facetiousness is the prevailing note. Rule XVI provides a typical example. It reads, "There shall be no Rule XVI." The initiation ceremony is very much like that of the House of Lords. It is the habit for the brethren to introduce their guests, in a speech, one by one. It is traditional to insult one's guests. The more distinguished the guest, the less veiled the insult. Vyvyan Holland once remarked of a well-known publicist, "The main advantage of the Sette of Odd Volumes is that it enables one to entertain persons to whom one owes hospitality, but whom one cannot very well invite to one's own house." The wittiest introduction that I remember was that of Eustace Hoare by Maurice Healy, that entertaining Irishman of law and letters. "My guest is a member of the second oldest profession in the world. Mr. Hoare is a banker."

The Sette was made gentle fun of in *Brideshead Revisited*. "It was a surprising association of men quite eminent in their professions who met once a month for an evening of ceremonious buffoonery. Each had his soubriquet —Bridey was called 'Brother Grandee'—and a specially designed jewel worn like an order of chivalry, symbolizing it; they had club buttons for their waistcoats and an elaborate ritual for the introduction of guests; after dinner a paper was read and facetious speeches were made."

André Simon's cognomen was "Vintner." In Novem-

ber, 1931, he read a paper to the Sette which was subsequently privately printed in an edition of 199 copies, under
the title "Wine in Shakespeare's Days and Shakespeare's
Plays." It is the ninety-third of the Opuscula that have been
issued to the Sette; it is one of my half-dozen favorites. The
information that it contains is spread among his other
books, but the concision necessary for its delivery within
forty minutes gives it a unique pace and vibrance.

In Shakespeare's day, he pointed out, nobody drank
water. It was not fit to drink. Beer and ale were drunk at
breakfast and at midday, wine in the evening. No one who
was not a vintner, a licensed taverner or a peer was allowed
to keep wine in his own house. The streets were ill-lit and
dangerous, and the inn was the natural meeting-place for
men after dark. The better taverns were large, with a big
public room on the ground floor and a number of private
rooms upstairs where men could exchange ideas on politics
and religion. Wine was abundant and cheap. It cost four-
pence a quart at a time when a rabbit cost a shilling and
beef two shillings a stone. It was young wine, shipped in
wood and drawn from the wood. Bottles existed then, but
corks did not. Corks did not come till James the First's day,
and bottles were only used to carry the wine from the cellar
to the table. There was no laying down of bottles in a cellar,
as the shape of the bottles would have made the binning of
them impossible. Nobody, in consequence, wanted old wine.
Young wine, a year old and freshly broached, was highly
prized. Although the population of England was a tenth of
what it is today, more wine was imported into England than
there is today, and this wine was not sipped but quaffed,
because of its youth. It was sherry, not table wine, that was
sipped.

The Elizabethan age was in terms of wine as of so
much else a golden period. With the accession of James I,

the state began the interference with the rights of the individual which has continued, deepening and strengthening
through the centuries. Chancellors of the Exchequer have
consistently taxed simple pleasures, battening on man's right
to innocent enjoyment. Although Elizabeth was desperately
in need of money, she did not unduly tax her subjects; she
believed in their right to happiness. Wine cost more in England than it had a generation earlier, but that was due to
a legitimate desire on her part to encourage the building of
ships and the training of sailors. She was anxious that English merchants should fetch wine from Bordeaux in English
ships. The King of France was equally anxious that his
ships should carry the wine to England and placed an export
tax on all wines shipped in English bottoms. This tax was
ultimately paid by the English consumer. But even so, four-
pence a quart was not a lot to pay.

This golden age ended with the accession of James I.
James liked claret but he liked gold more. He allowed his
subjects to sell wine at whatever price it would fetch in the
open market. This may have seemed an act of generosity
on his part, but he had ensured that the price would be high
by taking his own profit first. Elizabeth had regarded wine
as she had regarded bread and ale, as a necessity of existence, and had fixed its price by law. James I was indifferent
to his subjects' interests. Instead of limiting the right to sell
wine to vintners and to the aristocracy, he sold licenses to
anyone who could afford them. He also leased to individuals not only the royal privileges of prisage and butlerage,
but a number of other impositions which had previously
been collected by royal officers. These men were speculators.
They bought from the King at a lump sum rights whose value
they hoped to increase tenfold from the public, whom they
harassed under the protection of the King's authority.

Within a few years, wine was starting to become a luxury, and the poorer people were turning to a cheaper form of stimulant, to spirits, which anyone could distill at home without interference. There was no excise duty in Shakespeare's day; the excise duty was first imposed as a temporary measure during the Civil War in 1643, and nothing is so permanent as restrictive legislation passed in wartime "for the duration."

There are few references in Shakespeare to "strong waters." In *Twelfth Night* they are referred to as a midwife's tipple. In *Romeo and Juliet* it is the nurse who asks for them. Spirits were not sold in taverns, but hawked in the streets by "brandy-women." Spirits were homemade and untaxed. They were presumably exceedingly unpleasant. The technique of distillation was in the process of being learned and "burning waters" were made out of whatever lay to hand—wine dregs, sour ale and beerwash. You used for the still whatever was unfit to drink. Before James the First's reign was old, the high cost of wine had forced taverners to sell the spirits that had before only been found in dram shops.

It was not till later, however, that the full effects of such taxation became evident. During the Stuart period, the distillation of spirits in England was still small. Charles II, during his twelve years' exile in France, had learned to appreciate the qualities of French table wines, and a court is the center from which fashions spring. Moreover, his wife, Catherine of Braganza, introduced a taste for tea. But it was very different after the "Glorious Revolution" of 1688, with William and Mary on the throne, William a Dutchman who hated everything French because France protected the exiled Stuarts.

A few years earlier, a Dutch chemist, Professor Sylvius of Leyden, who died in 1672, distilled in Schiedam from rye a spirit that he flavored with juniper and called geneva after the French word *genièvre*—juniper. It had medicinal qualities and at first was sold only in apothecaries' shops. So popular a medicine did it prove that many apothecaries established distilleries. A poem dated 1729 by a distiller, Alexander Blunt, attributes to William of Orange the introduction of this geneva into London. The English soldiers, when they went to the wars in the Low Countires, sampled it and liked it. William's ministers, resolved to keep brandy out of the country because it was French, passed a law prohibiting the importation of spirits from all foreign countries and allowed anyone who gave notice to the excise to set up a distillery. Within a very short time the English had created a very tolerable imitation of geneva and shortened its name to gin. Its effect on the populace was calamitous.

Between 1684 and 1727 the production rose from half a million gallons to more than three and a half million gallons. Retailers hung out a board which read, "Drunk for a penny, dead drunk for twopence, clean straw for nothing." The situation became so serious that in 1736 the Gin Act was passed to restrain the sale of spirits. Opposition was fierce. There was widespread rioting. The death of Madame Gin was lamented in mock funeral processions. The Act was a failure and the yearly consumption of spirits rose in eight years from thirteen and a half million to nineteen million gallons.

Not only did the Whigs legislate against French wines and spirits but in 1703 they signed the Methuen Treaty with Portugal, which admitted Portuguese wines into England at a greatly reduced rate, an arrangement which, as a later chapter will show, was highly unsatisfactory.

Excessive and unwise taxation turned the wine-loving men of the Tudors' "Merrie England" into the gin-sodden crones and the gout-ridden country squires of Hogarth's drawings.

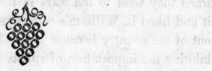

I HAVE WRITTEN over forty books and not one of them has turned out in quite the way I had expected. This one is proving no exception.

When I am asked, "Do you work out a synopsis of a novel before you start? Is it all planned in advance?" I give this answer. "I am standing on a hill. I see on another hill, ten miles away, a house that I want to visit. I know what direction to take, I know whither I am bound, and how long roughly it will take to get there. But I cannot tell the exact route that I shall follow. I cannot see the intermediate country. There may be rivers or marshes or a hidden range of hills. There may be a charming village which will tempt me to make a detour. It is in that way I write a novel. I may suddenly get a new angle on a situation, become absorbed in a character that I had meant to make a minor one, lose interest in another. I have the general scheme in mind. I know where I am headed. I know how long the book will be. But I may re-route myself at any moment."

That is what is happening with this book. I had planned to tell the story of wine in terms of periods of history, describing in turn the drinking habits of the ancient world, the Dark Ages, the medieval world and then our own, but before I had written many pages I had come to realize that the history of wine is not so much the history of centuries or of countries but of the wines themselves, or rather of certain great wines whose special qualities the world has come slowly to recognize and appreciate at their worth. For the real magic and mystery of wine lies in this: that though wine can be grown in innumerable areas, so many areas that there is at this moment a danger of over-production, great wines can only be produced in special places and in minute quantities.

The Romans and the Greeks spread the cult of it, but their own wines were not of transcendental quality. They cannot compare now—and they cannot have done then— with the great wines of Burgundy and Bordeaux, of the Rhine and of the Moselle.

Most forms of snobbery are tiresome, though some can be amusing, and the wine snob is one of the most tiresome. I beseech the reader to be patient with me for two more pages. "What!" I can hear him, or her, declaim. "Has this superior creature never, after a tramp through the Tuscan hills, washed down a great dish of spaghetti with a flask of vigorous Chianti? Has he never by the Lake of Geneva counterbalanced the midday heat with a light *pétillant* white wine from Neuchâtel? Has he never in California after an afternoon upon the golf links sat down to a great T-bone

steak with a bottle of Napa Valley Inglenook or Almadén
Chablis at its side?" Yes, of course he has and thoroughly
enjoyed them. I like wine, I need it with my meals, usually
all I ask is that there should be enough of it. In the 1930's
when wine was less expensive and those who cared for wine
more affluent, I often, when I listened to amateur connoisseurs dilating on the respective excellencies of this vineyard and that year, felt sympathy with Disraeli's Mr. Mount-
chesney's exasperated complaint, "I rather like bad wine, one
gets so bored with good." I chuckled as much as anyone over
James Thurber's cartoon in the New Yorker of a host offering
his guests a wine with the remark, "It's a naïve domestic
Burgundy without any breeding but I think you'll be amused
by its presumption."

The man who cannot enjoy a clean pure local wine is
not a wine-lover. André Simon has put it very well. "The
world, we know, is made up of all sorts of people; young
and old, good and bad, dull and brilliant. God loves them
all, but there are very few of them whom we like at all
times of the day and night, yet many do we welcome when
in the mood for them; there are also quite a few for whom
we have no use at any time. It is the same with wine. There
are all sorts of wine, young and old, good and bad, still
and sparkling. There are times, moods and occasions when
young wine will give us greater pleasure than the old; others
when we shall enjoy the company of the old far more than
that of the young. There are people who have been known to
prefer bad wine to good, just as there are men who are
fascinated by bad women."

But the fact that we can enjoy casual wines, must not
blind us to the superiority of the few great wines, and these
great wines come from four areas: Bordeaux, Burgundy, the
Rhine and the Moselle. The Rhone produces two noble, but
scarcely supreme wines—Hermitage and Châteauneuf-du-

Pape. Champagne, in many ways the greatest of all wines, is in a special category. It is not quite a natural wine and it is a recent discovery, to the extent that though it has been in existence for four hundred years, it is little more than a hundred years ago that dry champagne was put upon the market, and we should probably not be greatly impressed by the wine that Charles II introduced into England. Champagne is in a sense an unnatural wine, since it is subjected to a special process that will be described in a later chapter. Yet champagne shares the characteristic with Burgundy and claret that it is only a great wine when produced in its own area. You can get mediocre champagne from Épernay and Rheims, but you can never get a great champagne from anywhere else. Gold Seal's New York State champagne is very nice, so are Burgundy's Vin Mousseux, the Blanc de Blancs Champagnisé of Provence and certain South African sparkling wines, but they are an altogether different thing from even a non-vintage Krug.

In addition to those natural wines, there are the fortified wines of Spain, Portugal and Madeira. They are mixed with brandy and they, like champagne, are late arrivals, because in the classic days the technique of distillation was not understood; they too are special because nowhere else can sherry, port, and Madeira be produced.

The vineyards that produce great wines are jealous of their good name. If the wines of a certain year are poor, their owners do not sell them under their own label. They will use them for blending or sell them under the name of a district. A bottle of Pauillac may be a Lafite of a poor year. Port shippers will not declare a vintage year unless the wine of that year is excellent. The big wine manufacturers of Algeria and Provence extract 3000 gallons an acre from their vineyards, the owners of Chambertin are content with 120.

The big manufacturers aim at a standardized product. The owners of great vineyards take pride in the fact that no two of their wines taste the same.

The fact that no two wines taste alike is responsible for the snobbery that goes with wine. It is fascinating to guess at the wine that one is drinking. In New York the other day I mentioned that I was engaged upon a book on wine. A Frenchwoman asked if I could tell the year and provenance of a Château-bottled claret. "Of course I can't," I said. "A Frenchman could," she answered. I hope that my reply was tactful. "Some could, I know." I did not add, "but very few."

An expert in the wine trade, can, I am prepared to believe, make a shrewd guess. He has innumerable opportunities. He has a cellar at his disposal from which he can take samples at no cost to himself. He and five of his colleagues can say "Let's see how the '52's are getting on. Let's look at a Margaux, a Latour, a Poyferré and compare them." They may have the bottles up for lunch or they may sip them in their office, with a piece of hard cheese and a dry biscuit to clean their palates. They need not finish the bottles unless they want to; you and I cannot do that. We cannot afford to. How often in a month, or rather how often in a year do we get an opportunity of comparing four or five bottles against each other in the company of amateurs of wine. Before the war a few of my friends—Vyvyan Holland, Sir Thomas Barlow, Curtis Moffat, A. J. A. Symons, E. G. Boulenger—used to give dinner parties at which we could taste one claret against another. Vyvyan used to number the glasses so that one did not confuse the wines. I have not been to a dinner of that kind in London since the war.

In *Brideshead Revisited*, Evelyn Waugh described Charles Ryder's education in wine. Charles Ryder had a unique opportunity since he and Sebastian Floyd had the run during the long vacation of a cellar to which its owner was not expected to return.

We had bottles brought up from every bin and it was during those tranquil evenings with Sebastian that I first made a serious acquaintance with wine and sowed the seed of that rich harvest which was to be my stay in many barren years. We would sit, he and I, in the Painted Parlour with three bottles open on the table and three glasses before each of us; Sebastian had found a book on wine tasting, and we followed its instructions in detail. We warmed the glass slightly at a candle, filled a third of it, swirled the wine round, nursed it in our hands, held it to the light, breathed it, sipped it, filled our mouths with it and rolled it over the tongue, ringing it on the palate like a coin on a counter, tilted our heads back and let it trickle down the throat. Then we talked of it and nibbled Bath Oliver biscuits and passed on to another wine; then back to the first, then on to another, until all three were in circulation and the order of the glasses got confused and we fell out over which was which and we passed the glasses to and fro between us until there were six glasses, some of them with mixed wines in them which we had filled from the wrong bottle, till we were obliged to start again with three clean glasses each, and the bottles were empty and our praise of them wilder and more exotic.

". . . It is a little shy wine like a gazelle."

"Like a leprechaun."

"Dappled in a tapestry window."

"Like a flute by still water."

". . . and this is a wise old wine."

"A prophet in a cave."

". . . and this is a necklace of pearls on a white neck."

"Like a swan."

"Like the last unicorn."

Few of us have had so fortunate an experience. It is as I see it a question of mathematics. There are only fourteen meals in the week. There is a limit to what we can drink at any meal. We need to drink only half a glass of a great wine to appreciate its quality. We are a guest more often than we are a host. We cannot always drink what we would prefer. We are limited by our purse and company. We do not have enough chances of comparing one wine with another. Only very rich men and experts in the wine trade have this privilege.

I do not want to over-labor this point, but it is one about which I feel strongly. I have been exposed to a good deal of pretentiousness by amateur connoisseurs. Let us take a parallel from poetry. If the manuscript of an unpublished Victorian poem was put into my hand, I might not be able to spot its author, but I would make a reasonable guess. I might attribute a minor Swinburnian lyric to O'Shaughnessy or Dowson, but I could not mistake a blank verse line by Browning for one by Tennyson. I can say this with confidence because whenever I am in the mood, and that is not too seldom, I can, turning the pages of the *Oxford Book of Victorian Verse,* savor the bouquet of the era's poets. I can constantly remind myself of each poet's special idiosyncratic quality. I cannot do that with the wines of the Médoc and the Côte d'Or.

Before the second war, when I was in England three-quarters of the year, drinking two or three glasses of vintage port a day, I could as often as not guess the year of a vintage. The range of choice was not so very great. I was unlikely to be offered anything as young as a 1927 and I was not likely to be offered anything older than 1899. '04's and '08's were rare. If my host was offering me a special treat, I would expect a 1912. The only other wines were the '17, '20, '22, '24. Offley's was the only firm to ship a '23 and no one ever spotted my Boa Vista. It was, in the mid 1930's for the port-lover a question of distinguishing between eight wines all of which he had sipped many times. It was not too difficult to guess right fairly often, but I would never have attempted to guess the shipper, as an expert would have done.

Recognizing the year of a claret or a Burgundy is an altogether different matter. If you have set before you a Chambertin of '52 and a Margaux of '47 the difference between the two is obvious. There would be a discernible difference between two Burgundies of the same year, one from the Côte de Nuits and one from the Côte de Beaune; by that I mean that if you are given two different wines, you can recognize that they are different. But when a glass of red wine is poured out of a decanter, only an expert can do more than make a quite rough guess at it.

It is, I repeat, a question of mathematics. Let the amateur connoisseur, a man of moderate means who drinks his liter of wine a day, study the list of the sixty-one classified Châteaux of the Médoc. Let him ask himself how many of these he has ever looked at. Let him then reflect on the number of different wines of mark that each Château has produced over thirty years. Let him then remind himself that wine is a living thing, changing from year to year and that a Léoville-Poyferré of '29 would taste very differently today, could he unearth a bottle, from the way it tasted in '36. Then let him remember all the other great wines that are not included in this list: the wines of Burgundy and Graves, of St. Émilion and Pomerol; and in addition to those there are the wines of Germany and of Épernay. It is a very formidable list; how can the man of moderate means drinking his liter a day have more than a slight acquaintanceship with this vast subject?

Raoul Dahl in a highly amusing and sinister story recounts how a wine snob claims to recognize the provenance of a certain claret. It is thus that all of us would wish to talk, but the character in question had surreptitiously, unknown to his host, examined the bottle first. If I were offered a glass of Chambertin 1945 and asked to say what it was, I would consider that I had acquitted myself very creditably, if I were able to say, "It is a Burgundy. I think it is a good one, but I think it is a little old."

The vastness of the subject is, indeed, one of its great attractions. We need not be intimidated by the wine snob because we know that, in the last analysis, he is only putting on a front. He may know more than we do, but how little he knows in comparison with what there is to know! We are learning all the time; the wider our knowledge the keener our appreciation.

There is this point also to be remembered. A Frenchman may claim that he can recognize the provenance of a wine, but he is familiar with far fewer wines than the American and British wine-lover. He is familiar only with the wines of his own country, whereas we have a range that covers the vineyards of the world. We do not have such a deep knowledge of wine as the French but we have a wider one. Frenchmen would dismiss this statement as a heresy, but it was endorsed by André Simon in an article that he contributed to the London *Times* wine supplement a few years ago.

A brief examination will prove its truth. Wine-producing countries protect their own products with tariff walls. They consume their own produce and export the surplus, if they can find a market. In recent years every European country has sought markets overseas. The competition is heavy and they have not dared not to export their best. In addition there are local rivalries, each province boasting the superiority of its own wares. In a good Paris restaurant —but how often are we assured that Paris is not France!— you will be offered your choice of the best wines of France but you would be foolish to ask for a German wine. It would be very expensive and it might not be very good. The proprietor would have bought it reluctantly, so that he could have it on his list. He is uninterested in German wines and not informed about them. He would suggest an Alsatian wine. The wines of Alsace are clean and pleasant but they are not the equal of Moselle wines.

In Paris, port is an *apéritif*. It comes from Portugal; it is preferable to Byrrh, Suze and Dubonnet, but it has not been aged more than six or seven years in wood. It lacks the qualities of a fine tawny. How many Paris restaurants stock vintage port? You are denied what is for many of us the best climax to a meal. Sherry is to be found in France, so is Madeira, but they are neglected items in a wine list. You can eat better in Paris than anywhere, but you do not have such a wide choice of wines as in New York or London.

And Paris is an exception. In other cities, in other districts of France you will have a smaller choice. One of the great charms of France is its regional quality; its insistence on local excellence, its local dress, its local cuisine. France has never become standardized. Wherever you go in France, you find something that is new to you, something that is deep-rooted in tradition. It is one of the reasons why one can never weary of France, if one has the love of her in one's heart. But in terms of wine, this charm has its limitations. It means that in Bordeaux you drink the wines of the Médoc; in Rheims champagne, on the Côte d'Or, Burgundy; and in the Jura, in Alsace and Anjou you are wise to drink the wines in which the proprietor takes most pride.

The part of France that I love best is the coastline between Cannes and Menton, and the villages that perch on the hills behind it: Tourette, St. Paul-de-Vence and Èze. When I am housekeeping in Nice in my own establishment, I buy my wines from Félix Potin. I have found that the Algerian—Domaine de la Trappe—provides the best value;

when I spend a little more money, I buy a Mâcon or a Beaujolais; when I give myself a treat I order Châteauneuf-du-Pape.

There are those who maintain that Burgundy is too full-bodied a wine for the sun-soaked Midi. I have not found it so, but no one could call Mâcon heavy. There is a direct connection between Algiers and Nice and for centuries there has been a tradition of wine being brought to the coast down the valley of the Rhone. There is plenty of claret chez Félix Potin. But I have not found it too satisfactory. It seems a little hesitant, a little uncertain of itself, as perhaps it should. It is a newcomer on the Côte d'Azur.

My favorite restaurant is La Poularde Chez Lucullus. Michelin lists as its cheap local wines Bellet and Pierrefeu, the seat many centuries ago of one of the most famous courts of love. They are both excellent white wines, at the start of the meal. The white and rosé wines of Provence seem to me much better than the red ones. The Château de Selle's particularly and Gallardi's of Nice have an excellent *Blanc de Blancs*. But when I move on to the big wines—and it seems pointless to patronize an expensive restaurant, if you are not going to order wine that is worthy of the food—I find that the list of Burgundies is far more impressive than the lists of clarets. In Bordeaux, at the Chapon Fin, the opposite would be true.

The fact that each area has its own specialties in wine as in everything else makes traveling in France a perpetual adventure, but it does confirm the fact that you have a wider choice of wines in the U.S.A. and Britain; and that those of us who are interested and instructed in wines know more about wines—though not more about wine—than the untraveled Frenchman.

# THE WINES OF BORDEAUX

**T**his book has become, as I prophesied, a history of individual wines and, as an Englishman, how can I do better than start with the first great wines that were brought to England—the wines of Gascony?

They could not have had a better-omened provenance. Bordeaux was a flourishing city when Crassus and his Roman legions reached it, to be welcomed with good wine. The traditions of wine-making there have never been interrupted. The vineyards of Provence were pulled up under the orders of Domitian in 92 A.D., because the need of grain was paramount and Italy herself could supply the Mediterranean coast with wine. The amphorae of Italian wine found outside Marseilles are a proof that Provence was not then

producing wine. But the vineyards of Bordeaux were left intact, and Ausonius, that graceful poet of the silver age, who
was born at Bordeaux the son of a Roman senator, retired
after a successful career as a lawyer and colonial admin-
istrator to a villa outside the walls of St. Émilion, to pay
his tribute of verse to its full-bodied wines. Above the ruins
of his villa stands today Château Ausone—the home of
unique wines.

The wines of Bordeaux are the most natural in the
world. Nothing is added to them, no sugar, no spirit. The
grapes ripen and are pressed; the juice ferments; the wine is
racked and then left to mature. The *département* of the
Gironde produces 80 million gallons of wine a year.

Three kinds of wine were shipped from Bordeaux to
Henry II's England—red and white and *clairet*. There are
those who consider that *clairet* was either a *rosé* or a mixture
of red and white. Maurice Healy insists that one of the chief
beauties of the red wine of Bordeaux is its delicate color,
which contrasts strongly with that of other French red wines.
He points out that it was not uncommon for Bordeaux
merchants to strengthen the red wine they exported with
Rhone wine, Hermitage in particular—André Simon found
described in an 1830 catalogue a wine designated as "Lafite
Hermitages"—and it was blended wine that was shipped as
red, and that it was pure, clear, light-coloured wine. We welcome this to-day as Château Margaux or Latour that Henry
Plantagenet called "clairet." Maurice was a man of great
charm, who argued so persuasively that it was easy to forget that the Irish are noted neither for the logic nor for the
accuracy of their arguments, but for their wooingness. His
enthusiasm was contagious, but it is necessary to check his
statements. It is enough to record that our word "claret"
comes from "clairet."

At this period, it may be noted the people of Paris had

few opportunities of drinking claret. There were tolls and taxes between one province and another and there were highwaymen. Parisians were dependent on the vineyards of the Seine and Marne and Orleans. It was not till the exiled Duc de Richelieu in the reign of Louis XV developed a taste for claret, that it became popular at Court. Until then Burgundy, which became available early in the sixteenth century, was preferred.

At the end of this book there is a map of the Médoc area, showing how the great Châteaux cluster the left banks of the Gironde and the Garonne, and the right bank of the Dordogne.

"Wherever fine wines are produced," wrote Raymond Postgate, "the soil is poor and difficult. In the Gironde, it is gray, light, shallow, dusty, stony or dry—often all six. Some of the most famous clarets come from stunted vines on land where a carrot would not grow. Left to themselves they would support heather, thistles and a little clover; before the vines came they generally did."

But the visitor is not conscious of the poorness of the soil as he motors northwards from Bordeaux along the D. 2 road, toward Cantenac and Margaux, St.-Julien and Pauillac, names long familiar to him on wine lists, passing the Châteaux of which he has seen reproductions on the labels of well-cherished bottles. It is a green and friendly countryside.

I have only once stayed in a Château, at Loudenne. It is owned by the house of Gilbey and I went there in 1952, for the launching of White Gravette, then being put upon the market at the price of six shillings and sixpence a bottle. Some twenty members of the press made the excursion, with Ian Mackay as the *doyen* of the party.

It is a great experience to visit the Bordeaux countryside. There is a sense there of immemorial custom. Many

changes have taken place in recent years in the actual making of the wine. The grapes are no longer trodden by the
human foot. The work of many men is now done by
an *égrappoir*. Wine is often transported to London by tanker
to be bottled there. Every year science discovers some new
method of preventing waste without damaging the quality
of the wine. But in the vineyards themselves life has not
greatly changed since the founder of Eton College lost his
French possessions. The women still move between the narrow alley of the vine rows, snipping the bunches, and tip-
ping their baskets into the huge shoulder-buckets which the
*porteurs* empty into vast tubs which are drawn to the *chais* by
dun-colored slow-moving oxen—the "sacrificial victims" of
which Varro wrote. I do not think the old Roman poet would
feel he had returned to an alien universe if he could be
there in late September to attend the *"Bal du vendange."*
The town hall of every village would be crowded. There
would be local dances and gaiety till the early hours.

It would be hard to find a more charming setting for
a party than Château Loudenne which the Gilbeys bought
from the Vicomtesse de Marcellus in 1875. It is typical of
the countryside. It is not impressive and historic like one of
the Châteaux of the Loire. It is a comfortable country house
(the word "château" does not mean "castle" in the English
sense) in which a family of gentlefolk could live and supervise their property. It has charm, dignity and intimacy; it is
long and low, of faded rose-colored stone, slate-roofed with a
rounded tower at each end. From its long, stone-flagged terrace that is in shade after the early morning, you look across
a quarter of a mile of lawns and vineyards to the broad brown
river and the boats, large and small, that ply between Bordeaux and the Atlantic. Long avenues have been driven
through the woods. Bowered in roses and set in elms, the
Château crowns a little hill from which can be seen the spires

of thirteen churches in which pious Bordelais give thanks
for the gift of wine.

Typical, too, of the countryside is the part it plays in
the wine trade. The wine it produces is classified as bourgeois, which does not mean that it is poor but that it cannot
stand comparison with the *grands crus* of Pauillac and
Margaux. André Simon classes its wines with those of Livran
and Laujac as being distinctly superior to their neighbors
because of the greater care that has been given to their production.

The classification of wine in the whole area is thor-
ough and easily comprehended. The Médoc is divided into
Haut Médoc and Médoc—the *vignerons* of the western reaches
having objected to the original name Bas-Médoc. All the finer
wines come from the Haut Médoc which is divided into
separate communes, twenty-nine in all, each containing a
number of Châteaux, some producing great, others ordinary
wines. The nomenclature is simple to grasp. Margaux is a
commune which contains the Château Margaux. Four of
Margaux's neighbors, including Cantenac, are also allowed
to label their lesser wines as Margaux. The name St.-Julien
*tout court* in a wine list might not promise greatly, but the
commune of St.-Julien contains the Léovilles, Langoa, Tal-
bot and Beychevelle.

In 1855 a committee of Bordeaux experts classified the
clarets of the Médoc into five growths. The list is set out in
an appendix to this book. Only four wines were included
among the first growths: Lafite, Margaux, Latour and Haut-
Brion, which was added later and is not actually a Médoc
wine but a red Graves. The classification still stands, though
Mouton-Rothschild is now generally regarded as a first growth.
The wine brokers who drew up the list arranged it in terms of
the prices that the various vineyards had received over the
years. They assumed that "the higher the price the better the

wine" was a sound yardstick and in recent years Mouton-
Rothschild has often fetched a higher price than the four
first growths. The placing of a wine in the fifth growth does
not suggest that the wine is fifth rate. Only a professional
could detect the difference in quality between a Pontet-Canet
that is classified as a fifth growth and a Brane-Cantenac
that is classified as a second growth.

An experienced palate should however be able to detect the difference between a classed and an unclassed Médoc.
Not that the wines which are sold as Pauillac, St.-Julien or
Médoc are not excellent. There are no poor wines in the
Médoc. Some of the grapes come from small proprietors who
sell to a co-operative. Some of these vineyards keep their own
names, as Château Loudenne does. Citran and Beauséjour are
also well-known in England.

In addition to Haut-Médoc and Médoc there are Graves,
St. Émilion and Pomerol, and the area between the Dor-
dogne and the Garonne which is known as *Entre Deux Mers*
and produces white wines of little breeding. St. Émilion lists
Château Ausone and Château Cheval Blanc as *Premiers
Grands Crux*.

Graves wines are not accorded the respect that they
deserve. People talk of "Grocer's Graves" and convey by
that a thin, sweetish white wine. Actually more red Graves
is produced than white—880,000 gallons to 330,000 gallons
—and the red Graves include, in addition to Haut-Brion,
Pape-Clément, Smith-Haut-Lafitte, Domaine de Chevalier;
White Graves is often dry. There is Carbonnieux and I remember Margaret Lane offering me an excellent white Haut-
Brion. I have never seen on a wine list under "Red Wines"
the word Graves *tout court*, but faced with a choice between
Médoc, Pomerol and St. Émilion, I would choose St. Émilion. The district of Pomerol certainly includes Château
Petrus, but St. Émilion includes two of the greatest wines in

the world, Château Ausone and Château Cheval-Blanc. They are heavier than the Médoc wines, and Cheval-Blanc 1921, a freak wine in that very hot summer, tasted like a Burgundy and fetched fantastic prices. It seemed to me much simpler to buy a Burgundy and have done with it. But Cheval-Blanc 1921 was at its peak when "winemanship" was in its fullest flower, 1932-1938. St. Émilion, because of its extra strength, was always popular in England. Henry VIII's courtiers were so fond of it that the vineyard road is paved with the cobblestones that were brought back as ballast to replace the cargo of oak barrels that had sailed from the Dordogne.

Médoc wines are largely made from the *Cabernet* grape; St. Émilion and Pomerol prefer the *Merlot*.

The imprimatur of Château-bottling in the Médoc means more to English and Americans than it does to the French, in the same way that republicans have a greater respect for titles of nobility than those who live under a monarchy, and it should be remembered that Château-bottling is a recent innovation. At the beginning of the nineteenth century, the bottling was done by wine merchants, who put their name upon the bottle. Château-bottling only began when the merchants demanded it, so that they could offer "something very special" to a special customer. Not until 1869 was an entire vintage of Lafite Château bottled.

There is another point, too, that we should not forget: that the very bottling of wine is not of such long standing. We always forget to what extent we take for granted the amenities that would have astonished our grandparents. I can remember staying in houses where candlesticks were left on the hall table to light one to bed. In 1907, my father moved from West Hampstead into a new house on the edge of Hampstead Heath and I remember my excitement at finding myself in a house lit by electricity. I ran from room to room, switching the bulbs on and off. We accept what we find in the world on our arrival in it as having been here from time immemorial. We cannot picture an age that had not discovered the wheel and a boy in his teens today would find it incredible that the bottles of soft drinks were not always fastened with a tin cap, that in 1910 stone ginger-beer was corked and wired and that fizzy lemonade was enclosed in glass bottles by a ball that was forced into position by internal pressure. A schoolboy, lacking the appropriate gadget, opened it with a pencil and the bottle had two flanges to catch the ball when he lifted it to drink. Presumably some museum has an example of this type of bottle, but I doubt if anyone under forty would recognize the purpose of the wooden gadget with which storekeepers pressed down the ball.

When I began to write this book, I was surprised to find how recent an invention is the corkscrew. An ode written in 1732 contains the lines:

*The bottle screw whose worth, whose use*
*All men confess that love the juice:*
*Forgotten sleeps the man to whom*
*We owe the invention, in his tomb.*
*No publick honours grace his name*
*No pious bard records his fame.*

We do not know when the invention came, but it must have been somewhere in the seventeenth century. There was no need for one in the sixteenth. It was not till the close of Elizabeth's reign that they were used in England. Rosalind says to Celia, "I prithee take the cork out of thy mouth that I may drink thy tidings." Beer was bottled in Charles I's reign. Heywood's satire on drunkenness published in 1635 contains a passage about frothing bottles, but the corking of wine bottles was not introduced till early in the eighteenth century.

The lack of corks explains many things that might puzzle the modern student. It might well seem an abuse of privilege that in Elizabeth's reign only a peer or a person of high office could keep wine in his own house, but in point of fact, when wine was bought in barrels, a private citizen with a simple family establishment would have no need for a cask in his cellar. It would go bad before he could finish it. It pays very few Englishmen today to keep beer on draught. I made the experiment before the second war when we had frequent week-end guests, but even then it proved more trouble than it was worth. An Elizabethan of modest means could only need a cask of wine if he were trading it to his friends, or if he were using his house as a Club, perhaps to further some conspiracy. It is only in the last two hundred years that, through the use of bottles and corks, we have learned how to mature wines in bottle. Three hundred years ago wines were drunk young, usually within a year of their fermentation; if they were left in cask, there must have been evaporation and the casks must have been replenished, possibly with wine of the same vintage. The use of corks revolutionized the world of wine. I am surprised that so few writers on wine have stressed this fact. The aged wines that we drink today are very different from those which the Elizabethans drank, and very certainly are a great deal better, whereas the sherry to which Falstaff devoted such attention—because it is a fortified wine—is much the same as we drink now.

The imprint and date on the cork of a Château-bottled wine gives a guarantee that no other wine can have. It is a birth certificate. If the cork reads: CHÂTEAU MARGAUX/GRAND VIN 1929/MIS EN BOUTEILLE AU CHÂTEAU, with a picture of the Château itself, you are assured that that wine was made from grapes grown from the vines of Château Margaux in that year. You have not that guarantee with any other kind of wine, except with certain estate-bottled hocks and Burgundy, and in the case of hocks the nomenclature is so complicated and the range of sensation so great that even a professional cannot be sure of the precise flavor he is going to enjoy.

Château-bottling is one of the charms of claret drinking. You can taste the wine of one Château against that of another. You can memorize the dates and in retrospect compare the bouquet of one with that of another. In the 1930's, a certain kind of guest felt insulted if the wine you offered him was not Château-bottled. In the United States the distinction is still valid. It is a major project to ship wines in wood across the Atlantic and there are at present inadequate facilities for bottling imported wines. Moreover, the memory of Prohibition remains. Where bottles were tampered with, what may not happen to a cask? In point of fact I do not remember ever seeing in America an imported wine that had not been bottled in the country of its origin.

In England the situation has changed. Firstly, there is a very great difference in the cost of wines that have been imported in bottle and in wood. Secondly, the Channel is narrow and we ask ourselves why a competent London or Bristol merchant should not import hogsheads and bottle his wine himself. He may even bottle it better than the owner of a vineyard, who has so many other things with which to be concerned. Some individuals indeed buy their wine in casks.

The Belgians are great lovers of Burgundy and if a bottle of Chambertin is Liège-bottled its merit is enhanced. Of the classed wines of the Médoc Pontet Canet never indulged in Château-bottling, and Langoa-Barton have. Château-bottling is a guarantee of authenticity but so is the name of a good wine merchant. There is no more honorable profession. It is inconceivable that firms like Justerini & Brooks, Dolamore, Hankey Bannister and a hundred others could buy a hogshead of Château Latour and sophisticate it with Domaine de la

Trappe. It is possible that in England a virtue is being made out of necessity; we are so anxious that the cheaper wine should be as good as the expensive, that we are trying to persuade ourselves that it is. But I do think that fewer and fewer Château-bottled wines will be seen in England during the last half of the century, unless the laws are altered.

The Bordeaux area produces nearly two-thirds of the entire output of France—80 million gallons—in comparison to Burgundy's half a million gallons. Bordeaux not only produces red wines, but a great deal of white, some of inferior quality which cannot stand comparison as a table wine with that of Burgundy, Alsace, the Rhine, the Moselle, or Switzerland. It is as well to avoid any bottle of white Graves or Bordeaux that is not labelled *appellation controlée*. But the Médoc also produces the great Sauternes. Château d'Yquem is a wine that is set apart by itself, as a grand first growth. But Peyraguey, Rayne-Vigneau, Rieussec are only less good because d'Yquem is more than good and they are classified as first growths. It is surprising to find Filhot marked down into the second class. Sauternes has an exquisite golden color, and an immense fragrance. It is sweet and strong and must be sipped very slowly. Sauternes is made in a special way. The vintage is late and the leaves are stripped from the vines so that the grapes can enjoy the last gleam of sunlight. The grapes are allowed to ripen till the skin has begun to shrivel, till only a few drops of juice remain and what is called a *pourriture noble* is achieved. The wines have sometimes as much as 17 per cent alcohol. The grapes are picked with the greatest care. The laborers will go over the vines six or seven times, leaving behind every grape that needs an extra day of sunshine. The production of these vineyards is small and Château-bottling is essential.

The story has been told that d'Yquem's excellence was

discovered by mistake. The owner of the Château Marquis de Lur-Saluces had to leave his estate before the time of vintage. He gave instructions that nothing was to be done till he came back. He was delayed and on his return was horrified to find that his orders had been carried out literally and that the shriveled grapes were rotten on their stems. He shrugged and decided to make the best of a bad job. To his astonishment and delight the resultant wine was of an altogether different quality from anything that he had tasted. It was unique in color, richness, scent and flavor.

Chemists have since discovered that this excellence is due to the activity of a mold called *Botrytis*, whose filaments can pierce the skin of the grape and draw off the water, without damaging the taste of the wine. The remaining juice has 60 per cent of sugar. The *Botrytis* is the fruit-grower's greatest enemy but it is responsible for the particular richness of Sauternes and certain Rhineland wines. Normally grapes are picked before the *Botrytis* can get to work on them. It is from the *Sauvignon Blanc* and the *Sémillon* grape that the great Sauternes are made.

In poor years the great Châteaux do not accord the imprimatur of Château-bottling. They use their grapes for blending, to be sold as Sauternes or Barsac. I was once sold by my very good friend John Knight of Dolamore's an excellent bottle simply labeled Barsac; but normally the risk of ordering an unguaranteed bottle is too great.

Sauternes is out of favor at the moment. There is a prejudice against sweet wines and it is, or should be, very sweet. Perhaps cigarette-smoking and dry Martinis have blunted the palate for it. If one is ordered off alcohol for a little, one usually finds oneself wanting to drink chocolate and ice cream sodas. I do not smoke, I ration myself on Martinis and I like Sauternes, but it is a difficult wine to serve, both because some of one's guests may not like it and

because you can take only a very little of it at a time.
Eighty years ago it was the fashion to serve it with the fish
course, but it is too heavy and too sweet to take so early in a
meal. It kills the red wine that should accompany the roast
or game. It should come at the end of the meal with the
sweet course or with fruit, possibly instead of port. In England the majority of men prefer vintage port, and though the
Saintsbury Club owns some d'Yquem 1921 our cellarer re-
fuses to serve it at our dinners because the majority of our
members prefer port and there is no other point in a short
meal where it can be placed.

Usually, when I am in New York, I give a dinner-party
for eight, at the Châteaubriand. Eight is the right number
for a bottle of Sauternes, a glass to each. But Monsieur
Hounie shakes his head when I suggest it. "I think your
guests would like a Moselle to finish off the meal. Or perhaps champagne." I daresay he is right, but in the spring of
1958 since Dorothea Biddle and Charles Rolo were among
my guests, I overruled him, and ordered a d'Yquem 1949.
Charles Rolo was, I fancy, noncommittal but Mrs. Biddle
and I were delighted with the result.

I do not drink nearly as much Sauternes nowadays as
I would like too. I cherish particularly those friends who
share my taste for it, one especially. During the first blitz in
London, she lived in a flat near mine, in Buckingham Street,
and once or twice a week we would dine at Boulestin's,
which was only five minutes' walk away and deep underground. Not many people were dining out in London at that
time, the full effects of rationing had not been felt, and
Boulestin's excellent cellar was intact. We always finished
our dinner with a half-bottle of Rayne-Vigneau. We sipped
it slowly, appreciatively, lingering over its excellence, lingering longer perhaps because we did not know what manner
of tornado awaited us in the street above.

More fine wine comes from Bordeaux than from any other part of the world. Maurice Healy with typical Healian exaggeration remarked that while you will, drink only four or five bottles of truly first-class Burgundy in your whole life you can drink claret of the highest class several times in the year, claret that should be drunk kneeling.

The discerning who can afford to indulge their preferences have always insisted upon drinking the best claret, no matter what it cost.

William and Mary, the Hanoverians that followed them and the Whig politicians who served their interests did their best with restrictive legislation to drive French wine from the British table. Ordinarily tastes follow taxes. The war of the Austrian succession, for example, so damaged the sales of Spanish wine in England that while in 1734 over 9,000 tuns were imported, the year 1749 only required 5,000 tuns; after that the sale rarely exceeded 3,000 tuns. A taste once lost is not easily recovered. Before the First World War Turkish cigarettes were very popular in London. During the war they were unobtainable and the English developed a taste for American tobacco. In the late 1940's the distillers of Scotch whisky were afraid that the English would lose their taste for it, so hard was it to obtain, and that a generation would grow up with a preference for gin; which in fact it seems to have done.

This fate never befell claret. The aristocrats continued to drink it, though it is not certain whether they filled their cellars with wine on which duty had been paid or with wines that had been smuggled. The smuggler was a popular hero of the century and the long low beaches of Lincolnshire offered him ample opportunities for his activities. In Scotland the supporters of the Stuarts passed their claret glasses over their finger bowls and drank to their King across the water.

The superiority of French wine was never questioned. A doggerel verse-writer in 1720 was referring to

*"Foreign wines of every sort,*
*From costly French to common port."*

Swift was writing at about the same time to Stella, "I love white Portuguese wine better than claret. . . . I have a sad vulgar appetite."

Claret during the eighteenth century may be compared with Beluga caviar in the 1950's. We all know how good caviar is, but we can rarely afford it. In 1784, whereas 12,642 tuns of Portuguese and 3,319 tuns of Spanish wines came into England, France and the Rhineland only supplied 882 and 178 tuns respectively. But the high excellence of Bordeaux wines was never questioned.

A few years ago I was offered a pleasant assignment by the House of Gilbey. In 1957 the firm celebrated its centenary and I was invited to write its history. The assignment was pleasant not only because it brought me into close touch with four extremely sympathetic families, the Gilbeys, the Grinlings, the Blyths and the Golds, in whose hands the fortunes of the firm have rested since its start, but because it taught me a great deal about wine, particularly about claret. The late Sir James O'Connor once remarked, "If you know nothing about a subject and want to learn, sit down and write a book about it." And in writing the Gilbeys' centenary volume I learned much.

The firm began in the simplest way after the Crimean War in 1856, when two young men, Walter and Alfred Gilbey, who as civilian clerks had been employed uncomfortably, if unromantically, over their desks in the pay department of the army base at Gallipoli, returned to England to found their fortunes. They came of sound Essex stock, but they were penniless. Their father had been a coach-proprietor on the London-Bishop's Stortford run, and like Sam Weller's father had been ruined by the steam locomotive. He had refused to believe that there could be any competition from a form of transport that "wouldn't stop to pick up passengers." When he died in 1842 he left his family nothing but his name and an example. The example was more valuable than the name. For if the success of the House of Gilbey can be attributed to any one characteristic, it is to an instinctive ability to anticipate change and adapt its policy and program to it.

When the Crimean campaign ended, Walter Gilbey was twenty-six years old and Alfred twenty-four. Since their elder brother Henry Parry was employed with a wine firm which still bears an honored name in Oporto, Smith Woodhouse, they decided to go into wine concentrating, so their brother counseled them, on table wines from South Africa. Three years later he would not have given them that advice, for in 1860, just when the young firm was beginning to make headway, Gladstone, indifferent to the claims of the British colonials in the Cape of Good Hope and anxious to encourage French economy, decided to reduce the duty on French wines from twelve shillings a dozen to two.

It is curious to compare this act of Gladstone's with that of Sir Stafford Cripps eighty years later. One does not associate either with an atmosphere of hilarity, though I have been assured not only by his friends but his acquaintances, which in the last analysis is more revealing, that in his family Cripps was witty, lively, gay and that his self-imposed austerity was the outcome not of choice but a weak digestion whose frailty was accentuated during the First World War. Cripps, as Chancellor of the Exchequer, reduced duty on French table wines imported in bulk and thereby made daily wine-drinking a possible habit for families of moderate means.

## ✤ *The Wines of Bordeaux* ✤

In January, 1958 I traveled to New York in the *Queen Mary* with Everard Gates, an old friend of the cricket field, who was M.P. for Midleton and Prestwick from 1941 until 1953. He told me that he was the only Conservative who went on a Parliamentary mission to Bordeaux shortly after the war when a Labor government was in power. The Labor members of the mission were at the start strongly "against wine." They thought it "flim-flam" and a rich man's luxury. But when they realized how much the economy of France and the happiness of the French workers depended on it, how "democratic" in fact it was, they resolved that "Stafford must do something about this"; and the duty on French wines was lowered.

From Gladstone's budget the Cape wine trade received a blow from which it did not recover for three-quarters of a century. The extent to which Gladstone's budget altered the drinking habits of the English can be judged by comparing the kind of hospitality offered by Dickens's characters in the middle of the century with that offered at its close in George and Weedon Grossmith's *The Diary of a Nobody.* There is not a great deal of wine drunk by Dickens's characters. They are for beer and grogs, punches and mulled brews. It was on Brandy and water that Mr. Jorrocks and James Pigg made the classic discovery that the night was "hellish dark and smelled of cheese," though it was, admittedly, "old port—claret—good—very good," at the cricket dinner at Dingley Dell, according to Mr. Jingle, that made Mr. Snodgrass look so poorly. "It wasn't the wine," murmured Mr. Snodgrass in a broken voice, "it was the salmon."

Mr. Pooter on the other hand, the Grossmiths' "Nobody," a suburban member of the less affluent white-collar class, half a century later, invariably entertains his guests with champagne. Port and sherry are on his sideboard. The champagne that he acquires from his grocer is labeled "Jackson Frères," it is non-vintage but it costs only three shillings sixpence a bottle. Sherry, "dry and nut," is one shilling threepence. Whisky is offered at two shillings sixpence with twopence back on the bottle. But it is only because he has a cold that Mr. Pooter orders whisky.

Robert Druitt's *Report on the Cheap Wine*, published in 1865, is interesting in this connection. Smith was a Doctor of Medicine and he was concerned with the effects these changes would have on the health of the nation. "One thing," he argues, "that should go with the greater use of Bordeaux wine would be the custom of drinking it in its proper place *during dinner* as a refreshing and appetizing draught, to entice the languid palate to demand an additional slice of mutton. . . . Now we can say, 'Drink what you please at dinner, but don't sit and drink after dinner.' "

In between the passing of Gladstone's budget and the publication of *The Diary of a Nobody*, a pestilence was to strike the vineyards of France, the *phylloxera vastatrix*, a species of vine louse. Eventually the scourge was beaten, first by soaking the soil with sulpho-carbonate and later by grafting European vines onto North American stock which had become largely immune to the phylloxera, but many vineyards were destroyed before recovery was completed, particularly those vineyards which were not backed with capital. In 1884, Alfred Gilbey wrote in his diary, "The sad state of affairs in the Bas-Médoc on the properties of the smallholders, in comparison with the healthy and productive appearance of the vineyards adjoining large estates, would afford the strongest argument which could be adduced against the establishment in England of small peasant proprietors as a measure against the present agricultural depression," and two years later he was to write, "The small number of properties in the Bas-Médoc which have escaped destruction could be counted on two hands." Eventually the pest was eliminated and the slopes of the Médoc were green again, but no great wines were produced till 1899 and the economy of the country sustained a greater loss than it did from the Franco-Prussian war.

The pest struck in 1879, and experts hold that it was not till 1899 that a vintage was produced to equal the great years of '74, '75, '77 and '78. Moreover, the new wines are shorter-lived than the pre-phylloxera ones. There cannot be many pre-phylloxera wines left in the world today. I have never owned any myself. In the 1930's, I drank several bottles of '75 at Vyvyan Holland's house; they were magnificent; and in 1952, when I visited Château Loudenne, I was offered Margaux '75 from the Château's private cellar. It was still magnificent, but twelve bottles were opened before six were found that satisfied the exacting standard of Camille Gombeau, the guardian of the Château. The wines of 1929, if there are still any left, may not be alive at the turn of the century. Very certainly the 1952's will not be. There is a change today in the methods of wine-making: account has had to be taken of the fact that men can no longer lay down wines and forget about them for twenty years. Bordeaux wines have to be made that can be drunk between four and six years old, which can be arranged without destroying claret's claim to be a natural wine. It is not a question of employing chemicals, but of discarding through the *égrappoir* the husks and stalks which give the wine a harsh flavor at the start but insure its liveliness in age. The fermentation is also hastened by a different period of exposure to the air.

There are always those who will praise past times in preference to the new, and in the '30's my older friends always assured me that there was no comparison between the wines that we were drinking then and the '75's and '77's that they had enjoyed when they were young. In 1936, tasting a '75 against a '20 I could not see that superiority. But I am not an expert.

In the 1880's the reputation of claret admittedly stood low, not only as a result of the phylloxera. Two other considerations, the prevalance of cigarette-smoking and a taste for whisky—particularly the medical belief in the curative efficiency of whisky—had their effect on English habits. In the eighteen-sixties the English had indulged in the habit, very puzzling to the French, of drinking their best claret after the meal. In Saintsbury's *Notes on a Cellar Book* the menus of the eighteen-sixties invariably have a red wine following champagne, though preceding port. And Frank Harris, who, though not the most reliable of witnesses, has his value as a guide to the social habits of the *Fin de Siècle,* refers in *My Life and Loves* to the abandonment during the nineties of the habit of drinking claret after dinner. He attributes this to the emancipation of women, and their refusal to allow their husbands to "sit and soak" over their glasses till their servants carried them away. This is no doubt partly true, but the cigarette played an important part. A cigarette affects the palate and removes the wish to drink anything as delicate as claret. Virginia Cowles, in her account published in 1956 of *The Life and Lively Times of Edward VII,* puts as early as the eighteen-seventies the decline of port-drinking after dinner—what is true of port was true of claret. The Prince of Wales, she records, was the first host to permit smoking in the dining room—after the ladies had withdrawn, of course—instead of restricting it to special smoking-rooms, to be enjoyed only in quilted jackets and with a tasseled cap to protect the hair from the smell of tobacco. Cognac stood up better than port to the rich, oily smell of Havana leaf, and cognac—Miss Cowles suggests —began as long ago as that to usurp some of the after-dinner status of port.

André Simon gives another reason for the diminished consumption of claret, a reason that was a direct corollary to the phylloxera attack. Good red wine was scarce in the eighteen-eighties, and what little there was should have been expensive, but a number of short-sighted shippers, in order to retain their customers, supplied inferior wines at the ear-lier price. The poor quality of this wine destroyed the con-fidence both of the wine buyers and the public. Moreover, at the very time when the scourge of the phylloxera was render-ing difficult the enjoyment of good claret, dry champagne was making its first appearance on the market.

The story of champagne is told in a later chapter, and students of *The Forsyte Saga* will remember how in the first volume, *The Man of Property* which was set in the late 1880's, champagne was the invariable table wine.

Claret was not restored to its high position till the Edwardian era.

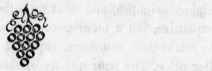

# THE AGE OF PORT

I**T WAS** 1688; the days of civil war were over; the Stuarts were in exile, the Papists in hiding.

"There followed," wrote Geoffrey, "a time of security for England, a time of German kings and contempt for France, of fox-hunting squires and comfortable churchmen, of coarse manners and cruel sports, of slow thinking and fast living, of Georgian houses and great gardens. This was the age of port."

The Englishman and his port; what a world of Galsworthian tradition those five words evoke: of London clubs, and college common rooms and "stately homes"; the pipe laid down at a son's christening, the cool dark cellars where the wine matures, the ritual of decanting, the bottle carried from the bin with cradling care, the funnel in the decanter's mouth, the light under the shoulder of the bottle; finally the strict conventions of the actual drinking, the decanter that must pass always to the left—clockwise, or the way of the sun—the cigarette that must remain unlighted.

Many tributes have been paid in literature to this noble wine. George Meredith's in *The Egoist* is the happiest, and a wine merchant might do worse than send to his customers as a Christmas card the twentieth chapter of that now neglected comedy. It has the much-quoted phrase in reference to the crust that great wines throw: "Old wine, my friend, denies us the full bottle." A phrase that is followed by the perfect duologue between guest and host:

"Another bottle is to follow."

"No!"

"It is ordered."

"I protest."

"It is uncorked."

"I entreat."

"It is decanted."

"I submit."

The perfect juxtaposition of pressure, reluctance and gracious, grateful and well-timed surrender.

The same chapter contains the happiest definition of a cellar: "Cellars are not catacombs. They are, if rightly constructed, rightly considered, cloisters where the bottle meditates on joys to bestow, not on dust misused."

But it is in his weighing of the separate excellences of port and Burgundy that Meredith crosses the borderline between prose and poetry.

"Hocks, too, have compassed age. I have tasted senior hocks. Their flavors are as a brook of many voices: they have depth also. Senatorial port! we say. We cannot say that of any other wine. Port is deep-sea deep. It is in its flavor deep; mark the difference. It is like a classic tragedy, organic in conception. An ancient Hermitage has the light of the antique; the merit that it can grow to an extreme old age; a merit. Neither of Hermitage nor of hock can you say that it is the blood of those long years, retaining the strength of youth with the wisdom of age. To port for that! Port is our noblest legacy! Observe, I do not compare the wines: I distinguish the qualities. Let them live together for our enrichment; they are not rivals like the Idean three. Were they rivals, a fourth would challenge them. Burgundy has great genius. It does wonders within its period; it does all except to keep up in the race; it is short-lived. An aged Burgundy runs with a beardless port. I cherish the fancy that port speaks the sentences of wisdom. Burgundy sings the inspired ode. Or put it, that port is the Homeric hexameter, Burgundy the Pindaric dithyramb. What do you say?"

"The comparison is excellent, sir."

"The distinction, you should remark. Pindar astounds. But his elder brings us the more sustaining cup. One is a fountain of prodigious assent. One is the unsounded purple sea of marching billows."

It is generally held that the age of port began with the signing of the Methuen Treaty which admitted Portuguese wines, in return for certain concessions with regard to English woolens on a duty of seven pounds a tun whereas French wines had to pay fifty-five pounds. But André Simon has argued that the Methuen Treaty did not so much create a taste as continue and confirm one. He quotes from the poems "In Search of Claret" published in 1691 and "Farewell to Claret" published in 1693.

*"Some claret, boy!"*
*"Indeed, Sir, we have none.*
*Claret, Sir. Lord! There's not a drop in town.*
*But we have the best red port."*
*"What's that you call red port?"*
*"A wine, Sir, comes from Portugal.*
*I'll fetch a pint, Sir."*

To the author the change was far from welcome.

*"But now—with what regret the now I name*
*The wine we drink is now no more the same . . .*
*Mark how it smells, methinks a real pain*
*Is by its odor thrown upon the brain*
*Fetch me a pint of any sort*
*Navarre, Galicia, anything but port."*

Alexis Lichine, author of *The Wines of France*, however, is of the opinion that Bordeaux wines had at this time lost their quality and the English would no longer drink them. And it may well be that when the three hundred years' connection between Gascony and England was severed there was a deterioration in the wine. It is a point on which it is impossible to be certain at this late date. What is certain is that before the Methuen Treaty, England was starting to drink port.

In 1648, so we are assured by that sound historian, F. A. Cockburn, two young sons of an English wine merchant who had been sent to Portugal to learn the business, were entertained at a local monastery outside Oporto with a wine that so delighted them that they shipped back to their father as much of it as they could buy, having fortified it first with brandy; it had a considerable success.

Moreover the traditional source of supply through Devonshire had been resumed when the brief unhappy period of Spanish rule was ended. The Devon traders still took their penitential cod to Portugal; Portugal was a colonial power before England was, and at the start of the sixteenth century they had exchanged their woolens and salt fish for sugar and colonial products; but when England herself owned colonies in the Caribbean which supplied her with spices, sugar and ebony, the Devonians took wine instead.

It is hard to tell at this distance of time how much the

lessened demand for claret at the end of the seventeenth century was due to changing taste, to economic causes, to political pressure. A mixture of all three, most likely, with patriotism playing a definite if minor part.

Patriotism takes strange shapes. During the Spanish Civil War of 1936, English supporters of the elected government refused to drink sherry. At that time, a member of the Savile Club wanted me to sign a letter suggesting that patriots, instead of asking for "Gin and It," should ask for "Gin and Imp"—for Imperial rather than Italian vermouth. In the First World War it was considered unpatriotic in France and England to drink German wines, although the wines had been bought before the war, and might go bad if they were kept. The Saintsbury Club owned in 1939 some very fine German wines. André Simon on his own authority had them sold for the Red Cross to remove a blot from our cellars. In the eighteenth century, Swift was writing:

*Be sometime to your country true,*
*Have once the public good in view.*
*Bravely despise Champagne at Court,*
*And choose to dine at home with Port.*

It is curious though that he should have been talking of "Champagne at Court"—in view of the Hanoverian dislike of everything French.

The Methuen Treaty was aimed at killing the taste for light French wines and making the English drink Portuguese wines instead. It failed in this latter respect. It may certainly have driven a final nail into the coffin of the general public's interest in claret, but it did not replace French table wines with Portuguese for the simple reason that nobody much liked them. They were not very good; even today it is very hard to find Portuguese wines that are palatable. A few weeks ago in the Braganza restaurant in Soho I was given a *rosé* wine, Mateus Rosé, slightly *pétillant*, that I found most agreeable, but in Portugal during a week's stay when I was the guest of the wine trade, the wine that I most enjoyed was a light, young greenish wine with an alcoholic content of nine per cent. I found the strong red table wines rough and harsh; but perhaps I should have drunk them with the heavy, oleaginous bean stews that are the traditional fare of the workers in the vineyards.

The young merchants to whom Mr. Cockburn referred had fortified their wine before shipping it and though the wines that Portugal shipped to Britain may have been indexed as beverage, by the time they passed the lips of county squires they had become a highly fortified post-prandial brew.

Samuel Johnson said, "Claret is the liquor for boys, port for men, but he who aspires to be a hero must drink brandy." But there is no reason to consider him a qualified judge of anything but the alcoholic content of what he drank. His port was sweetened with sugar, laced with brandy and then warmed. They called this blackstrap "Negus."

A certain Dr. Fenner made the ingenious suggestion that the name "Negus" may have a punning connection with the line in *Paradise Lost* (xi, 397)—"Th' Empire of Negus to his utmost port," but there is little doubt that the christening of the eighteenth-century concoction was a tribute to the reputation of Colonel Francis Negus who died in 1732.

In his day he was a man of considerable distinction. From 1685 to 1688 he was secretary to the Duke of Norfolk and in that capacity made the acquaintance of Elias Ashmole. He served in the French wars under Marlborough, reaching the rank of Lieutenant-Colonel in the Twenty-fifth, or Suffolk Regiment of Foot. In 1715 he was appointed Joint-Commissioner, and on June 25, 1717 Sole Commissioner, for executing the office of Master of the Horse, an office which he held until the death of George I.

He was appointed Clerk-Marshal to George II on June 20, 1727 and Master of His Majesty's Buckhounds on July 19 of the same year. He represented Ipswich in Parliament from 1717 until his death, which occasioned a copy of verses in the Ipswich Gazette, beginning: "Is Negus gone? Ah! Ipswich, weep and mourn!"

He was also Ranger of Swinley Chase, Lieutenant and Ranger of Windsor Forest and one of the Commissioners of the Lieutenancy of Middlesex and Liberty of Westminster.

He was a man of tact and on one occasion when the bottle was passing more rapidly than good fellowship seemed to warrant, over a hot political discussion in which a number of prominent Whigs and Tories were taking part, he averted a fracas by recommending the dilution of the wine with hot water and sugar. Attention was diverted from the question at issue to a discussion of the merits of wine and water which ended in the compound being nicknamed "Negus."

A correspondent of the *Gentlemen's Magazine* (1799, i., 119) stated that the term first obtained currency in Negus's regiment. A contemporary, Thomas Vernon of Ashton (1704-1753) thus recommends the mixture: "After a morning's walk, half a pint of white wine made hot and sweetened is reckoned very good. Col. Negus, a gentleman of taste, advises it, I have heard say." (Notes & Queries, 1st. Series, x. 10). Malone, in his *Life of Dryden,* definitely states that the mixture called "Negus" was invented by Colonel Negus in Queen Anne's time.

Johnson and Boswell each drank a bottle of Negus every night, and most evenings they would order an extra bottle which they would divide. When Boswell complained of the bad effects this heavy drinking was having on him, a friend assured him that it was better to be palsied at eighteen than not keep company with such a man.

Those were the days of three-bottle men, when most dinner parties ended with the men under the table. On one occasion an author who was anxious to continue his work next day simulated drunkenness and slid to the floor. He soon felt a pair of small hands at his throat, and heard a treble voice whisper, "Sir, I'm the lad that's sent to loosen the neckcloths." Raymond Postgate wrote, "Our ancestors who spent whole days fox-hunting were three-bottle men no doubt, but we don't live their lives, also they died young, purple or yellow, gouty, savage-tempered and inflamed; the memoirs of the eighteenth century are full of the results of port-drinking."

There are many reasons why a man could wish he had been born in the eighteenth century instead of in the twentieth, but none why a wine-lover should. The eighteenth century is indeed the dark age of wine, the day of the barbarian. And yet out of evil, good emerged—the discovery of the port that we enjoy today.

At first, the wines of Oporto were less palatable and sold more cheaply than those from Lisbon, although the wines of the Douro were richer in sugar at the time of the vintage. It was eventually recognized that because of this excess of sugar, the must fermented too fast, in fact fermented itself right out. There was only one remedy: to check fermentation with alcohol, but when such drastic measures are taken, the wine has to be allowed to mature. For several years after it has been fortified, it is undrinkable.

A new process was demanded. Such wine could not be casually sophisticated as the beverage wines had been, the taste softened with treacle, the color deepened with elderberries. It had to mature either in cask or bottle, and it was lucky that the discovery of a bottle that could be binned coincided with this need for a new technique. A bottle in which wine matures must lie on its side so that the cork is in contact with the liquid, otherwise the cork will grow dry and shrink. The right kind of bottle was evolved only in 1780. Up till then bottles were squat, short-necked, wide in the beam so that they could stand firmly on the table. Without a bottle suitable for binning, there would have been no vintage port.

There are today two main types of port: port which has matured in bottle and port which has matured in wood. Two kinds of port are matured in bottle: vintage and crusted port. Vintage port is the wine of a particularly good year which is kept in wood for two years in Oporto, then shipped to England where it is bottled and put away to rest, remote from noise, light, vibration and changes of temperature, to acquire merit during ten, twenty, thirty, maybe fifty years. During the period of rest, it throws a crust inside the bottle, and great care has to be taken over its decanting. It must be carried from the bin to the decanting shelf in a wicker basket, so that it may be held horizontally all the time. A glass or silver filter must be used. Very often the cork breaks. When it does the wine can be strained through muslin but there are many who deplore its use. A light needs to be held under the neck of the bottle to watch for the moment when the wine ceases to flow clearly. It cannot be poured to the last drop.

How long the wine should be kept in the cellar is a doubtful point. It was believed when I was young that vintage port had to be twenty years old. But things have changed since the second war. Such wine as was then available was drunk too quickly. In 1945 there was a universal shortage. And people were reluctant to lock up their capital, if they had any spare to lock up, in an uncertain period.

Most of us began to drink younger port. Those who did excused themselves by quoting the author of the Ingoldsby legends, the Rev. R. H. Barham—

*Though Port should have age,*
*Yet I don't think it sage*
*To entomb it, as some of your connoisseurs do,*
*Till it's losing its flavour, and body, and hue;*
*I question if keeping it does much good*
*After ten years in bottle and three in the wood.*

—while those who withheld their wine contended that their patience has been rewarded.

I am writing this chapter in October, 1957. When I am at Edrington I drink Dow's 1924 and Cockburn's 1927. They are both excellent. When I tasted the Cockburn in 1938, it seemed a little raw. I foolishly did not lay down either the '34 or '35. But Lear-wise I gave to each of my sons six dozen of Crofts 1945, which I hope that they will share with me. My younger son opened one of his bottles the other day, and we agreed that it was not ready yet. On the other hand, two or three years ago I tried some Graham's 1942 at Pratt's and was delighted. I gave a dozen bottles of Croft's '45 to the Saintsbury Club. I am curious to know when our cellarer André Simon will decide to open it.

Crusted port which is sometimes described as vintage character, is also matured in bottle, but it is not made from the grapes of a single year. It is a mixture of several wines, bottled after four or five years in wood. It has no guarantee of quality, except the shipper's name, which in the case of port is adequate. It is often excellent but it is a cheaper wine and of a definitely lower order. It throws a crust and needs to be decanted carefully.

Wood port, as its name implies, matures in cask and includes the *porto* which is drunk as an *apéritif* in France, the ruby wine which is offered in saloon bars to young ladies who ask for a "Port and Lemon" and the magnificent tawny port, rich in age and color, which so perfectly with cheese and a slice of cake rounds off a lunch party. There is also white port, which is served in Portugal and in France as an *apéritif*. When chilled it is pleasant on the palate; but it is idle to pretend that it is a substitute for sherry; served with soda water it can make, on a hot day, an agreeable alternative to the "Hock and Seltzer" that the early Victorians favored. Between ruby and tawny port, the difference is only one of age. Both are blended wines to insure a uniformity of taste and color. Ruby is seven or eight years old, tawny port is twelve. Ruby is said to improve in bottle, tawny does not, and in fact deteriorates occasionally. In the past, tawny port was "manufactured" by blending ruby and white port, but such practices are uncommon now.

In Britain no wine can be sold as port that has not been made from grapes grown in the geographically limited region of the Douro and shipped from Oporto with a certificate of origin and from the Instituto do Vinho do Porto. The Portuguese are very jealous of their high reputation. A winegrower is fined forty shillings if an elder tree is found near his vineyard and imprisonment is the penalty for mixing berries with grapes. The Portuguese travel office in New York issues a pamphlet with the following statement about port:

Port is a wine fortified with wine brandy through a process that can be duplicated in any other wine-growing country. The qualities responsible for port's taste come, however, fundamentally from the climate, soil and other conditions under which the grapes are grown in the Douro Valley. It is on such ground that the Douro growers claim their rights as sole producers of an exclusive type of wine whose reputation they built through over three centuries of trade.

Their claims have been subject to controversy and are not fully respected, as a consequence, in a few countries. One of the drawbacks of the Douro as a wine-producing region is, however, the very low yield of its vineyards. Quality in the Douro is opposed to abundance. Yields are therefore considerably lower than in almost all other wine-growing regions of the world.

AVERAGE YIELDS PER ACRE, IN GALLONS

Douro region ........................120
Portugal ...........................158
California ..........................183
Australia ..........................277
Union of South Africa ...............223

Port could not compete therefore, where wines are offered for consumption under its borrowed name, except through quality.

The pamphlet then explains the position of port in the U.S.A. Genuine port is offered, in the U.S., under the simple designation of port, while all other fortified wines must carry the name of the producing country, as California Port, New York State Port, etc. Consumption of genuine port comes only as a minute fraction of the total.

I was first offered U.S.A. port, in 1951, in California. I reserved judgment because I had no means of knowing how long the bottle had been kept open in a cupboard. When I went to the MacDowell Colony in 1958 to work upon this book, I bought from the New Hampshire liquor store, for $1.30, a bottle of New York State port wine, containing 19 per cent of alcohol. It was a dark brownish-red. I raised it to my nose. It can't taste the way it smells, I thought. It did. The first sip was one of the biggest shocks my palate has sustained. I cannot imagine what I would have thought it was, had I been offered it without a warning. It bore no resemblance to anything, unmedicinal, I have ever tasted. Had I been offered it by someone whom it was essential for venial reasons that I should placate perhaps, I should have had the tact to say, remembering Baghdad's Habdah, "Like something out of the Arabian Nights!"

The sipping of that wine was in one way a sad experience. What a pity, I thought, that a country that enjoys a fortified dessert wine should not pay the few extra cents that are involved and which it can so well afford and savor the pleasures of a really noble wine, particularly when the makers of that wine are such a gay and gallant people whose economy depends so much upon its sale overseas. Moreover there is the danger that young Americans interested in wine who have sampled this concoction, will decide that they do not care for port, thereby depriving themselves of a great pleasure. Yet on the other hand there is this consolation: that New York State, with its great wealth and all the aids of science cannot produce a wine comparable with that which is stamped out by the short-limbed sturdy Portuguese in their dark *lagares*. Great wine is the gift of the Almighty, bestowed capriciously where sun and soil are clement. It is well to be reminded of that now and then.

The Athenians grew tired of hearing Aristides called "the just," and port in its time has been overpraised. In consequence it has had its enemies. It is always well to hear the other side. And no one has put that other side with greater force than Cyril Redding whose book *On Wine* published in 1854 is an often quoted classic.

A certain type of literary critic feels that he can best praise one writer by attacking another. How much praise of Tchekhov in the early twenties was not prefaced by a disparagement of Maupassant's machine-made plots with their punch in the last line (a device that in point of fact he in-

frequently adopted) and Redding, an enthusiastic apprecia-
tor of French wines, attempted to heighten his tribute to them
by an assault on port.

No wine is worthy to be drunk in a highly civilized community which
is not made of grapes alone, carefully selected from vines upon
which practised labor has bestowed the proper culture. . . It would
almost seem as though the Portuguese made their wine a vehicle for
disposing of their brandy. . . no valid excuse has ever been made
for the practice of adding such a quantity of brandy to the wines of
Oporto. . . . The brandy is bad, distilled from figs and raisins of
which no other use could be made.

I have tasted the brandy which is mixed with the must
in the Douro, and fiery most certainly it is. The grape-tread-
ers take it, neat and on an empty stomach, first thing in the
morning, as a stimulus to work. It serves that purpose admirably no doubt, but I should question if it is employed or
employable for any other. The brandy that I drank in the
cafés as a *pousse-café* was very different. It did not strike
me as inferior to the Marc de Bourgogne that I have drunk
in France.

Redding continues his attack on port in the manner of a
school debate, where the speaker's object is less to reveal the
truth than to score laughs and discomfit the opponent with
eloquence and ridicule.

A just proportion of brandy exists in southern wines naturally, and
from the same consequence, in those of Oporto. What is added to
such wines by nature of so much strength must be injurious, and can
never assimilate, as the natural alcohol does, with the wine even during fermentation. The trade may talk of fretting in, "working" and
what not, the commingling is never perfect, and the alcohol un-
combined is so much more noxious to the stomach of the drinker,
who, in fact, drinks not water and brandy, but wine and brandy.
What then, is to be said of the addition of brandy to wine naturally

strong, and that, too, during the process of fermentation when the
must or wine is in the most delicate state of transition and the least
interference is destructive of its quality? This has been done with
the Portuguese wines in the teeth of better knowledge to the extent of
four and five gallons per pipe at the beginning of the present century. Now no less than twelve gallons are thrown in during fermentation! Then, the color of the skin of the grape not being deemed
deep enough, elderberry coloring is added, according to fancy, and
four gallons more of brandy with it. The wine now goes into Oporto,
is racked and receives two gallons more of brandy, and often when
only nine months old is considered fit to go to England, another
gallon of brandy being added on shipping. In all, twenty-four gallons of brandy are added per pipe. . . . When sent thus immature
they are sweetened and softened. . . . This adulterate consists of
dried elderberries, coarse brown sugar and treacle and unfermented
grapejuice.

It is a lively piece of invective but Redding weakens it
when he says that he drank with a Portuguese diplomat a
wine from Oporto, that was natural as opposed to the export wines, *vinhos separados,* which he found excellent, with
"all but the delicacy of France." I do not know what he can
have drunk, but in terms of my own experience I can only
say, "If you think so highly of that wine, your failure to
appreciate vintage port is unimportant, you are an argu-
mentative partisan."

In 1952 I had the good fortune to be one of a group of
writers taken out by Gilbey's to Portugal to see the vintage.

In Oporto we were entertained to dinner at the Factory
House, the hundred-and-fifty-year-old club for the member
firms of the British Association of Port Shippers. Forty of
us sat down to an excellent straightforward dinner; a dry
white port as an *apéritif,* a white Graves preparing the way
for a Pontet-Canet 1929, cheese straws cleaning the palate

for a tawny port. At that point, so the menu informed us, we
were to be offered two vintage ports, a 1917 and a 1927.
The chairman rose to his feet. The bouquet of vintage port
could not, he told us, be properly appreciated in an atmosphere that was tainted with the fumes of food; would we
move into the adjoining room, bringing our napkins with us.
There a second table awaited us, set with forty places.

It was a lovely sight, a gleaming stretch of mahogany
under a cluster of chandeliers, bowls of red roses, high-piled
fruit; a Doulton dessert service, cut-glass decanters, a
cherry-colored carpet to match the china; a delight to the
eye, but an even greater delight to the senses of touch and
smell. It is always difficult, if not impossible, to describe a
physical sensation; it is enough to say that coming into that
cool-fresh room, its air scented with fruit and flowers, I had
the sense of being transported to another planet; a moment
later I was thinking, "I'm living in another century."

It was a feeling that I had often during the next few
days.

Our party was taken to the Quinta da Roeda at Pinhao.
By rail it is under a hundred miles from Oporto, but the road
winds along the steep hills that flank the Douro, rising at the
Marao Pass to a height of three thousand feet, and the
journey took five hours. Much of the countryside appears
barren, with only olive and cork trees flourishing in that
slaty soil—schistose is the geologists' word for it—and
with an occasional pine tossing its feathered headdress. But
as one climbs, one reaches areas of recent afforestation.
There is considerable terracing, and the tiny hamlets on the
way are as charming as they are lovely. Smoke curls
through the tiled roofs of the cottages, scenting the air with
the smell of the brushwood that burns under many an old
iron pot.

Portugal produces a great deal of table wine for its

own consumption, and vineyards line the roads. But by official demarcation the wine of only one small area can carry the name of port; there, the manufacture of the dessert wine is restricted by the Casa do Douro, the official body that controls the district, so as to avoid over-production. Licenses are granted yearly to the farmers, specifying the amount of wine that can be made into port, and the necessary brandy is allocated accordingly.

The wine not made into port remains as table wine, referred to as Douro Consumo, a good deal of which is taken over by the Casa do Douro for distilling into a brandy which will be used, in its turn, for the making of port. Generally speaking, the actual Douro district is divided by the river Corgo, immediately above the chief town of the district, Regoa. Wines from below the Corgo, where quantity is achieved, are referred to as Baixo Corgo. Ports of quality come from Cima Corgo, "above the Corgo."

The Douro district is a narrow stretch of territory, roughly a hundred miles in length. It has been called Portugal's gold ring: if that is so the Quinta da Roeda might be called its diamond, for it lies in the very center of the Cima Corgo.

The word *quinta* means farm, and there is nothing elaborate about any of the *quintas* that you will see dotted along the hillside of the Douro with their names standing out in large black lettering against the long low white-painted walls. Even now, after the extensive rebuilding and replanning of the past thirty years, the Quinta da Roeda is in appearance a modest-seeming property—a one-storied bungalow, set about with outhouses. But the house, offices and staff living quarters are new; the lodge where the wine is made and collected has been rebuilt and extended, and there are new farm buildings and stabling for the oxen. Tunnels have been driven into the side of the hill for water, and pumping machinery lifts water from the river to irrigate the staff's vegetable garden. The *quinta* produces above two hundred pipes of port a year, and about twenty pipes of olive oil.

The permanent staff is small: only about twenty or so, but the dormitories are nearly always full; except for six weeks in late July and August, there is work to be done among the vineyards: the spraying, the weeding, the grafting, the general maintenance of the roads and terraces, and it is one of the peculiarities of the Douro that there should be separate workmen, specially recruited, for each particular operation, and that after their month or six weeks at the *quinta* they should return to their own village to attend to their own fields and spend the money they have earned. For the vintage itself, a mixed gang of men and women is recruited.

The vintage takes place at the beginning of October and it is the region's festal period. For a *quinta* like Roeda, a foreman will collect forty men and women, sometimes from his own, sometimes from neighboring villages. It will be the same foreman every year, bringing the same team with him. They arrive like schoolchildren back for the holidays. They have traveled on foot as much as thirty miles over a rough road; but their entrance will have a ballet-like quality; they will be in two separate lines of men and women in single file: they will move at a quick jog, a musician at their heads, leading them with an accordion, a whistle or a flute. The women will be carrying their personal possessions on their heads in identical wicker baskets under a black shawl, the men carry hoes over their shoulders; they shout and sing and wave as they move into what will be their living quarters for the period of the vintage; the men and women, even if they are married, occupy separate quarters.

This atmosphere of ballet is continued right through the harvest. It is a period of exceedingly hard work: all day long the women are in the vineyards, picking the grapes under the brilliant sun, and they never squat upon their heels. The baskets in which the men carry the grapes to the *lagares* weigh 130 pounds. Whereas in the past wine was made by continual treading, nowadays treading is limited to the "first-cut" treading that pulps the grapes. After that all pressing is done with wooden appliances.

Everything goes to music. The men carrying baskets move in line, at a jog-trot, as Africans do, to keep the weight off their feet, with a musician blowing the time for them on a whistle. There is a special music for the men working in the *lagares,* and in the evenings, when the girls come down and dance till midnight, the music gets keener as the men are refreshed with tots of *bagaciera*—a potent brandy. The vintagers do not only look as though they were having the time of their lives: they are in fact having it. It is the big three weeks of their year. When working for the port shipper, they are better fed than at any other time. They have comfortable quarters: they have their liter of wine with every meal. It is a break with the routine of their existences; they meet old friends and make new ones. It is a great courting time. The joke about "June babies" may not be founded on too strong a basis of fact, but many marriages can trace their origin to the evenings of the *lagares.*

They leave, as they arrive, with an air of ballet. The girls parade before the *quinta,* in single file, their spokesman at their head carries a symbolic wand decorated with grapes and paper flowers (a *Rama*), which she presents to the lady of the house with a flourish of *viva's*—"*Viva Portugal,*" "*Viva Inghliterra,*" "*Viva Quinta da Roeda.*" There is a fine litany of names and finally with a charming candor she shouts *"Viva myself."* I fancy that I shall always enjoy vintage port and the ritual that goes with it the more for having seen the ritual and happiness that are the prelude to its long passage from the stalk upon the vine to the rich dark wine that twenty years later is reverently brought up from the cellar.

The same ritual exists in all the other *quintas*. With one or two exceptions, all the big shippers who are members of the British Association of Port Shippers have their own *quinta*, but they use it as a center of operations, for the amount of wine produced on a shipper's own *quinta* bears little relation to his total requirements, and he buys a great proportion of his yearly total from Douro farmers, often from families he, or his own family, has known for generations. The shipper will usually buy the whole of a farmer's production while it is still on the vine, sending a foreman to superintend the picking of the grapes and the making of the wine.

One of the chief responsibilities of a shipper is the supervision of the various estates. He checks the cleanliness of every piece of equipment in a farmer's property. The *lagar* in which the wine is made, the vats in which it is stored, pumps and all minor pieces of equipment are inspected. In checking the vats the foreman always observes the ritual of putting his head through the small slit in the head of the vat, and beating with his hand, or with a "flogger," upon its side to stir up the air inside, so that he can test its aroma. Any acidity or uncleanliness shows itself immediately. If you followed his example you would be surprised at the extent to which your nostrils would be stung by the powerful bouquet of wine with which the wood is soaked.

There is no equivalent here for the local co-operatives of the Bordeaux districts and it is fascinating in vintage

time as one strolls through a quiet village to turn a corner
and see through a dark archway a couple of peasants treading out their grapes in a stone tank.

Yes, it was all like living in another century. And there
are those who will argue that in the middle of the twentieth
century, in a mechanized age, grapes should not be trodden
by foot, and carried on men's shoulders up and down steep
slopes, that lorries should replace the oxen with the curious
bowler-hat padding between their horns—their harness is so
arranged that they push their load instead of pulling it—
in the same way that lorries and the Douro railway have
largely displaced for the purposes of transportation to
Oporto the curious flat-bottomed square-sailed boats (*bar-
cos rabelos*) that alone, in the old days, could satisfactorily
navigate the shallow Douro and which are now maintained
chiefly for reasons of sentiment. One day the peasants of the
Douro may grow weary of their work in the vineyards; the
young people may want to live in cities, and a shortage of
labor may enforce the installation of machinery. One hopes
that that day is distant. The port might lose its flavor, and
certainly the life of the Douro would be the poorer without
the festal weeks when the grapes are plucked and trodden.

The vintage takes place late in September and early in
October. In February the wine is brought down the river
either by boat or rail to the shippers' lodges at Oporto
which are now concentrated on the south bank of the river at
Vila Nova de Gaia, where it is measured, tasted, analyzed,
blended according to type and to the shipper's requirements,
and then stored in vast vats, some of which hold as much
as two hundred pipes—a pipe contains 672 bottles. Here the
real work begins. If the wine of a certain year is found to be
of exceptional quality and the shipper decides to treat it as
a vintage year, then he will allocate a portion of the vin-

tage, the "pick," to be shipped eighteen months later, to England, to be bottled, the corks being branded with the date and his name.

The shipper has done his task, and much now depends on the bottler's experience and loving care. The bottler rests the wine and chooses the right moment to bottle it. He corks, capsules and waxes the bottles. It takes specialized cellarmen, too, to bin the wine into its resting place, where it will mature quietly in the dark, safe from oxidization, throwing its crust, perhaps for twenty or thirty years.

The bottler of a vintage port should have his bottling completed before the second Christmas following the vintage—in a little over two years from the vintage.

The wine that matures in wood—destined not to be "vintage" port but ruby or, as it loses its color, tawny—presents a very different problem. Oxygen seeps through the wood: the wine loses its alcoholic strength, it needs to be refreshed, it needs something to feed upon, and it has to be replenished with more wine. The problem of the shipper is a constant one: he has to maintain on the market a constant homogeneity of taste and color for his different brands. They must always look and taste the same. Otherwise the customer would reasonably complain that the wine differed in quality or type, bottle from bottle.

This homogeneity can only be maintained by constant care and accurate blending in the hands of experts. It is not till a wine has been eight years in cask that it loses its ruby and gradually acquires its tawny color; until then it is shipped as a ruby port, excellent in its way, but with the inadequacies of all young wines. A tawny port is usually at its greatest after twelve years in wood; by that time even an expert could not tell of what wines it had been blended, and in what proportions. These tawny ports, aged in wood, are lighter than vintage ports, and more popular. Being freshly bottled, they should be ready to serve at any time, in brilliant condition, a pleasure to the eye, as to the palate.

The care of wine in a cask for a dozen years involves endless labor, and it is fascinating to go round the lodges and watch the men at work on their various tasks. You will find two men rocking a cask back and forth. There will be a chain inside the cask, and this, they say, is the best means of cleaning it, for the deposits loosened by the chain are flushed out with jets of boiling water. In the cooperage department half a dozen men will be repairing the casks; they are made by eye out of memel oak, New Orleans oak and native oak, to exact measurements. There is the cooper, one of the most important artisans, who goes around the casks with a light and hammer looking for leakages. He can tell by the sound whether the level of the wine has sunk below the stipulated height: he measures that height with the palms of his hands. Port is always shipped in fresh shipping casks of 117 gallons and a man will be going around with a wide class tube from which he takes samples to sniff the bouquet of the wine and to make sure that it is clear. A lodge like Croft's will keep a hundred and twenty men in permanent employ, and sons succeed fathers for generations.

Tawny port is as different from vintage port as claret is from Burgundy. They are both great wines and they are both expensive, because they involve locking up capital for a long time. I fancy that those who prefer Burgundy to claret will prefer vintage to tawny port. I have always been a Burgundian myself and during my four wineless years in the Middle East during the war, I would reflect on those famous vintages, '22, '24, '27, that were quietly maturing for me in an English cellar.

For me, myself, vintage port is the greatest of all wines. There is so much that is delightful about it, in addition to the actual drinking of it, particularly if you have a cellar. It has in that respect so many advantages over tawny port. There is the storing of it in the first place. Tawny port does not improve in bottle and in fact needs to be drunk quickly. You have not the pleasure of looking at your bins and thinking, "What treasures I have laid up for myself in ten years' time." There is no drama about the decanting of tawny port: it is merely a matter of drawing a cork and pouring out the wine. There is no cherishing of the crust. Nor with tawny port do you have the interest of testing one year's wine against another's, of suddenly deciding to open a bottle that is several years too young "just to see how much difference there is between it and what we've been drinking."

Yes, a whole lot of fun goes with vintage port; at the same time I cannot help feeling that the ritual involved in the enjoyment of it has robbed tawny port of much of its merited prestige. They are two different wines and round the drinking of vintage port there has grown up inevitably an atmosphere of *chichi*, of assumed superiority, a snobbery of connoisseurship, which has in the long run acted against the best interests of the port trade, for it has made the man who enjoys wine but has no cellar where he can lay down wine, feel self-conscious about serving tawny port. He feels he does not "know about port" and offers his friends a cognac.

During the week I spent in the Douro, I only once drank vintage port—at the banquet at the Factory House. At the *quinta* we drank a dry white port as an *apéritif;* sometimes when we were hot and dusty after a morning in the vineyards we were recommended a dry white port and soda and were astonished to find how refreshing it was. After lunch and dinner we drank a twelve-year-old tawny. It was naturally better suited to a hot climate than vintage port would have been, but even so, as I appreciated its body, its delicacy of flavor and of bouquet, I could not help wondering whether it is not the wine of the future.

In England the proper conditions for the drinking of vintage port are now fast vanishing. The owners of houses in the country have no security of tenure. They are reluctant to mortgage the future by the purchase of wine that they will not be able to drink for twenty years. In houses—and that is in most houses now—where there is no help, or simply someone "who comes in," or a couple who want to get off "to the local," there is far less sitting over the table. There are the insistence of the radio and the demands of television and you cannot drink vintage port in the dark: you want to look at it. Moreover you want to talk or listen to talk when you are drinking it. Tawny port is, perhaps, more suitable to our day and age. And perhaps the trade would be wise to concentrate upon wood port: presenting it not as the "poor man's port" but as the chic wine for informal parties. An attempt might even be made to revive the Victorian habit of a glass of wine and a slice of cake at eleven in the morning. In most offices, at that time of day, there is a break for coffee. How much pleasanter to be greeted by the manager with a glass of Croft's or Sandeman's; it would make the conduct of business very harmonious and it would certainly tend to re-establish the magic evocation of those five words "an Englishman and his Port."

# THE KING OF WINES

At the age of twenty, as I have already told, I believed that the first duty of a wine was to be red, the second that it should be Burgundy. During forty years I have lost faith in much, but not in that.

I am a Burgundian still, and the entries in that catalogue of wines at Edrington over which I brooded with the keenest anticipation during my exile in the Middle East were those of my three great Burgundies, of two great years, Chambertin, Richebourg and La Tâche of 1923 and 1926. Alas, when I came to drink them, I found that of the '23's only the La Tâche had stayed the course. That is one of the troubles about Burgundy, as Meredith long ago complained. It has to be drunk young, particularly nowadays.

In 1957, when I was the guest in Beaune of Louis Latour, I drank a superb Chambertin 1929. It was a much bigger wine than the Cortons of 1952 and 1947 which had preceded it. Its bouquet was staggering, but I very much doubt whether the wines of 1957 that I had sipped earlier in the day and which were sold that afternoon under the auspices of the Hospices de Beaune, will be alive in 1985. Louis Latour told me that after the first war his father had concentrated upon making wines that could be drunk young. The period of fermentation was cut down from two weeks to six days. This robbed the wine of some of its strength but also of its early harshness. It became a gracious wine within six or seven years. Most shippers have followed the same procedure since.

The Côte d'Or is a small area, composed, so writes Camille Rodier, High Chancellor of the Brotherhood of the Knights of Tastevin, of the chain of hills facing eastward and southeast, which under the expressive name of "Golden Slope" forms the furthest border of the Massif Central.

"This old cliff, straight and traversed with dells at whose entrances are gathered wine-producing villages, is an uninterrupted strip of land 60 kilometers in length and with an average width of 650 meters, spreading from Dijon to Chagny. The great vineyards are situated halfway up the gentle and ample slopes which are lit by the first rays of the sun. Over these regular spaces, with a gravel soil, untouched by muddy deposits, clayey, rich in iron ore, prevails a stillness of atmosphere which favors the blooming of the vine and the ripening of the grapes." He describes the wines, the product of the Pinot grape as "rough and hard in their youth, divesting themselves, softening with age and when years have ripened them, shining bright, pure, soft, perfumed and delicious in all the splendor of a magnificent glory."

The Côte d'Or is divided into two sections. The Côte de Nuits, immediately south of Dijon, which contains the best red wines and the Côte de Beaune, which contains Corton and the great white wines, Montrachet and Meursault. Only 60,000 gallons are made of the great red Burgundies a year, and 35,000 of the white. Bordeaux produces by contrast 80 million gallons of wine of *appellation controlée* quality.

Burgundy has never been an easy wine for Englishmen. It has always been expensive. "Poor Jorian," said one of Meredith's characters. "I know no man I pity so much. He has but six hundred a year and a passion for Burgundy."

In early days it was awkward to transport it. It was much simpler to ship Rhenish by river boats, and claret from Bordeaux, which is the kind of fact that we in the twentieth century tend to forget when picturing life in the thirteenth. It is as simple to import wine from Beaune as from Bordeaux. When we weigh the cost of one wine against another, we think of the duties levied against the produce of certain vineyards. We do not consider the cost of transportation. To us that is a negligible factor. It was not so six centuries ago. The Englishmen who fought at Crécy had had little chance of appreciating the excellence of Burgundy and indeed Parisians themselves did not have many opportunities until the sixteenth century when Charles V of Spain and the Holy Roman Empire handed over the Duchy of Burgundy to the crown of France.

In Shakespeare's day little of it can have come to England. The two references in *King Lear* are far from fortunate:

> *"to whose young blood*
> *The vines of France and milk of Burgundy*
> *Strive to be stressed. . . ."*

and later,

> *"Take her then, France:*
> *Not all the Dukes of waterish Burgundy*
> *Shall buy this unprized precious maid of me."*

One would have imagined that Charles II after his long exile in France would have introduced Burgundy along with champagne to the English court, but in Steele's *Tatler* there are no Burgundian advertisements though Bordeaux, Spain, the Canaries, Florence and the Azores announce their shipments. An incident in Swift's *Journal to Stella* shows how expensive a luxury Burgundy was then. Peterborough wrote to Swift that he had sent Bolingbroke ten dozen flasks of Burgundy from Dijon, of which Swift was to have his share. Bolingbroke drank it all. "I tell him," wrote Swift, "that he owes me thirty pounds"—at that rate a flask must have cost ten shillings.

In *Tom Jones* a gambler's extravagance is instanced by the fact that "though he had contented himself with simple claret before, nothing but the most precious Burgundy now serves his purpose." This was in the days when the duty on French wines was very high, and smuggling was in vogue. It was obviously simpler to launch a bootlegger's operation from Bordeaux than Beaune. Peacock refers frequently to Burgundy, but no distinction is made between one Burgundy and another. Stephen Gwynn contends that the drinking of Burgundy in England was not general till the end of the nineteenth century and that its vogue was aided by the spread of the restaurant habit. "It was," he wrote, "the fashion to know of a little restaurant in Soho where a good bottle of Beaune was to be had."

It was always expensive and it still is even though transportation has ceased to be a problem; there is an immense demand for it, but the supply is inadequate, and this has led, in the past, to a number of dubious dealings. Wines were sold as Beaune and Pommard that had never seen the Côte d'Or. The word Burgundy is not a trademark as port is. Wines from Spain and Australia have been put on the market labeled Burgundy. Eighty years ago certain wine merchants were not as scrupulous as they should have been. In the nineteenth century it was the admitted custom of the Bordeaux shippers to strengthen their weaker wines and a great deal of wine falsely labeled Burgundy appeared on the market in England and America. It is no use trying to pretend that the student of Burgundy is not faced with a number of initial problems.

Larmat's section in his *Atlas de la France Vinicole* that is devoted to Burgundy opens with this definition of the nomenclature of Burgundies.

In Burgundy there are very many names. This is due to the different types of land that stretch over four departments, to the variety of *cépages* (the species of vine) which are cultivated and the extent to which the properties are divided. There are five types of grape: The *pinot noir* from which the best red wine is made and the *gamay* which produces an abundance of cheap red wine. The *chardonnay* and its cousin the *pinot blanc* from which the best white wines are made, and the *aligoté*, the white equivalent of the *gamay*.

On the Gironde there are large estates whose wines are known under the name of the separate Châteaux. This practice constitutes a trademark. In Burgundy, particularly on the Côte d'Or, the dividing up of vineyards, the difference of soil and climate have prevented the establishment of large estates with wines of a fixed and settled nature. Instead there are a number of *lieux-dits* [localities] whose vines belong to a number of different owners. These *lieux-dits* called *climats*, [vineyards] many of them very small (*d'une très faible superficie*), produce famous wines which have been classified by the Chamber of Agriculture at Beaune.

In 1860 the best known communes and the most famous *lieux-dits* were registered under their names of origin—this explains the great number of Burgundian surnames.

If one omits the names of the *climats*, one finds in Burgundy as in all other areas that produce fine wines, regional names such as Bourgogne, Bourgogne Aligoté, subregional names like Mâcon and Beaujolais and names taken from that of the commune, Chablis,

Aloxe-Corton. At the same time there are certain peculiarities that should be noted before examining the conditions which control the names of origin.

Four points are made.

1. There are different kinds of Burgundy—Bourgogne, Bourgogne-Passe-tout-grains, Bourgogne-Aligoté, Bourgogne Grand-Ordinaire and Bourgogne Ordinaire. Of these the label Bourgogne has to satisfy the sternest tests.

2. In the geographical area of Burgundy are two sub-regional names, Mâcon and Beaujolais, which have to satisfy less exacting demands and are only entitled to the name Burgundy when they do so.

3. The *cépages* demanded for the name Burgundy are not the same over the whole area; they differ depending on whether they come from Yonne, the Côte d'Or, Saône et Loire or the Rhone. Great importance is attached in Burgundy to the kind of grape that is grown.

4. The name of a *climat* is more famous than the name of a commune. Chambertin is the superior of Gevrey-Chambertin. When a name is followed by that of a *climat* its status is higher and stricter standards are applied, Vougeot-les-Cras being more honored than Vougeot—except in the case of Chambertin, Charmes-Chambertin being of lower standing.

The best wines are known as *Tête de Cuvées*, then come the *Premières, Deuxièmes* and *Troisièmes Cuvées*.

All this sounds relatively straightforward and up to a point it is—but the essential difficulty remains that two bottles labeled Château Margaux 1947 which have lain in the same cellar are identical, while two authentic bottles of Chambertin 1947 may not be identical, even though they carry the name of the same shipper. They may have come from wine-growers who owned different sections of the area;

the vines of the one may be younger than those of the other, the picking of the grapes may have taken place on a different day. A fold in the land may have protected the one from the full violence of a late spring hailstorm. The two wines will have basic resemblances in color, in body and in flavor, but they may be different wines.

To the neophyte who respects and values the guarantee of the stamped cork, the absolute assurance that the wine he is drinking was made out of grapes grown on a certain hill, in a certain year, this sounds highly unsatisfactory. "How," he asks desperately, "can you be certain about Burgundy?" There is only one answer to that. "You must trust the shipper and your wine merchant."

When the Saintsbury Club was entertained in Paris at the Pré-Catalan in 1938 by the Club des Cents, it was given as their chief wine, to which a Mouton-Rothschild 1924 had been the predecessor, a Burgundy which appeared upon the menu as Beaune 1923. That on an English or American menu might mean anything. All that can be certain is that the restaurateur was sufficiently aware of his responsibilities to have put a date against the bottle.

The nomenclature of Burgundy is difficult, and as has already been pointed out has been made more complicated by the practice of certain communes of adding to their own names that of their most famous vineyard, in the same way that men marrying into more distinguished families hyphen their wife's surname to their own. The commune of Aloxe becomes Aloxe-Corton; Gevrey, Gevrey-Chambertin; Chambolle, Chambolle-Musigny; Nuits becomes Nuits-Saint-Georges. Beaune, Volnay, Pommard and Santenay have not followed this practice. Each commune produces some very great wine, each also produces some sound but undistinguished wine.

All great table wines except those of Graves grow on a

slope: the grapes on the peak of the hill do not ripen properly and the soil in the plains and valleys is too rich and
heavy. Louis Larmat's *Atlas de la France Vinicole* shows in
red, yellow and green the areas that produce first-, second-
and third-class wines. The red areas come halfway up the
slope. The commune of Beaune contains over twenty estates
that are painted red. The names of very few would have
significance to anyone but a born Burgundian—Clos de la
Mousse, perhaps, *Les Bressandes,* Sur les Grèves, but for the
most part it is simpler to sell first-class Beaune abroad as
Beaune Supérieur.

The small supply of good Burgundy in relation to the
demand for it is a great problem for the wine merchants
and many of them have partially solved it by following the
example of the champagne shippers, ignoring the names of
communes at making blends which can be marketed under
a merchant's name—Louis Latour, Louis Jadot, or Léonce
Bocquet. The wine is sound and its cost reasonable. At the
same time some vineyards are now shipping their wines under
their own names. An attempt is being made to establish estate-
bottling. Most of this wine is being sent to the U.S.A.

On the Côte de Nuits the nomenclature is more difficult
than on the Côte de Beaune. On the Côte de Beaune the only
cause for confusion is that between Corton and Aloxe-Corton, but the commune of Vosne-Romanée presents many opportunities for misunderstanding. It contains several of the
great vineyards in the world—La Tâche, Richebourg, Ro-
manée, Romanée-Conti and Romanée-St.-Vivant. A bottle bearing the label of any of those would be supreme, but wine
labeled Vosne-Romanée might well be of the second class.
Vougeot on the other hand is in a different position. It is a
small commune. Most of it is painted red on Larmat's maps
and is occupied by the vineyards of Clos de Vougeot. Its
southern neighbor, Flagey-Echézeaux, is small; it contains

Les Grands-Echézeaux and Echézeaux de Dessus, most of it
is painted red, but no wine is put on the market bearing the
name of Flagey-Echézeaux. The commune of Morey hyphened
to itself the name Saint-Denis. I have never seen Clos Saint-
Denis, but the commune contains the great wines of Clos de
Tart. The word "Clos" derives from the medieval habit of
setting a wall around a vineyard.

It is curious that some vineyards should be so well
known out of France and others not. It is probably the question of a name; some impinge upon the memory, other do
not. Chambolle-Musigny is a misleading name upon a bottle. The commune contains Les Musigny, Les Petits Musigny,
Les Charmes Musigny and Les Bonnes Mares, but it also
contains a great deal of second-class wine.

The greatest confusion, however, occurs further north
in Gevrey-Chambertin. Chambertin is a great name. It rolls
on the tongue, suggests the well-loaded table, it is evocative
of full-blooded pleasures. It rode beside Napoleon into battle. It is a big *climat* too, including Chambertin Clos de
Bèze. It produces with Clos de Vougeot two-thirds of the
great red Burgundies, 40,000 gallons a year, but the large
commune of Gevrey-Chambertin produces much wine that
did not make the grade even as a third class in the classification by the Beaune Committee of Agriculture a hundred
years ago. I would not disparage a bottle labeled Gevrey-
Chambertin, but it is not Chambertin.

I would not disparage a bottle of Gevrey-Chambertin,
nor would I disparage a bottle labeled Bourgogne-Passe-
tous-grains or Bourgogne Aligoté or Bourgogne Grand-Ordinaire. It would come from the Côte d'Or, from that succession of gently rounded hills, some of them wooded at their
summit, that face the sun and shut out the northern winds
and that lie on your left as you travel by the railway, north
to Dijon. They may come from areas that are shaded gray

or are left blank in Monsieur Larmat's Atlas, but if they are entitled to the imprimatur *appellation controlée,* they partake of majesty.

Always in the wagon restaurant of a French train, I take the bottle with the sloping shoulders. It will have been subjected to grievous treatment, shaken over points and curves, exposed to changes of temperature, and before it had started on its journey it was no doubt an unpretentious wine but even so, it began its life on the Côte d'Or, on those hills which have cherished the vine since the dawn of culture.

In 311 A.D., the Rhetor Eumenes spoke of the wines of Beaune with their standing of several hundred years. All true Burgundians maintain, basing their assertion on the discovery of Greek pottery and articles along the Côte, that the vine was introduced by the Greeks coming from the East through passes in the Jura, and that the Roman legions as they marched northwards up the Rhone were welcomed with wines richer than their own.

Stephen Gwynn, in his book on Burgundy in 'Constable's Wine Library,' claimed that the vines of Burgundy, shedding their deposits over many years, had created their own special soil. He quoted a poetic passage by M. Gaston Roupnel, in a preface to M. Camille Rodier's monograph "Clos de Vougeot": "It is with the vineyard as with the wine. Age makes it. Time alone can bring into being the delicacy of the bouquet, the aroma and the velvet texture of our great vintages. But however old it may be, the great vintage dates from far away beyond the year of its birth. Long before the starting point of its brief existence, the shaping forces were in play; it draws its excellence from origins deep buried in the earth from which it came. Before it could begin to be born it was necessary that the earth where it was engendered should become a thing ancient in use, and that its cradle should be a tomb full of ashes of the years and

dust of the centuries." Roupnel also spoke of "this sump-
tuous flank of land which the mountain with a shrug of its
shoulder throws to the plain in a gesture of grand and list-
less grace."

Burgundy is called the king of wines and claret the
queen, and there is a regal quality about great Burgundies,
just as there is a regal quality about the town of Beaune, the
capital of the Côte d'Or, in terms of wine.

Bordeaux is a great city, with its docks and its proud
river, with its Opera House and unmatched restaurants and
its links with history; but its very greatness diminishes its appeal for the wine-lover. Bordeaux is so many more things be-
sides being the center of the Médoc's wine trade. Beaune is
dedicated to wine alone. It has a population of only thirteen thousand. In summertime its streets are noisy with traf-
fic hurrying southwards to the Midi but in winter it has a
monastic calm. So few cars are parked in its *grande place*,
that you can appreciate its proportions. Its houses are stone
built and stucco fronted, with irregular gables and tilted
roofs which have sagged during the centuries. The ramparts
that contained it as a fortress in medieval days remain, and
the immense low rounded bastions serve as cellars. The
present and the past are co-existent there.

The building of the Hospices de Beaune was begun in
1443, under the instructions of Nicolas Rolin. Louis XI said
"he has ruined the people with his taxes; it is fitting that he
should provide them with an almshouse." It is a fine example of Gothic architecture, with its high, long roof and
its bright pattern of yellow and black tiles. It contains much
of interest: the superb fifteenth-century tapestries which are
brought out to decorate the cloisters during the weekend of
the November wine sale; the imposing chapel with its red-
curtained beds running each side of the wall, so that the patients who were too sick to rise could watch the ritual; Roger

van der Weyden's magnificent "Last Judgment." In the center of the polyptych, an angel is weighing the dead who have
risen from their tombs; on the right the guilty are descend-
ing to eternal torment, on the left the virtuous are being
elevated to perpetual bliss. There are many more figures
on the right than on the left. Was this, I wondered, because
the artist considered that there was a higher proportion of
sinners in the world or because he found it easier to paint
misery than beatitude? Every novelist knows how hard it is
to make a "virtuous" character convincing.

In addition to the tapestries of the Hospices there is a
delightful fifteenth-century tapestry showing the life of the
Virgin Mary that is shown now in a special room. The flower
decorations at its foot are particularly attractive; the colors
after five hundred years have a vernal freshness. The wine
museum is placed in a reconstructed house and courtyard
where the Dukes of Burgundy used to live. Its high raftered
hall has old oaken wine presses and the museum itself an outside fifteenth-century gallery. The museum contains the most
complete existent encyclopedia of viticulture. It has full-scale
models showing every implement that is used in the vineyards.
It shows the different kinds of glasses that have been used for
wine, and I noted that in the early eighteenth-century pictures,
the glasses are held not by the stem but by the base. This practice is followed now by wine experts and I have always thought
it an affectation, an impractical one at that as it is less easy to
put the glass back on the table afterwards, but the experts have
clearly the authority of a long-based tradition on their side.

There are examples of the carafes, *pichets,* that were
used to carry the wine from the casks to the table; there is a
collection of bottles from the seventeenth century (*trapu et
arrondi*) to the nineteenth century bottle (*élancé et cylin-
drique*) as we know it now, which shows that there can have

been no binning of bottles, no maturing of Burgundy in bottle till the end of the eighteenth century.

There are no decanters in the exhibition; a notice explains that at the start of the nineteenth century amateurs of wine liked to present a dusty bottle to their guests as a proof of the wine's age, and I noticed that in private homes the wine was poured straight from the bottle. There is little, if any, sediment in Burgundy nowadays. On the Côte d'Or it does not hold good that a great wine denies us the full bottle. It is probably because we have been trained in port and claret, both of which need decanting, that in England we like to see wine in a decanter, and a fine decanter does accentuate the color of the wine. But there were no decanters in Beaune's museum.

There was much else of interest there: old wine bills, a collection of the silver wine-tasting cups showing the texture and the color (*la robe*) of a wine, a collection of labels that show how rapidly the custom became elaborate. At the start of the nineteenth century there was affixed a mere slip of white paper, barely larger than a postage stamp—no date, no shipper, just the name of the wine. Later came the shipper's name, after that the date as well. There was a Meursault designed as Château Comte de Moucheron. The final room of the museum contains a fine modern tapestry by Lucat which was made to fit the wall. It has symbolic passages of the rabbit and the fox growing wings as they savor the bouquet of a bottle; it has a tiger who typifies the strength that comes from wine; there is sunlight pouring through bottles onto a sheet of music suggesting that wine inspires the arts; on the left-hand side there is a skeleton, head downwards, a vine wreathing its tendrils among its bones, suggesting that we are born again in wine.

I went to Beaune in mid-November, to attend the wine

sales of the Hospices de Beaune. The sales of wine topped sixty million francs (the official rate of the dollar to the franc was 420 and the pound sterling 1120). This sum was realized from the auction of roughly 240 *pièces*—a *pièce* containing 288 bottles. Wine is sold by the *tonneau* which is two *pièces*, though no such container as the *tonneau* exists. The small town of Beaune had not a hotel bed unoccupied and I was quartered five miles out on the road to Dijon. I was glad I was; the hotel was at the edge of Aloxe-Corton and my bedroom looked onto the wooded hill of Corton.

I arrived after a ten-hour train journey from Nice, at about half-past six. The hotel was recently established and it was less a hotel than a family pension, three agreeable small children being much in evidence. The bedroom which I was allotted contained a bath that was unprotected by any curtain from general scrutiny. Next morning I investigated the rest of the hotel and found that the undraped bath was a *specialité de la maison.* I have never before been in a bedroom that faced straight upon a bath. It was an arrangement, or lack of arrangement, that might, I fancied, have embarrassed a Victorian English couple.

I was treated like a guest in a private house. I was asked when it would be convenient for me to dine. I suggested that I should come down for an *apéritif* in about half an hour. "You shall have an *apéritif du pays,*" I was told. I was presented with a large wide-mouthed glass containing a pink cool liquid that was, they told me, compounded of a white local wine and a vermouth that came from Corgoldin. It was agreeable and refreshing but I should not have wanted two glasses of it. This was the only form of *apéritif* that I saw in Burgundy. At none of the parties that I attended was an *apéritif* served. I was not conscious of a *mauvais quart d'heure,* however. I think that my fellow guests were so

confident of the excellent fare that they would receive at a
Burgundian table, that they could converse easily in happy
anticipation. The wine I was served at dinner was an Aloxe-
Corton 1952. It was a sound full-bodied wine and cost 800
francs. Stephen Gwynn, writing of Burgundy thirty years
ago, was impressed by the cheapness of everything. I was
not. Dinner cost 1200 francs. It was a sound bourgeois dinner, but I could have fared more sumptuously in Nice, at
"la Poularde chez Lucullus" for 1000 francs.

In the morning I was called for at nine o'clock by Louis
Latour: he wanted to be at the tasting of the Hospices de
Beaune's wines when it opened at ten o'clock. He motored
me in a détour around the hill of Corton. The history of Corton is curious. The actual strip of land that is designated
"Le Corton" is too high up the hill to produce the greatest
wine; it is marked green and yellow on Monsieur Larmat's
map, and it is mostly white wines that are produced from
the vines immediately below the wood, but the name Corton
caught the public fancy and the *climats* below, Bressandes,
Clos du Roi, Renardes and Charlemagne decided to hyphen
the name Corton before their own. If you meet in a wine list
a wine labeled Corton-Clos du Roi you can be sure that it will
be better than one labeled simply Corton. At the same time,
to avoid confusion, a shipper would label his wine Corton,
instead of Corton-Renardes, a name that would only have
significance for a Burgundian.

The wines of Corton-Charlemagne are mainly white
and they come from grapes grown on the south side of the
hill, which gets the maximum of sun, the minimum of wind.
The name of Charlemagne lingers here, because after the
Saracens had sacked Saulieu, Charlemagne gave a vineyard to the distressed clergy. I drank twice at the Latours'
table a white Corton-Charlemagne 1952. It was as noble a

white Burgundy as I have ever drunk, with the exception of certain Montrachets.

The sale at the Hospices de Beaune is claimed to be the largest sale for charity in the world. For five hundred years the upkeep of the almshouses has been maintained by the sale of wine from the vineyards that have been bequeathed to it. These vineyards are scattered over the whole stretch of the Côte de Beaune from Aloxe-Corton to Meursault, and the wines are sold under the names of 29 different *crus*. Nicolas Rolin made the first bequest, and the almshouses now own 120 acres of vineyards. The quality of the wine has been maintained and the administration has disposed of any vineyards which it has been bequeathed that produced inferior wines. In 1953, 500 casks fetched $53,-000. The wines may be bought by anyone who has a qualified sponsor, on condition that they are sold with an "Hospices de Beaune" appellation. The occasion is a mixture of charity and publicity. The prices offered in the sale by experts are taken as a guide to the quality of a certain year.

It is always a big weekend for Beaune. This time it was a sunny Saturday and the tapestry-decked Cloisters were bright with chrysanthemums. The fee for entrance to the sale was 500 francs. The tasters brought their own silver goblets. It was impressive to see the long rows of casks, each with its famous name above it. By each cask stood a man, by one or two casks a woman, who drew the wine out of the cask with a glass filter and released the wine into the silver cup. I watched the experts roll the wine round the goblet, judging its color and texture, raising it to their lips, rinsing their mouths, and spitting it on to the floor.

There was a pleasant vinous smell in the long low cellars, but the wine itself was singularly unpleasant. It was difficult to believe that it would have achieved greatness in less than a decade. It is even harder to understand how the

experts can recognize which wines will be good and can recommend this sour substance to their clients.

How often do they make mistakes? There is the often
quoted instance of the 1928 clarets. So much promise was
held out for them. "A much bigger wine," the experts said,
"than the charming '29's." But some '28's never fulfilled
that promise. The experts, when questioned, shook their
heads and shrugged. "They are hard now, but wait," they
said. They were still shrugging ten years later. "Yes, they
are still sulky. Be patient, wait." It was after the war that
they were saying that, when most of the '28's had been drunk
in desperation, in a time of shortage. In fifteen years' time
they will be saying, "The '28's are now at their prime. If
only they had not been guzzled, improvidently, during the
era of austerity." I have my counter ready. In 1935 I
bought two dozen Léoville-Poyferré '28 in half-bottles, most
of which I drank after the war, and very enjoyable they
were. I also bought a case of Latour, a wine over which Mr.
Gage, the wine waiter at the Athenaeum, sadly shakes his
head. I have been unlucky with that case. I have barely had
a chance to look at it. My elder son in my absence took
down to my cellar a fellow cadet at Dartmouth. "I am sure
my father would like us to have the best he's got." His
friend thought the Latour label promising; and that was at
the start of a weekend. Once my daughter decanted a bottle
for a bright young people's party in the belief that it was
vintage port, to the subsequent dismay of her guests, an error that confers no credit on my tuition. Surely she should
have missed the sealing wax? But I have four bottles left. In
1965 I am going to open one of those bottles, and present it
unobtrusively to an expert. It will have a bouquet certainly,
and a rich clear color, but I shall expect it to be harsh upon
the palate. What will be his guess? "A bourgeois claret, a
little too young as yet?" I hope he will not say, "Something

you picked up in Nice." But of course there is the chance
that the experts were right all along, that the wine will en-
chant the senses, and I shall be mourning the eight victims of
hastiness and mischance. I hope that that is what will happen. Wine tasters are not like picture dealers. They organ-
ize no racket, they exploit no artists, they minister to the
needs and delights of man. Their mistakes, if any, are made
honestly. I am confident that they are right in prophesying
such high things of the Burgundies of 1957.

At the wine tasting there was a young and charming
couple, three months married, about to start a life abroad.
"Where will we be," they were wondering, "when we drink
this at its prime?" I prayed that they will be still together
when it is. Was there the motif for a short story there, I
asked myself. A young couple in the first flush of love spitting out a wine that would mature while their love was wan-
ing—the tender becoming sour, the harsh becoming smooth.
Might there not be a happy ending—an estranged couple
brought back to one another by the sharing in 1964 of a
Volnay Santenots that they had sipped together in Beaune
in 1957, by the long deep wealth of symbols and associa-
tions that were involved in that?

By the time that we were through with the tastings,
Louis Latour and I, the cellars were becoming crowded and
we drove back to Corton, to his Château in the center of the
commune. The colors were changing now from their first
fierce autumn coloring to a gentle ocher. The vineyards were
bare and no one was working in them. It was the idle season. We walked through the great cellars, silently as though
they were the cloisters of a church. I was shown the gadget
that Monsieur Latour's father had invented for withdrawing
the sediment from young white wines. His father must have
been a considerable mechanic. He had also invented a sil-

ver ring to put around the mouth of a bottle to prevent the
wine's dripping on the tablecloth.

That afternoon there was a second tasting, a more democratic one, where, so I suspected from the demeanor and
behavior of the company, the wine was not always spat out;
there was a sandwich bar—at 80 francs apiece—to provide
the appropriate "blotting paper."

This was announced as the *85ᵉ Exposition Générale
des Vins de Bourgogne*, and was presented in the adjuncts of
the Hôtel de Ville. Here was offered an immense variety of
wines, not only from the Côte de Beaune, but from the Côte
de Nuits, from Mâcon, Beaujolais and Saône et Loire. A
number of sober experts were no doubt taking stock of what
the year had to offer, but the general atmosphere was one
of Bacchic celebration.

That was on the Saturday. On the Sunday there was
the sale of the wines in the Hospices. I did not stay long; the
heat was fierce and I had no interest in the bidding, but the
atmosphere was special and peculiar. The bids were decided
by "candlelight"—that is to say, tapers were lit and when
the taper burned out, the last bidder had the prize. This is a
practice that was general in England in Queen Anne's day.
It was thus that wines were sold at Crutched Friars and
in Lloyds' Coffee House. But I am told that only in Beaune
and on this day will you hear the auctioneer's call *"Deuxième
et dernier feu."* (Second and final light.)

That night there was a festal dinner in one of the high-
arched bastions of the town's defense. It was an informal
gathering, in that we wore dark suits but not black ties, and
that there were no speeches. It is known as the *Dîner aux
Chandelles* because at one point the electric lights are
lowered and the halls are illuminated by servitors carrying
candlesticks. It will surely be of interest if I set out the menu
of a supremely typical Burgundian meal.

Le Consommé à la mode de l'Auxois
Beaune Blanc 1955

La Truite saumonée braisée au Vin de Meursault
Beaune Clos des Mouches 1955
offert par l'Office du Tourisme de Beaune

Le Coq au Vin de Beaune

Les Mousserons de la Côte à la Crème
Beaune-Bressandes 1953
offert par l'Ambassade des Vins de France

La Gigue de Chevreuil de la Forêt de Cîteaux
Grand Veneur et sa Garniture
Corton 1945 Cuvée Charlotte Dumay
offert par les Hospices de Beaune

Les Fromages du Pays

Le Parfait Glacé des Ducs

Le Puits de l'Hôtel-Dieu

Les Friandises
Bourgogne Mousseux Blanc

Le Café

Le Vieux Marc de Bourgogne

La Prunelle de Bourgogne

In addition to these wines, on the left hand page of the menu
was set out a list of wines that *"Nos hôtes pourront de-
mander à déguster, suivant les disponibilités, un ou plusieurs
des grands vins ci-dessus"* which amounted to meaning that
if you were at the right table—and everybody was—you
were given an opportunity of tasting one or two great wines.
I was shown, and I regard the tasting of it as a high privilege that life may not send my way again—a Beaune Clos

de la Mousse 1947, offered under that long-honored name Bouchard Père et Fils.

There were no speeches at this dinner, but there were many intimate informalities. There was music and there were Burgundian songs, and when such a song is sung there is the *Ban Bourguignon*, the guests beating time, turning their hands first one way then another, then clapping out the rhythm. Our party contained a Nigerian lady of youth and charm. The Mayor of Beaune was fascinated by the contrast between her dead-black face, her brilliantly white teeth and her long-fingered hands with their gray-white palms. Would she mind, he said, conducting the *Ban Bourguignon?* So she stood up with all the spotlights on her, and her hands, alternating white and black, turning to the music. That gesture seemed somehow typical of the universal imperial quality of the wines of the Côte d'Or.

Louis Latour, before he took me into the cellars of the Hospices de Beaune, handed me a small silver goblet in which to taste the wine. It is called a *tastevin* and its use is the particular privilege of the Burgundians. To produce one at a Bordeaux tasting is, I have been assured, a serious oenological solecism. "The *tastevin* is silver," wrote Alexis Lichine, "so that no foreign taste will be imparted to the wine; it is dimpled along the sides so that you can see the color of the wine at different depths. Some *tastevins* have ridges along one side to reflect the shimmer of light through the wine. The grooves of the 'taste' darken quickly because of the wine. The handle has a silver ring, often with a thumb-rest on its top edge."

In 1932 the universal economic crisis coinciding with three bad vintages caused serious dismay to the minor vine-growers of the Côte d'Or. The big firms with their well stocked cellars of noble wines could afford to ride out the storm, but the small men were in danger. In January 1933 under the leadership of Camille Rodier and Georges Faiveley, a number of businessmen founded the *"Syndicat d'Initiative de Nuits-Saint Georges"* to decide how best to rescue these floundering vessels. A year later the *"Confrérie des Chevaliers du Tastevin"* was founded.

Over the bar in the Chateaubriand Restaurant in New York, and in the halls and studios of many wine-lovers—including mine—you will see a framed vellum document announcing that such a one has been elected to that *Confrérie*. At times you may see at a gourmet dinner a man with a red-and yellow-ribboned boutonniere which a Spaniard would think indicated devotion to the Royal Family and an Englishman would take as a tribute to the M.C.C. Over the framed testimonials in the Chateaubriand to Alexis Hounie and his partner hang broad ribbons that carry a large silver *tastevin*. These ribbons are worn by Chevaliers at their chapter meetings.

The Confrérie was founded to publicize and popularize the wines of the Côte d'Or, and it is, André Simon writes, "to the undying credit of the Chevaliers that they have made of that mid-November sale, a wonderful triptych with the Hospices de Beaune's Sunday auction in the centre panel, the Confrérie's Saturday banquet on the left and the Monday's *Paulée de Meursault* on the right, three festive days, now known all the world over as *Les Trois Glorieuses,* three days devoted to the glory of the wines of Burgundy."

At the *Dîner aux Chandelles*, I sat opposite Louis Latour's niece, Christiane Latour; on her recommendation I was admitted into the *Confrérie des Chevaliers* that December and in the following June I went to Dijon to be installed.

I went with two good friends from the south of France.

We took the *Mistral,* I believe the fastest train in the world,
and certainly one of the most comfortable, with its rubber-
ized seats and cozy bar. It was raining hard as we waited on
the platform at Antibes; a wind was blowing off the Alps
and we were grateful for the warmth of the wagon-restau-
rant, but late in the afternoon the weather cleared and a soft
amber sunset lay over the golden slopes as we read through
the windowpane that succession of noble names: Beaune,
Volany, Gevrey-Chambertin, Clos de Vougeot.

Throughout that whole weekend the goddess of an in-
clement spring relented; we were able to saunter in comfort
through the narrow streets of that charming medieval city,
sip an *apéritif* in the half-circle of low two-storied buildings
that had once been the stables of the Dukes of Burgundy, and
look onto their palace through the windows of the Trois Fay-
sans restaurant while we sampled such regional dishes as
*escargots, quenelles de brochet* which is poached pike,
ground and shaped into a rissole and covered with cream
sauce, and *boeuf bourguignon,* which owes its richness to the
red wine in which it has been soaked.

The initiation ceremony was scheduled for half-past
six and at ten past an autobus drove off from the Hôtel
Cloche d'Or. The bus needed careful manipulating along the
narrow vineyard roads. Burgundy is the country of the snail
and to appreciate its beauties you must travel at a snail's
pace. The Château de Vougeot looked very regal, among its
vines, with its low wall guarding them. It was easy to understand why a French colonel had ordered his men to salute it
on their way to battle. "Soldiers of France, it is to defend
beauties such as these that you are called upon to fight."

About fifty new Chevaliers were to be initiated and the
large upper room was crowded with guests and sponsors.
The ritual was reminiscent of that of the Odd Volumes.
There are those who find a little ridiculous the  spectacle of

middle-aged men arrayed in fancy dress, indulging in archaic diction, and indeed it often is, but the whole drill of
the initiation was so well done that it was neither absurd nor
boring. There were huntsmen in pink coats and black caps
to sound a fanfare on hunting horns; the Grand Masters,
the Grand Chancellor and the senior officers wore the long
Doctors' robes and hats of the days of Rabelais; each novi-
tiate was summoned separately; each of us was welcomed
with an address. When my turn came, a friendly reference
was made both to my books and my brother's. We had both
paid tribute to Bacchus. It was hoped that I would "hold my
pen in trust" to what I had rightly called the "King of
Wines." I then stepped onto a dais, my hand was shaken,
the Grand Master tapped me on each shoulder, saying something in medieval French. I was duly embraced upon both
cheeks; the red and gold ribbon of the Order with a silver
*tastevin* at its end was hung round my neck, and I signed my
name in the Golden Book. The ceremony lasted ninety minutes. When it was ended, the Burgundian *apéritif*—chilled
white Burgundy with Cassis—was served in an adjoining
room, and we were free to walk around the Château and ad-
mire its ancient presses. In the courtyard I was delighted to
find my old and dear friend Alexis Hounie, of the Chateaubriand Restaurant in New York.

We sat down to dinner at eight-thirty; we did not rise
till half-past one. Five hours may seem an interminable time
for a meal to last, but it did not seem so. There were at
least four hundred of us, seated at long tables in the large
high raftered room that had contained the cellars of the
monastery. Usually at public dinners a long and heavy
meal is served too quickly, and one is left over-replete, with
one's digestive powers strained, at the mercy of self-impor-
tant oratory. But this dinner was skilfully organized. At

the end of the hall there was a stage, decorated with the
motto of the association, *"Jamais en vain, toujours en
vin,"* and set with chairs and barrels; here sat the *cadets de
Bourgogne* to enliven the proceedings with songs glorifying
wine and love. The cadets were men in middle life, some of
them in advanced middle life, who have worked in the vineyards, they and their fathers before them, since earliest days,
forming an hereditary choir for the embellishment of such
occasions. They wore white shirts, black trousers, black
sleeveless jackets and long peaked black caps; they had
strong, lined faces and long noses; they sang with gusto,
summoning us every so often to raise and clap our hands,
turning them in the *Ban Bourguignon.* Between their songs,
they drank from a row of emptying bottles. And in between
their songs, and between courses, speeches were delivered
from the stage. The Grand Master delivered an address of
welcome to the four Ambassadors, American, Norwegian,
German, Swedish, who had honored the occasion with their
attendance. Camille Rodier made an eloquent and literary
speech on the civilization of the vine. Another high officer
spoke wittily and salaciously on the aphrodisiac properties
of wine in general and Burgundy in particular. I could not
follow all of it and my thoughts wandered. I remembered
George Moore's tribute to Pommard in "The Lovers of Ore-
lay":

> *"Quand on boit du Pommard, on devient bon, on aime,*
> *On devient aussi bon que le Pommard lui-même,"*

and I remembered Hilaire Belloc's speech at a Saintsbury
Club dinner over which he was presiding and at which we
had been enjoying a bin of Chambertin 1911. Its peroration
was as follows: "And when I depart from this earth to appear before my belovéd Lord to account for my sins, which

have been scarlet, I shall say to Him: 'I cannot remember
the name of the village; I do not even recollect the name of
the girl, but the wine, my God! was Chambertin!' "

At the end of the evening the ritual of initiation was re-
peated, so that the four Ambassadors and a few other distinguished guests might be enrolled as Chevaliers.

There was in fact a continual non-stop cabaret performance. This served two excellent purposes. There was a
long pause between courses and there was also a long pause
between speeches. We had the opportunity to digest our food
and savor our wines, and it was possible to appreciate the
speeches when each speaker could make his separate, personal contribution. How often have I not heard a speaker
say after a public dinner, "It's terribly difficult having to
follow———." The five hours of the dinner passed more
swiftly than many a three-hour banquet I have attended.

The creator of Pantagruel is the presiding spirit of the
brotherhood and at the foot of the menu, which was set out
in archaic French, was printed, *"Salut à tous en notre bon
Maître François Rabelais!"* The left-hand sheet was headed
*Disnée* and the right hand sheet *Escriteau.* Under the names
of the four Ambassadors was written, *"Seront pourtez sur
les tables à banquet des très prétieux Chevaliers du Tastevin six services en l'ordre qui suit, présentés par le maître
Queux Georges Garin . . . chef ordinaire des rôtissoires,
coquemars et aultres quincailleries de gueule de ladicte
bachique confrérie."*

The six courses consisted of two kinds of *pâté,* hot
salmon, chicken cutlets, braised ham, cheese, fruit and ices.
I was surprised that ham should have been the main dish,
and that early in the evening the hams that we were later to
enjoy were carried on stretchers shoulder-high between the
tables, but game was out of season and ham is a regional

dish; certainly it was very excellent, flanked by hearts of artichoke, adorned with peas.

There were two desserts, a model in nougat of the Château's winepress, and an immense ice snail, surrounded with Melba strawberries.

The wines that accompanied these courses were set out wittily and unpretentiously. The Pouilly-Fuissé Les Chailloux 1957 was described as fresh and pleasing (*frais et gouleyant*), the Meursault-Genevrières 1956 as subtle, the Santenay 1953 as silken, the Nuits-Saint-Georges *premier cru* 1953 as nectarlike, the Clos de Vougeot 1949 as godlike. The coffee was encouraged with a Vieux Marc or Prunelle de Bourgogne; and during the ritual of initiation there was a sparkling white Burgundy.

In the course of that five hours I had consumed a considerable amount of food and wine, but I had no sense of having overeaten, nor was my vision clouded. Next morning my head was clear.

# A WINE TRIP TO CHAMPAGNE

My visit to Clos de Vougeot was the first stage of a wine trip which I had planned to include the Rhineland with the champagne area of the Marne and the cognac area of the Charente. Unfortunately time forced me to omit the Rhineland and I must apologize to the reader for the very little that this book contains about two of the four supreme table wines—Moselle and hock. The trouble is that I do not know enough about them to write informatively.

My acquaintance with them is fond but slight. With the interruption of two wars, they have always been difficult to come by, they are expensive: partly because they are scarce, partly because the steepness of the ground along the rivers makes their cultivation costly—in many places animals

cannot be used, partly because the vineyards lie so far north
that the soil needs elaborate treatment. In addition, their
nomenclature makes it difficult for the inexperienced to tell
what kind of a wine he is ordering, whether it will be dry or
heavy, light or sweet and with which part of the meal it
should be served. In consequence, when I have ordered a
special meal, I have preferred to play for safety, choosing
a French wine of which I could be sure.

Moselle wines are easier than hocks. They are gay and
fragrant. They are usually light though it is possible to
meet one that is rich and luscious. They are of the same
family as the Alsatian wines with which most of us are familiar and which are known not by their locality of origin
but by the grapes from which they are made: *Riesling,
Traminer, Sylvaner* and *Muscatel.* Under the German occupation from 1871 to 1918, the Alsatian vineyards were not
neglected but their wines were denied identity and were used
for blending. The French raised their social status. They are
now pleasant enough; they are standardized; you can rely on
them, but they do not seem to me superior to the best white
wines of South Africa, California or New York State. They
have not the character of the best Loire wines—Pouilly Fumé,
for example. Certainly they have not the distinction of a fine
Piesporter or Bernkasteler. Anyone who enjoys Alsatian
wines will be delighted with Moselle. It rarely disappoints
you.

Hock is another matter. The first wine that I ever tasted
was, as I have already told, a hock and I was surprised by
its sourness. German wines have a tendency to be acid because the vineyards lie far to the north and are exposed to
frost. To counteract this acidity, sugar is often added to
the must. Such wines are known as "bettered" (*verbesserte*),
and can be excellent. There are, in fact, two distinct types
of hock. There are shippers' blends which are "treated"

and labeled Rüdesheim, Hockheim, Nierstein. Such names on
a bottle give little indication of its contents. The best known
name is Liebfraumilch; it is a pretty name but it means little. There is an area of vineyards near Worms called Lieb-
frauenkirsche and a bottle labeled Liebfrauen Stiftstein or
Kirschenstück has a definite territorial connotation. You do
not often meet such a bottle because the wines from that
area are usually used for blending. The name Liebfraumilch carries no guarantee. It can be excellent, it can be
flabby.

There are other wines, however, which are subject to the
most strict regulations and their purity is guaranteed by an
elaborate and precise nomenclature. Inside my copy of
H. R. Rudd's contribution to the "Constable Wine Library,"
*Hocks and Moselles*, are pasted two prewar labels. One is of
a Marcobrunner 1920. It has in the center the coat of arms
of the owner of the vineyard, Freiherr Longwerth von
Simmerache. In the bottom lefthand corner it has *Edel-
beeren*, in the righthand corner *Auslese*. In the top corners it
has *Cabinets Wein* which means "special reserve." The
other label reads Rheingau 1934, *Mittelheimer Edelmann,
Riesling Spätlese, Original-Abfüllung*, which means that it
was made from Riesling grapes that were gathered late and
was bottled in the cellars of the man who made it.

There are a great many other pieces of information
that you can find on a German label. *Auslese* alone means
a selected gathering of bunches. *Trockenbeeren Auslese*
means that overripe berries have been selected one by one.
Sometimes there is the number of the cask or Fuder, the type
of cask used on the Moselle. The word *Wachstum* often appears, which means that the wine is the growth of a certain
owner.

All these designatory phrases testify to the care with
which the wine was made. Every Teutonic device is employed

to ensure honest dealing and there are equally strict regulations about the branding of the cork, but the trouble about all this for the novice is that when he has studied a wine list or a label, assured though he is that he is going to drink a pure and noble wine, he has no idea how it is going to taste.

Hocks can be rich, dry, full-bodied, but they can also be overpoweringly sweet. One evening shortly before the second war, after a dinner at his house in Chelsea, Vyvyan Holland presented me with two bottles of a Rheingau wine; as I was getting out of my taxi one of the bottles slipped through my arms and broke upon the pavement. When I came down the next morning, the air was still perfumed.

If you want a dessert wine in France, you order a Sauternes and if you want a wine to go with fish you order a white Burgundy, and that is that, but in Germany it is not so simple. In terms of Sauternes you would imagine that a wine marked *Spätlese*—late gathered—would be sweet; but it is not always.

At the Savile Club in the 1930's we had in our cellars some superb German wines. I once arranged for A. J. A. Symons and Louis Wilkinson to meet there; after the lunch A.J. wrote in my copy of *The Quest for Corvo*, "For A.W. who has added, by proxy, an unpublished and probably unpublishable chapter to this authentic account; with deep gratitude for a remarkable bottle of Rauenthaler, an exciting luncheon and some excellent conversation."

During the last four years of peace, I began to learn a little about German wines, but when I was faced with a German wine list in January, 1939, I found myself sorely puzzled. I was traveling from New York to England in a German ship—the *Hansa*. War was imminent and I wanted to remind myself before the curtain fell of how very many pleasant things there were in Germany and how much there

was that was pleasant about the German way of life. I was
not disappointed. I retained till the war was over a sentimental memory of a Beer Garden evening, but I also retained the memory of how, at the end of each concert and
cinema performance, brown-shirted figures with Swastika
armbands stood in the doorway, ominous and sullen, making collections for some Nazi fund.

I had a table to myself and at each meal I ordered a
different wine, but I kept being surprised by the type of
wine that I received. What I had expected to be dry was
sweet, what I had expected to be sweet was dry. I speak very
little German, and was not in a position to consult the wine
steward. By the third day I had acquired a small battery of
bottles that I was able to apportion to their proper place in
the order of dishes.

It is over twenty years since I drank a great Rheingau
wine. The taste of it is unique. There seems to be a sequence
of sensations upon the palate, but it cannot be explained,
it must be experienced. It is too late for me to pick up the
threads of my apprenticeship, but I would strongly recommend the young readers of this book to start as early as possible a study of these noble wines.

I went to the champagne country under happy auspices.
In New York I had told my very dear friend Peggy Mann,
the author of that excellent novel *A Room in Paris*, that I
was planning to see champagne made. She said at once, "I
must introduce you to people who will help." Two lunch parties
followed, at one of which I sat next Maurice Hennessy, and
by the time I left New York, I was in touch with the respective
heads of the Comité Interprofessionel du Vin de Champagne
of Épernay and of the Bureau National du Cognac, in
Cognac. It was arranged that while I was in Épernay, I

should be the guest of Moët et Chandon in their Château de Saran.

The Comité Interprofessionel du Vin de Champagne collaborates closely with the French Ministry of Agriculture. It was founded during the German occupation in the autumn of 1941, when it was of obvious and supreme importance to protect an industry on which depended so much of France's future. Good came out of evil. It may not have been necessary in the case of cognac, but for champagne, for the good name and reputation of champagne, some form of rigorous control was needed.

No wine has been more ill-used. No wine has suffered more at the hands of malefactors. I am tempted indeed to parody the opening lines of *A Tale of Two Cities:* it is the best of wines, it is the worst of wines. It is associated with some of our most pleasant experiences and some of the most disagreeable—particularly in our youth, when we are short of money. It is an absurdly expensive wine, because Chancellors of the Exchequer treat it as a luxury, overtax it, grasping at an opportunity to soak the rich. How often have we not all of us been forced to buy it when we could ill afford it in nightclubs where it was *obligatoire* and by venial ladies in league with the headwaiter—and how bad such wine invariably was. How often have we not been embarrassed and exasperated by the ostentatious vulgarians who will say, "Let us have wine tonight," as though claret and burgundy were not wines. How often have we not been stinted because a host has considered the presence of champagne a sufficient token of hospitality and has let one bottle do the work of two. I will not say, "Of no other wine have I such unpleasant memories"; that would be unfair to wine. I will omit the "such."

And yet what a lovely wine it is, so fresh, so wholesome, so gay to look at, so rejuvenating; exquisite in color and in flavor, with such a sharp sting upon the palate; how it warms the blood and lightens the spirit. How quickly a party gets going under its influence. It is nearly as effective as a dry Martini and how much pleasanter to taste; how much more beneficent in its effects.

It is the one table wine that you can drink at any time. Thomas Walker wrote in 1835:

To give champagne fair play it ought to be produced at the very beginning of dinner or at any rate after one glass of sherry or Madeira . . . the advantages of giving champagne with whatever limit at the beginning of dinner are these: that it has the greatest relish, that its exhilarating quality serves to start the guests, after which they seldom flag and that it disposes people to take less of other wines after, which is a relative and sometimes even an absolute saving to the pocket of the host and it is undoubtedly a saving to the constitution of the guests.

Still champagne is suitable to a grave party talking over matters of state; but the sparkling is much better adapted to give brilliancy and joyousness and for that purpose, I believe, would be preferred by almost everyone.

I was told when I was young that it was vulgar to serve champagne at luncheon. I cannot think why it should have been. I suspect that this stricture was a post-first war form of snobbery to discountenance the *nouveaux riches*. I have often heard men say, "The best time for champagne is eleven-thirty in the morning after a heavy night, with a dry biscuit." It is excellent then, but to speak of that hour as the best one is to limit champagne, to deny it its full merits. Apart from the proviso that you cannot drink any wine for long without an exhaustion of the palate, champagne can be drunk at any point of a dinner, it goes with any food.

It is the supreme wine for middle age. Not only because
we are then better able to afford it, are no longer intimidated
by headwaiters and have taken the measure of the kind of
young woman who feels that she is not properly dressed if
her table is not decorated by a steaming bucket, but because
of a change in our metabolism. May I quote a passage from
a travel book that I published in 1952:

Middle age has its own rewards; its own matured and satisfying
preferences. A taste for champagne is one of them. In my twenties I
had despised it as a vulgar, ostentatious drink. In *boîtes* where it was
"obligatoire," I would tell the waiter in a lordly way that he could
put a gold-foiled bottle in a bucket if he liked and I would pay for
it, but I was going to drink a real wine, Beaune or Chambertin. In
my thirties I patronized it. It was all very well, I said, in its own
time and place, at eleven o'clock in the morning with a dry biscuit,
after a heavy night, or before a long several coursed dinner, instead
of a Martini with small hot sausages. But most men after forty, if
they have not switched to spirits, find that champagne does something for them that no other wine can do. I was lucky in that my
taste for it began to mature at the very moment in the late '30's
when Krug 1928 was moving to its majestic peak. I do not expect to
see a wine like that again—in depth of color, body, full-blooded
fragrance. But the Heidsieck '43 that I drank in the *Kampala* was
fresh and clean with a light April quality. "I'll remember our good-
bye," I said to Leslie.

The highbrows of the 1930's were inclined to be con-
temptuous of champagne. It was not a pure wine, they said.
It was manufactured. As though all wines were not manufactured; and certainly the wines of Épernay are subjected
to a process that has only been perfected in the last hundred
years, though the making of sparkling wines is far from being a new discovery.

There is extant a certain amount of misinformation
about the origins of champagne. It has been claimed for

Dom Pierre Pérignon, who was born in 1639 and from 1668 till his death in 1715 was cellarer of the Benedictine abbey at Hautvilliers, that he "put the bubbles into champagne," wherefore the French have long reverenced his memory with song and statuary. But that, the historians now inform us, is not altogether true.

Dom Pérignon was, they say, primarily a great blender. For many years the still wines, red and white, of the area had been highly prized. The slopes south of Rheims are planted with the same grapes as the Côte d'Or—the *pinot noir* and the *chardonnay*, and until Burgundy became a part of France, Parisians concentrated on the wines of Champagne, Touraine and the Loire. Dom Pérignon, who was blind, had a wonderful sense of smell and he taught the wine growers how to get the most out of their wines by blending them. He also replaced with a cork stopper the wad of hemp dipped in oil which had been used to keep dust out of the wine. That is why he earned the reputation of "putting the bubbles into champagne." It had long been recognized that if you bottled wine before the fermentation was complete you got an effervescent liquid. Such was the young New Testament wine that stretched and split the wine skins. The bubbles in champagne are drops of liquid agitated by escaping carbon dioxide and are a natural by-product of fermentation. Hemp dipped in oil kept the dust out of wine but it did not keep the carbon dioxide in. And the incompletely fermented wines that Dom Pérignon corked up retained their sparkle.

That, as I understand it, is the modern version of the legend.

In synopsis the making of champagne is simple. The wine ferments in bottle, not in cask. Because of its cold northern climate, the fermentation of champagne is slow and is not completed when winter closes down; the wine is treated at the beginning very much as any other wine; it is racked and fined and bottled, but since the fermentation is not complete, there is still sugar in the wine which has not been converted into alcohol. The second fermentation starts when the sap rises in the vineyards. Strong bottles have to be used and the corks have to be firmly clamped. The bottle is now kept for two, three or four years in the cold clammy chalk cellars of Rheims and Épernay. During this period the sugar ferments out, but in the process, the wine will have thrown off a sediment of dead wine yeasts. The problem is to remove this sediment without robbing the wine of its carbon dioxide.

The process is a long one. The bottles are set in a rack and pointed downwards at an angle. Every day the bottle is given a slight twist to the right and a slighter twist to the left and slightly tilted downwards: the bottle is at the end of the operation an eighth of its circumference further around and the particles in the wine have been shaken from the sides of the bottle. A highly trained man—*le remueur*—can turn thirty thousand bottles in a day. Eventually the bottle points straight downwards with all the sediment resting on the cork, and it is ready for disgorging; "throat-clearing" is Raymond Postgate's word for it. The cork, that is to say, has to be withdrawn, the sediment removed, and another cork inserted before the carbon dioxide has evaporated. It is an extremely difficult operation for which a man needs a five years' apprenticeship—longer than the tea ceremony in Japan. Before the second cork is inserted, the wine is liqueured (*dosé*) to fit it for the particular market for which it is intended. It is completely dry, or "brut," when the first cork is disgorged and a *dosage* may be administered. It is because of this *dosage* that the highbrows call champagne impure. The dosage may consist of cane sugar soaked in still champagne, or it may be laced with brandy. The amount of sugar inserted depends

on its future market. There are four kinds of champagne—
Brut which contains zero to one per cent of sugar; extra
sec, one to two per cent; sec, three to six per cent and demi-
sec, five to ten per cent.

Champagne is a blended wine; each shipper aims at a
uniformity of taste; in consequence vintage years are not
so important as they are with Burgundy and claret. Champagne does not improve after the second corking and it is
wise to drink it young, before it is ten years old; though
there are those who like a fading wine with little sparkle.

Champagne has had its ups and downs, historically. It
was introduced into England and thence presumably into
America, by Charles II at the Restoration, but it was a
sweet wine that he brought with him which connoisseurs
looked at askance, though the man-about-town liked it, in
modern parlance "for the hell of it." Lord Chesterfield's
favorite toast was,

> *Give me Champaign and fill it to the brim,*
> *I'll toast in bumpers every lovely limb.*

Etherege wrote:

> *To the Mall and the Park*
> *Where we love till 'tis dark,*
> *Then sparkling Champaign*
> *Puts an end to their reign;*
> *It quickly recovers*
> *Poor languishing lovers,*
> *Makes us frolic and gay, and drowns all sorrow.*

Matthew Prior, half a century later, was paying it the
tribute of:

*By nerves about our palates placed,*
*She likewise judges of the taste,*
*Else (dismal thought!) our warlike men*
*Might drink thick Port for fine Champagne,*

and Lady Mary Wortley Montague at about the same time
was saying:

*They sigh, not from the heart, but from the brain,*
*Vapours of vanity and strong Champagne.*

No matter what its cost, champagne was established as
"the wine for an occasion" but it was not until a modest
chemist of Châlons-sur-Marne published in 1836 a booklet
on the technique of controlling the carbonic acid gas produced in a bottleful of fermenting wine that the champagne
industry became organized. Up till that point the average
loss through exploding bottles varied between forty per cent
and twenty-five, so that still red and white wines were a
more profitable investment for the wine growers. No large
stocks were produced until the technique of production was
finally established; and it was not till the eighteen-sixties
that a general taste for dry wine developed. Champagne in
England ceased then to be a dessert or ladies' wine. W. E.
Gladstone, a temperate man, drank a quart habitually with
his dinner, and the consumption rose from seven million
bottles in 1861 to twenty-one million in 1890.

In this connection it is interesting to note the drinking
habits of the Forsytes in the first volume of the *Saga*. John
Galsworthy was himself vividly appreciative of the pleasures of the table. His man-of-the-world characters pride
themselves upon their palates. All the Forsytes except James,
and he kept a fashionable table, were good trenchermen.
They appear to have drunk nothing but champagne; they

had port and brandy, sherry and Madeira; but champagne was their table wine. Swithin Forsyte, in his last days deaf and stertorous, had always beside him on the dinner table in his club a steaming ice bucket. The two most memorable meals in Galsworthy are the Stoic's last dinner, and the din-ner given by Soames and Irene Forsyte to June and Bosin-ney. At the first Old Heythrop drank several subsidiary drinks; he had sherry with his soup—complaining that "no one drank Sherry nowadays, hadn't the constitution for it" —although he had previously drunk a glass of champagne with his oysters; with his cheese savory he had a glass of port, a '68. Finally he had brandy. But champagne was his table wine.

Champagne, of an unspecified year and shipper, was the wine chosen by Soames Forsyte for his cousin June and her fiancé. The dinner was remarkable, if not indeed unique in literature, as being both one of the most succulent meals served on the printed page, and an occasion of acute em-barrassment. Rarely can a meal have been chosen with greater care; rarely can a meal have provided less enjoy-ment. The dinner is also interesting as an example of the quantity and the elaborateness of the food provided at this time for the English upper-middle classes. It was a meal, it will be recalled, prefatory to the theater. Soup came first. "Bosinney, a glass of sherry with your soup." Then a fine fresh Dover sole, cutlets "each pink-frilled," spring chicken, asparagus, an apple charlotte. Olives from France and Rus-sian caviar were set upon small plates. Brandy accompa-nied Turkish coffee and Egyptian cigarettes. June and Bosin-ney went to the theater by bus. Three minutes' walk from Montpelier Square to the Brompton Road: at least fifteen minutes by horse bus to Piccadilly. One wonders at what time the meal began. There were of course no cocktails then. There was *le mauvais quart d'heure* instead.

Galsworthy was at great pains about that menu. It is a little surprising that Soames in his own house should not have "led up" to a big wine. He preferred, however, to serve champagne right through the meal. Clearly at that time the Forsyte classes considered that they could only trust one wine.

Before I went to Épernay I had a rough idea of how champagne was made, but there was a great deal more that I wanted to know; there were many questions that I needed to ask. I wanted to absorb an atmosphere; to see the countryside, to visit the cellars where the wine is stored; in particular I wanted to watch the process of "disgorgement." I had read descriptions of the operation, but I could not visualize it and I would like to express here my gratitude to the various gentlemen who gave up their time to me, to my Moët et Chandon hosts at their Château de Saren, to Paul Krug who produced from his cellars a bottle of 1928 that still retained the golden majesty I had so enjoyed during the first months of the war, to Victor Lanson who lunched me sumptuously in Rheims, to Comte Alan de Vogue who showed me his notable chalk cellars and to Monsieur Boudin who told me much of interest over an exquisite bottle of Perrier-Jouet.

The valley of the Marne is not a gastronomic area. Sheep were raised there once but now such land as is not suitable for vines is planted with beet sugar and wheat, but meal after meal was made memorable by the excellence of the wines that went with it, and I must not forget to pay tribute to two excellent local red wines named after their villages, who sound like two slovenly henchmen in a farce, Bouzy and Dizy, which are not put upon the market, which the shippers drink at their own tables and use occasionally to make pink champagne.

The fine weather that had gilded the golden slopes for the Chevaliers' chapter at Clos de Vougeot broke on the second day of my visit to the Marne, but on my first afternoon Monsieur Dargent drove me round the countryside. A large proportion of champagne is made from black grapes. He showed me how the *Montagne de Reims* rises between Rheims and Épernay. The white grapes grow south of Épernay, the black north of the Marne. He showed me how the vines ran in ribbons along the flanks of the hills, growing out of long layers of chalk; explained how the peasants restore in winter the topsoil that has been washed down the hills. The hills, like those of Burgundy, have forests at their summit.

I asked Monsieur Dargent whether there was any great difference between the wines that came from Épernay and those that came from Rheims. I seem to recall some music-hall song that made an unflattering comparison between the two. Monsieur Dargent was diplomatic. There was, he said, a great feeling of friendliness between the shippers. They were united in their devotion to the interests of their great wine. But there was inevitably and very properly an atmosphere of competition. There were rivalries in general and in particular between the firms that were based on Épernay and those that were based on Rheims. About seventy per cent of the world's champagne is produced by twenty firms, but there are about a hundred and twenty shippers who make wine that can be legally shipped as champagne. Monsieur Dargent was tactful enough not to say so, but it is the products of some of those less well-known shippers that are sold as *Champagne Obligatoire* in nightclubs, and one of the functions of his Bureau is to insure that the standards of champagne are maintained by the smaller firms. I also learned that four-fifths of the big shippers are based on Rheims. These shippers—or some of them—have use of the superb chalk cellars that lie under the city. These cellars were constructed by the Romans, who used them as mines for extracting chalk. They consist of long galleries, broken every now and again by what can only be likened to an underground and empty oast-house tapering to the open air. It is extremely cold there. If you scratch the walls, you see the clean whiteness of the chalk.

The shippers who are based on Épernay do not have the advantages of these cellars, but they have a recompense. They are nearer to the vineyards and it is possible for a house like Moët et Chandon to have the grapes carried straight to their factory. It is the practice here for the peasants to sell their grapes direct to the shippers, or to co-operatives or brokers, and the big Rheims shippers have presses scattered among the vineyards. The journey to Rheims is so far, that the grapes would be crushed and the color cells inside the skins broken, spoiling the clear color of the wine. But Moët et Chandon are able to complete the entire process of the wine-making inside their central factory. Once the grapes have been approved, and it is known from what hillside they have been gathered, they can be mixed with the grapes of other vineyards. There is no estate-bottling.

It is for this reason that the purists describe champagne as a manufactured wine, but it is only "artificial" to the extent that a very little sugar and brandy are added to it, and it is "manufactured" only in so far as greater care is devoted to its production than to any other wine.

I watched the bottling process in both the Veuve Clicquot cellars in Rheims and the Moët cellars in Épernay, and I realized that champagne would have to be an expensive wine even if it were not universally overtaxed as a luxury product. Until I paid those visits I had not understood the process of "disgorgement," and as I suspect that the majority of my readers do not understand it either and as it is the key point in the making of champagne, I would like to repeat and amplify what I have already written. Everyone asks, "What puts the bubbles into champagne?" The answer is that the fermentation takes place in the bottle, not in the cask. But the affair is not quite as simple as all that. There is still a certain mystery about the second fermentation that takes place during the spring following the harvest. The Marne lies far to the north. The grapes are harvested late, to increase their sugar content, and the generally accepted explanation is that the cold descends before the fermentation is complete, and all the sugar has been converted into alcohol. But the wine growers of the region still like to think that there is a special miraculous intervention of Providence on their behalf.

After Christmas, when the cellar doors are opened, the inrush of cold air causes a precipitation which enables the wine to throw off its impurities. It is at this point that the *cuvée* is prepared, that expert tasters decide how the various *crus*—*cru* is a hard word to translate; it signifies the gathering of grapes from a particular area—are to be blended to produce a perfect mixture. The shippers draw a simile from music; a harmony being created by the succession of different notes. Each shipper has his own special type of wine and he aims at making his non-vintage wines identical from year to year. He keeps in reserve a certain amount of old wine for blending. Sometimes, however, there is no need for the use of this old wine, sometimes the *crus* of a single year harmonize so well that he decides to declare it a vintage year. That is what the date on a champagne bottle means—that it has been made exclusively from the grapes gathered in a single year. With a few exceptions—such as the year 1928—there is not a very great difference between a vintage and a non-vintage wine. Shippers like to declare a vintage year occasionally and when they put a date upon a bottle, it means that they themselves consider it a better wine, but there is not the difference between a vintage and a non-vintage champagne that there is between a Château-bottled Margaux and a bottle labeled Margaux. A far more important date on a bottle of champagne would be—if it were ever given—that of its disgorgement, as I shall hope to show a little later.

When the *cuvée* has been made, either as vintage or non-vintage, the wine is bottled; sometimes a little sugar is added, if there is a lack of it. It is in the bottle that the second fermentation takes place, and bubbles are produced by the carbonic acid gas that is unable to escape. The bottles have to be very strong or they will break under the pressure of the gas. The bottles are left to lie on their sides for three or four years and during this time the wine becomes clear and sparkling but a sediment has been thrown onto the bottom of the bottle. This sediment has to be removed, without losing the effervescence. The operation of disgorgement is long and intricate. I have already described the process of *remuage*—by which the bottles are placed in shelves and by a daily twist lasting over three months are brought to a point where they are standing on their heads. They are now ready to be disgorged, but it is not necessary to disgorge them. They can be left pointing down, and during this period they will continue to mature. Once they have been disgorged, they will not mature; but after a certain time they will deteriorate.

I saw bottles being disgorged in both the Veuve Clicquot and the Moët et Chandon cellars. The process is basically the same but there are differences. The Moët method is the easier to describe. There is a long, low, narrow trough filled with a special freezing acid; the bottles, head downwards, are strung on a revolving chain that carries the neck of the bottle through the acid; by the time they reach the end of the trough there is about an inch of ice below the cork. Parallel with the trough is a line of workmen. One man turns the bottle right way up, and snips the wiring around the cork; the explosion of the carbonic acid gas forces out the ice and with it the particles of sediment that have collected; the workman wipes away the froth and smells the bottle to make sure that it was not corked. He is paid a reward for every corked bottle that he detects. He then places the bottle on a rotating line and a rubber nipple fits tight in its mouth, to prevent a further escape of wine. Only a very little wine has escaped, just enough to make room for the mixture of sugar and brandy which is to be added.

The morning on which I went around the Moët cellars, the bottles were destined for the South American market where a sweet wine is preferred and a little wine had to be withdrawn to make room for an extra supply of sugar mixture.

Because of the pressure of the carbonic acid gas inside the bottle, the corks have to be very strong, long and very thick. By law every cork bears around its base the word "Champagne," and the name of the shipper is printed on the bottom. Very powerful pressure is exerted on the cork to squeeze it into the bottle. The supply of cork, which comes from Spain and Portugal, is a considerable problem for the champagne trade. Experiments are being made with plastic corks and the kind of capsule that is used for beer bottles, prior to disgorging. But it is not yet known whether the results are satisfactory.

The wine does not improve once it has been disgorged. After five or six years it begins to deteriorate. It loses liveliness, and tends to "maderise," i.e., become dark and sour. It is unwise to order a bottle ten years old. It is possible, however, to find a bottle twenty years old that is full of charm and youth. This is very likely to be because the wine was not disgorged at the same time as the majority of the wines of that year that were put upon market. Shippers usually maintain in their cellars a quantity of undisgorged bottles. During my stay at the Château de Saran I drank 1898, 1906 and 1911 champagne. I cannot say that I particularly enjoyed them, but they were far from dead. On the other hand, I drank a '34 that was excellent. It had been only recently disgorged. That is what I meant by saying that the date of "disgorgement" could be more important than the date when the grapes were gathered.

The importance of the date of "disgorgement" is exemplified by the Dom Pérignon brand that Moët et Chandon market. I had wondered and asked whether shippers did not make special *cuvées* in special years for special customers. I was told that by and large they did not; they concentrate on the two types of wine, vintage and non-vintage, but in the same way that Roederer puts out a special "crystal" champagne, in a clear glass bottle without a punt—I have been told that this type of bottle was originally devised for the last Tsar—Moët in 1936 put out a special wine in an old-fashioned type of bottle, the accepted form of champagne bottle having been standardized under Napoleon III. This wine proved very popular, embarrassingly popular in one respect. Everyone wanted it and the supply was short. Because this particular-sized bottle existed, those who ordered Moët et Chandon wanted their wine in that bottle. The experiment was made again in 1947 and 1949. The chief difference between a Dom Pérignon and an ordinary vintage wine lies probably in this, that the Dom Pérignon wine stays longer in the bottle before "disgorgement." At the time of writing (June, 1958), the 1949 bottles have not yet been disgorged.

There is also made a certain amount of still champagne. We were served it every night at the Château de Saran as a first wine, before the red Bouzy or Dizy. It was popular in London in the 1930's but I always felt about it as I did about a red hock—why bother about it when there are better red wines elsewhere? It seems a pity that any of the grapes that grow on those fortunate slopes beside the Marne should not be made to sparkle.

There was a time when I mistakenly thought that Grande and Petite Champagne were brandies distilled from still champagne. The only spirit made in the area is De-daine—a *marc* de Champagne. I took a glass each evening at the Château but never managed to finish it.

The champagne was always served in a medium-sized tulip-shaped glass. Wine shippers view with horror the flat saucer-shaped glasses that are served in so many restaurants, and which remove the sparkle from the wine almost as quickly as a swizzle stick. The best glass of all, they told me, to retain the sparkle is one with a hollow stem. I was shown an old crystal glass whose stem was shaped a little like a bottle of Schiaparelli's "Shocking." The small waist at the foot sent up a surprising explosion of bubbles. They do not make such glasses now, but I foresee a pleasant hobby for my declining years searching for them in antique shops. I am prepared to go to quite a lot of trouble to increase my friends' and my own pleasure in this delightful, fascinating wine.

# SPIRITS

## *1. The Art of Distillation*

✤                                ✤

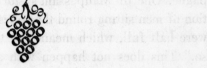

**F**ROM ÉPERNAY I went to Cognac, and through that visit a quite different section of this book begins. So far I have dealt only with wine, with the fermented juice of the grape, but now we are dealing with the spirits that are distilled from wine and other fermented compounds, and with the wines other than port—that is to say, sherry and Madeira—that are fortified by spirits. It is an entirely different subject.

I have done my best to foster in my children a love of wine, but to discourage a too early taste for spirits. Spirits are an intoxicant which the hot blood of youth can well do without.

The table of alcohol content tells its story. Table wines contain about ten per cent of alcohol. Fortified wines, ver-

mouth, sherry and the like, contain twenty per cent, but
spirits contain forty per cent; that is a vast difference.
Moreover, spirits are insidious. They "creep up on you."
Wine has a self-protective quality. After you have drunk a
certain amount, you have difficulty in swallowing, the epi-
glottis appears to close; this is particularly true of champagne. One of Maupassant's stories begins with a description of men sitting round the relics of a dinner: "The glasses
were half full, which meant that the guests were completely
so." This does not happen with spirits. You do not notice
how much you are drinking, and as the color of the liquid
darkens you miss the taste of it. I have seen a good deal of
alcoholism in my time, particularly in the U.S.A. as a result of Prohibition, and in every instance it has been due to
spirits.

A certain section of Françoise Sagan's public was disturbed by the casual morals of her heroines; I was shocked
by the amount of whisky they consumed, and before luncheon too. Whisky is too heavy a drink until the evening, and
even then I believe that one is better without it till one is over
thirty. At the same time how pleasant are the various pre-
prandial drinks that have a base of spirits.

During Prohibition in the United States, there were
those who suggested that partial repeal might be achieved
by allowing the sale of light wines and beers. In terms of
Europe that might have been a feasible suggestion, but in
terms of America it was unhelpful. It would be untrue to
say that America is a spirit-drinking country, since it stands
eighth in the list of wine-producing countries, and is one of
the chief importers of French wines, but "American Bar"
would not be such a universal appellation if you did not
find in U.S.A. the best drinks long and short that can be
compounded out of ice and alcohol. How often in the south
of France on a hot June morning, faced with *pastis* as the

only tolerable alternative to sticky *apéritifs* like Suze and sour ones like Byrrh, have I not felt envious of my fellow centurions and members of the coffee house who take their pick of any number of drinks, long or short, sweet or sour, compounded of rum or gin. I can imagine France and Italy subsisting very happily on light wines and beers, but I cannot picture the United States doing so.

Possibly, as is so much else, it is a question of climate. You need to hit back at the hard winters and the heavy summers. The Scandinavians have always been spirit drinkers.

Spirits present a problem to the unwary; let us leave it there, giving the last word to Saintsbury. "I think those who can drink them and do not, fools, but I think those who can't drink them and do, worse fools and unjust men too because they bring scandal on an excellent creature and consume that share of it that should go to others."

In essence the making of spirits is very simple; alcohol boils and becomes vapor at a lower temperature than water. If this vapor is collected in another vessel and cooled, the alcohol will resume its liquid form, without water. It is as simple as that; but it took the modern world a long while to discover it.

The ancient world was partially aware of it. Pliny describes a method of distilling spirits of turpentine from resin by cooking it in a pot covered with a fleece of wool, the spirits being squeezed out of the wool afterwards. There was also a method of distilling fresh water from sea water. But it occurred to no one to distill spirits from grape wine.

The West lost the art of distillation during the Dark Ages, but the East preserved it; though the Arabs were forbidden alcohol, they distilled perfumes and it was from the Arabs that the Spaniards acquired the technique, so that sherry as a fortified wine had a long start over its rivals.

Liqueurs were first discovered in the monasteries. Alchemists as a whole were secretive about their potions as they were afraid of being tried for sorcery, and chemists only sold their brews on a doctor's recommendation, but monks were above suspicion. Benedictine, which so delighted Francis I, was the first of the monastic liqueurs (it was invented in about 1510 by a Benedictine monk named Dom Bernardo Vincelli), and contains twenty-eight different herbs, including honey and China tea. The abbey was destroyed in the French Revolution and the recipe was lost for nearly a hundred years when it was discovered by Alexander Legrand in a collection of old papers. Chartreuse, green and yellow, is its greatest rival. The Chartreuse that I drank in London in the twenties had not the quality that the early nineteenth century had appreciated. It was originally produced in the monastery near Grenoble. But in 1860 a large distillery was installed and the quality dropped. Then in 1903 the Carthusian Order was expelled from France, and the liqueur that they produced in Tarragona was poor. They returned in 1931 and the Chartreuse that is marketed today, though a standardized commodity, is better than what was sold as Chartreuse in the 1920's.

Spirits can be distilled from almost anything: brandy comes from wine, rum from sugar cane, Calvados and applejack from cider. Whisky comes from grain, *Aquavit* from sawdust, schnapps and vodka from potatoes, the best gin from molasses, arrack from a dozen sources: rice, palm-sap, dates and grapes. But there are only three great types of spirits: brandy, rum and whisky; by that I mean there are only three types that you can inhale, sip, roll round your tongue; that can inspire poetry. Gin is the chief ingredient in many of the best cocktails and many of the best long drinks, but its qualities depend upon the ingenuity of man, on his skill in transforming its taste with other liquids, hard or soft. No one would sip straight a glass of London Gin and dilate upon its merits.

## 2. *Cognac*

Brandy was the first and is the most famous of all spirits. It is distilled from grape wine and the name is derived from the German *Brantwein,* burned wine. It was also called *Eau-de-vie.* Every wine-producing country produces brandy, but one brandy is supreme, that which is made from thin, new wine on the river Charente, a little to the north of the Gironde. It is called cognac after the town that stands upon its banks, and no other brandy can use that name.

In medieval days wine from these vineyards was shipped from La Rochelle to England, Denmark and the Low Countries, but the religious wars in the middle of the sixteenth century devastated the area, and when at the end of the century the vineyards were replanted, it was difficult to find a market for the wines. There is some doubt as to why this should have been. The new wines do not appear to have been strong enough to stand a sea voyage and André Simon suggests that during the years of war, the peasantry lost the art of wine-making. Robert Delamain, on the other hand, considers that the distress in which the wine growers of the Charente found themselves was due to high taxation, a heavy duty being laid on wines shipped by river, which placed them at a great disadvantage in relation to the wine growers on the coast, so that they were driven in their despair to distill their wine into brandy—this process having now become a recognized branch of the wine trade—since it could be shipped more economically when it had been reduced in bulk. At any rate, for whatever reason it was, the wine growers started to distill their wines into *Eau-de-vie* for which there was a ready market with the Danes and English. As time went by they discovered to their surprise and their delight that their brandy had a quality that was to be found nowhere else and that has been unchallenged through three centuries. Why this should be so, no one can tell. It is one of the mysteries of wine that one must accept as a miracle, as one accepts the wines of Burgundy and Bordeaux.

It was to see the scene of this miracle that I made the journey to Cognac. By the time I arrived the distilling was over, but I did not think that I should miss much by missing that. The process is very simple.

Cognac is distilled at the start of the year in a copper pot with a broad rounded bottom which tapers to meet a copper spiral tube. The first vapors to reach the condenser are called "the head," the last "the tail." It is from "the heart" that cognac is made. Cognac matures in wood, and it has no vintage year since it is a blend and since the cask in which it has been stored has to be replenished to meet evaporation. When a date appears upon a bottle, it refers to the year when the brandy was finally blended and put in a cask.

Seventy-five per cent of the crop is distilled by the vine grower himself; twenty-five per cent going to professional distillers and co-operatives of small growers. The vine grower takes samples of his brandy into Cognac and sells it to one of the big shippers. He may sell it when it is young and white or he may keep it in his cellars, while it gradually matures and takes on the color of the oak which comes from the neighboring forest of Limousin and is held to be responsible for its flavor. The small proprietors of the Charente do not leave their money in banks, nor hide it under their bed in stockings; they leave it in their cellars; it is liquid gold.

I have mentioned that cognac does not improve after it has been bottled. The best cognac has been matured for twenty years, but it can be drunk after three years. There are seven areas from which cognac comes: Grande Champagne and Petite Champagne; there are the areas of Borderies and Fins Bois, of Bons Bois, Bois Ordinaires and the Bois Communs. Wine merchants make their purchases in terms of these distinctions: to the public they recommend it in different ways. Three Star Brandy is over three and under seven years old. V.O. (very old) and V.E. (very extra) come next: they are seven to twelve years old. V.S.O. (very superior old) is from twelve to seventeen. V.S.O.P. (very superior old pale) from eighteen to twenty-five. V.V.S.O.P. (very very superior old pale) from twenty-five to forty. But that is a rough yardstick. Some shippers use a different nomenclature. In France one is wise to ask for a *Fine Maison*. It is invariably good.

I only spent two days in Cognac but they were enough to give me the feel, the atmosphere of the place. I went around two of the factories—Hennessy's, one of the two largest, and one of the smaller ones—Barnet and Elichagaray, a house of long traditions that makes a high quality cognac; on the second morning Maurice Hennessy drove me through the vineyards.

Cognac is a charming city; there is peace and dignity about its central rounded *place* with its equestrian statue of François I. There is an air of quiet, leisurely prosperity about it; in tune with the maturing wine on which its fortunes rest. They describe themselves there as "slow but wise." "Time is our life, not an enemy," they say. In the same way that a smell of oil hangs over the refinery at Aden, so does cognac scent the air around the Hennessy factories, and the

walls carry a dark patina, a fungus that the fumes have
set there. From the twilit shuttered cellars where the wine
matures, every day over twenty-five thousand bottles, as
much as is consumed in the whole of France, is lost in evaporation. "Angels' drink," they call it.

I was shown around the factory by a lively young
woman who provided me with the kind of anecdote that could
fit into such a narrative as this. "V.S.O.P., you know what
they mean?" she said. *"Versez sans oublier personne* (pour
without forgetting anyone) or *Vieux sans opinion politique*
(old without political opinion)." She showed me a picture
of the projecting hat that the local women wear. It was devised in Plantagenet times as a protection against the gallant advances of the British soldiers and is known as a
*Kichenot* (kiss-not). She pointed out the industry of the
women workers who take out their knitting during the fif-
teen-minute break in mid-afternoon.

I am not a scientific person. I did not understand by
any means all that I was being shown. When I was introduced to a refrigerating plant that was employed to prevent
sediment in the brandies destined for cold climates, I nodded
sagely, but I did not understand.

My chief impression was of the bulk of liquid that was
being stirred in vast vats and that was splashing through
pipes from one container to another. I had not realized that
cognac existed in such quantities.

Except that there is a bottling plant in Ireland, all the
bottling is done in Cognac. That afternoon the factory was
busily filling a demand from Venezuela for Three Star
Brandy. Each bottle had to bear the Venezuelan Customs
stamp. The order was accompanied by a supply of these
stamps, every one of which had to be accounted for. The
Venezuelans insist on their consignments being made in
wicker baskets. Americans want cartons, Britain wooden

cases. The Cognac firms are doing their best to convince the British that cartons are as safe as, and simpler to handle than, wooden cases. The American packages were stamped gift cartons. Inside they were wrapped for Christmas.

Hennessy is one of the great brandy firms of the world. Hennessy, Martell, Hine, Otard, Remy Martin are known everywhere, but before that afternoon I had frankly never heard of Barnet and Elichagaray; without, however, the ninety minutes that I spent there, my picture of cognac would have been incomplete. It is the equivalent of a small, solid provincial business producing a sound commodity for a small, loyal and gradually increasing clientele, and it was typical of that kind of business that at the end of the factory there should be a rose garden.

One of the rooms in the factory—a large high-ceiled room—is called *Le Paradis*. It contains a considerable quantity of demijohns, filled with old cognac. The brandy will not improve once it has left the cask, but it was moved into demijohns so as to avoid the loss through evaporation. Though it seemed so typical of a small and cozy house, I understand that even the larger firms generally have a room labeled *Le Paradis* also.

The grapes of the Charente are poor to eat and little wine is made there now. The table wine that I was served at the local hotel, L'Auberge—and incidentally a very good one—came from Jurançon (though I was interested to find there a bottle of the *vin rosé* that Alexis Lichine is making at Château Lascombes). But there is a local *apéritif* called Pineau, made in the same way as port, the fermentation being stopped by alcohol. I tasted it for the first time at Barnet's. It was called Pineau St. Martin. It had a poor nose, but it was not unpalatable. I should prefer it at the end of a meal rather than at the beginning.

Henri Martin, the director of Barnet's, opened his show-

case for me. He had a bottle labeled "Napoleon." "It is ridiculous, isn't it?" he said, "but if people ask for this kind
of thing they must be given it." He also had a bottle labeled
"Chef's Cooking Cognac." It had a chef on the label. "A
new idea of mine," he said. "It is just as good cognac as
three-quarters of the brandy that is sold as a liqueur, but
because it is labeled 'Cooking,' English and Americans
will scatter it freely in their sauces and much improve their
cuisine." But I am glad to say that the bottle he gave me as
a souvenir carried no fancy nomenclature; it had a very
simple crested label *"Vieille Réserve Grande Fine Champagne."* It came from *Le Paradis,* I suppose.

Next morning Maurice Hennessy drove me around the
vineyards. It was a two-hour drive, and during two hours
you can get quite a lot of talking done. I asked him what
had happened here during the second war; I had heard that
when the Germans retreated in the summer of '44, the stocks
of cognac were greater than they had been in 1940. The explanation I had been given was that the Germans had visualized the Charente vineyards as an essential contributor to
their planned economy of the Fortress Europe, to which end
they had conserved stocks of brandy till they could draw up
their blueprint, and that when the retreat began they had
no time to withdraw their stocks. Was this true, I asked
Hennessy? He shook his head. It was true that there were
bigger stocks in 1944 than there had been in 1940, but the
Germans were not responsible for that.

Maurice Hennessy is now in his early sixties. "In July
1940," he said, "I recognized that our export trade was
ended for the duration. I did not see where or how we were
going to sell our brandy. What was going to happen to the
wine growers of the Charente? I was very conscious of my
duty to them. For generations they had been the basis of our
business. They had to be protected. I went to Vichy, inter-

viewed the Ministry of Agriculture, and suggested a series of regulations that would safeguard their interests in a period of depression. That is what I anticipated, a slump in the demand for cognac. I could not have been more wrong." He chuckled. "For two months," he said, "there was complete stagnation, then we had the biggest succession of orders from all over France and Germany in the history of the cognac trade. If we had not had these regulations there would not have been a cask of cognac left. We made the regulations for one reason and used them for another."

I asked him where the cognac went. "Mainly down the gullets of the French, though the Germans got their share. Wine vanished, I don't know where, as things do in wartime. But there was always cognac."

I asked him whether there had been much black-marketing, much of what was known as the *Système D*—which after the war was so difficult to dislodge from the French economy.

"Naturally," he said, "but there is a gold book in our memories, in which are written the names of those wine growers who never let us down. Those men and their descendants can do anything they like with us. I'm going to take you to see one of them."

He took me to La Sentinelle, a vineyard that has been so fortunately placed by the curving of the hills that it has been spared the frosts that have hurt the crops of so many of its neighbors. It was run by three generations: the father, the son, the grandson. The father was in his middle seventies and complained of bronchitis, but he looked hale and cheerful; there was a mischievous twinkle in his eye; between himself and his grandson was apparent the difference that fifty years of progress has effected even in agricultural France. The old man was the perfect, the eternal type, of the vineyard owner, with his black cap and black scarf knotted around his throat and dark misshapen trousers; the young man was almost dapper, with well-cut trousers and smart shoes. He was a man, clearly, of the vines, but he would also have been at his ease in a Bordeaux dance room.

At La Sentinelle I saw within a few yards the whole process of making brandy: there were the large presses, idle now, and the copper pot stills shining, like heathen deities beside the red brick ovens where the wine was heated. I was taken into the dark cellar where the brandy was maturing in its casks. There were many casks there, waiting to be sold to the cognac shippers. That was the family capital. They gave me sips from the brandies of various years, the young white *Eau-de-vie*, and the dark mature wine that would be blended in cognac into a *Fine Champagne*. The white wine was fiery hot; a drop on the tongue was all that I could take; the dark wine I rolled slowly round my palate. I took a last look back as we left the cellar. How much more satisfactory to see one's wealth lying in the dusk in casks, growing more rich each day, than to scan apprehensively the lists in the stock market.

There is less *chichi* about brandy now than there was when I was young. We talked then about Napoleon brandy not realizing that there could scarcely be such a thing, or if there was, it might not be any good, since the important point about brandy is not when it was bottled, but how long it had been in wood. If it had been in a cask since 1811— the date of a great vintage—little would now be left of the original spirit.

In the 1920's there was much rolling round of thimblefuls of liquid in large balloon-shaped glasses, and I spent a ridiculous amount of time practicing the roll of the liquid, with water in the glass, so that a continuous flow could be maintained. A thick treacly brandy was then in vogue. Evelyn Waugh selected this English trait for a sharply pointed satiric passage.

In *Brideshead Revisited* Charles Ryder is entertained in Paris by that exasperating *faux bonhomme*, Rex Mulcaster.

"The cognac was not to Rex's taste. It was clear and pale and it came to us in a bottle free from grime and Napoleonic cyphers. It was only a year or two older than Rex and lately bottled. They gave it to us in very thin tulip-shaped glasses of modest size.

"Brandy's one of the things I do know a bit about," said Rex. "This is a bad color. What's more, I can't taste it in this thimble."

They brought him a balloon the size of his head. He made them warm it over the spirit lamp. Then he rolled the splendid spirit round, buried his face in the fumes and pronounced it the sort of stuff he put soda in at home.

So, shamefacedly, they wheeled out of its hiding-place the vast and moldy bottle they kept for people of Rex's sort.

"That's the stuff," he said, tilting the treacly concoction till it left dark rings round the sides of his glass. "They've always got some tucked away, but they won't bring it out unless you make a fuss. Have some."

"I'm quite happy with this."

"Well, it's a crime to drink it if you don't really appreciate it."

Cognac is the greatest brandy, but armagnac is very good. At its best it is better than a mediocre cognac. It comes from a smattering of vineyards south of the Garonne. France herself produces many other brandies. So does every other wine-growing country, for export or for home consumption. Many of them are far from being poor. The only thing against them is the same thing that is held against local wines in relation to the wines of the Médoc, Burgundy, the Rhine and the Moselle. They are not as good as cognac. Most of us who served in the Middle East during the war were exposed to Palestinian brandy. Even when diluted with

soda water it was barely palatable. Occasionally we found
a bottle of South African brandy. That was very different.
The best brandy that I have tasted apart from cognac and
armagnac is Domecq's Spanish Fundador. It is exported to
South America, to Cuba and to Mexico. I drank it for the
first time in New York in the autumn of 1945. Cognac was
then in short supply. I thought it excellent. When I was in
Spain a few years ago I thought even more highly of it and
was assured—a statement that L. W. Marrison confirms—
that the brandy which is retained inside the country is even
better than that which is exported. I confirmed this opinion
very definitely when I went to Jerez. Calvados, which the
French distill from cider, is a brandy rather than a liqueur.

Every wine-growing country and many a vineless one
produces its own liqueurs as its own *apéritifs*. I would not
recommend the traveler to make a habit of sampling local
brandies: they can be lethal in their effects on the nerves
and the digestion, particularly the Italian *grappa* to which
Ernest Hemingway's characters are so addicted. But local
liqueurs are a different matter. They are usually palatable,
since they are doctored to please the palate, not to give a
kick; they are also a great deal cheaper than imported
French liqueurs like Benedictine, Grand Marnier and Coin-
treau. Usually they are made from fruit—apples, plums,
cherries, apricots and strawberries. There is the Cherry
Heering of Denmark to which a later chapter will be devoted. Of Strega, the Italian liqueur, a gourmet whose name
I cannot recall remarked, "I never met a woman who did
not like Strega, yet I never met a woman who had ever had
it before I offered it to her." There are certain other excellent post-prandial drinks which, strictly speaking, should
not be classified as liqueurs since they are not and are listed
in France as *Eau-de-vie et spiriteux*. There is Kirsch in
West Central Europe; there are Framboise and Mirabelle

and how many others; there is Scotland's Drambuie, Slivo-
vitz from the plums of Yugoslavia. Each has its special
charm but the classic end to a dinner is a glass of cognac.

### 3. *Whisky*

Only a Scotsman will deny that cognac is the greatest distilled potation. No one will deny that whisky has the second
place.

Whisky is a late contestant, in this highly competitive
arena. In Dickens' novels, whisky is scarcely mentioned. "B
and S" (brandy and soda) was the drink for the smart man-
about-town, if he felt like spirits rather than such a light
drink as hock-and-seltzer. Whisky was something barbarous
from across the border, and until the eighteen-eighties it was
more likely to mean Irish than Scotch; in 1875 Gilbey's sold
83,000 dozen Irish to only 38,000 dozen Scotch. It was the
phylloxera's attack on the Charente that gave Scotch whisky
its chance. As soon as the English became familiar with its
excellence, and improvements in distilling methods were introduced, its popularity increased so rapidly that a for-
eigner today invariably caricatures an Englishman with a
whisky-and-soda or a tankard of bitter in his hand.

The juxtaposition is not inappropriate. For what
brandy is to wine, whisky is to beer; the one obtained by
distilling wine, the other by distilling fermented grain. To
each, moreover, has the same generic name been applied,
brandy being called *Eau-de-vie* and the word "whisky" (or,
in Ireland, "whiskey") being derived from the Celtic *uisge-
beatha,* later *usquebaugh,* meaning "water of life."

The oldest reference to whisky appears in the Scottish
Exchequer Rolls for 1494, where a Friar John Cor is issued

eight bolls of malt wherewith to make *aquavitae:* Burns, in his *Tam o'Shanter,* pays tribute in the same couplet to two-penny ale and to whisky:

> *"Inspiring bold John Barleycorn*
> *What dangers thou canst make us scorn!*
> *Wi' tippeny, we fear nae evil:*
> *Wi' usquebae, we'll face the devil."*

Just as wine varies according to the soil and climate in which it is produced, so does whisky. Each country's product is completely different. Many countries have tried by using identical methods to produce a so-called "Scotch" but without success. The soft burn-water off the peaty moors of the Highlands gives true whisky its inimitable flavor.

Sir Robert Bruce Lockhart in his book *Scotch* has written a poetic description of this countryside.

. . . the belt of land bounded on the west by the River Ness and on the east by the River Deveron. Here Nature has been generous in her gifts. The land, cold and hard in winter, but in summer warm to eye and heart, slopes down from the granite of the Blue Mountains through peat and heather moor to the rich farmlands which stretch to the Moray Firth and which grow the life-giving barley. It is peopled by a race which retains to this day the graces and natural manners of the Highlander. Wondrously beautiful are the summer evenings when sky and setting sun weave a kaleidoscope pattern of light and shade on hill and glen, until night in the form of a low white bank of cloud steals slowly like a wraith over the tops of Cairngorm and Braeriach.

To the average contemporary Englishman "whisky" means Scotch whisky. There has never been a great demand in England for either Canadian or Australian whiskey. American whiskies have rarely found their way to the English table, and though Irish whiskey was popular in the eighteen-sixties, and there are still many who appreciate its special qualities, most connoisseurs would agree that only the best bourbon whiskey from Kentucky can enter into competition for flavor, richness and purity with the malt whiskies of Campbelltown and Speyside.

Historians are not in agreement with one another as to the origins of Scotch. Was it the Greek barley-wine or the Egyptian Bolonachi? Mr. S. H. Hastie considered that it was the Irish spreading northward through Killarney who introduced the Scots to the excellence of pot-distilled whisky. He dates this to the middle of the eighteenth century. Bruce Lockhart states that the batle of Culloden (1746) not only opened the Highlands to the Lowlands but carved a road to the south for the passage of Highland whisky.

Culloden ruined the Jacobite chiefs and exalted the Whigs who had supported the Hanoverians. Civil wars are followed by injustice to the defeated, and as a British equivalent of the carpet-baggers who poured into the Southern States after the defeat of the Confederates, the Highlanders had excise men and gaugers levying taxes on their whisky. The English insisted that stills should have a minimum capacity of five hundred gallons, because the existence of such large stills could be checked. This naturally antagonized the Highlanders, who were further exasperated by a decree that whereas England and the Lowlands paid duty on each gallon, the Highlanders were taxed on the capacity of the still, whose produce had to be sold within the thinly populated Highlands. It is not surprising that during the last half of the eighteenth century and the first quarter of the nineteenth, smuggling flourished in the Highlands.

Few illicit industries have been more fortunately placed. The process of manufacture is not complicated. It consists, in the simplest terms, of malting the barley, mashing the malt, fermenting the resultant liquor (the wort) into wash and finally submitting it into two pots for distillation. It is then matured in wood. The distiller's task is to deprive the plant of its food and convert the starch into fermentable sugar. The malting process is performed by stimulating germination and then arresting it. Yeast is the fermenting agent. Malt is placed in the kiln—a chamber with a perforated wire floor below which a peat fire is burning. The smoke dries the malt slowly and gives it a peaty flavor. Not only did the Highlands provide with their water, peat and barley the essential ingredients for whisky, but the remoteness of their glens provided a perfect cover for illicit stills.

Bruce Lockhart's *Scotch* contains a number of stories of the devices that the smugglers employed to outwit their enemies. It is a temptation to quote some of them, but it is unfair to "pick plums" out of a fellow-writer's book—particularly when that writer is a friend—so I will content myself with warmly recommending to the reader that informative and fascinating book.

The war between the smugglers and the excisemen was waged for three-quarters of a century, until 1823, when the Duke of Gordon in the House of Lords assured the government that if it would sanction the manufacture of legal whisky of a quality equal to the illicit on the payment of a reasonable duty, he and his friends would do their best to suppress smuggling.

The Scotch which was distilled by the smugglers was a pure malt whisky and this fact delayed the universal popularity of Scotch; it is too strong a drink for Lowlanders and Englishmen, and it was the invention of the patent still that brought whisky to England. Neil Gunn dismissed this as "an affair of two tall columns heated by steam into which wash is poured at one end and out of which practically pure alcohol pours at the other," and malt whisky owners described as trash the grain whisky that it produced, but it was not until malt was blended with grain whisky that a mixture was produced which was suitable for the city dwellers of England and the U.S.A. Moreover, a patent still may be established anywhere. There are fifteen distilleries near Edinburgh and Glasgow. All spirits are colorless when they are distilled, and the pale yellow shade is produced by caramel. It is stored in wood, usually old sherry casks, for a minimum of three years. That is the legal limit. But it is usually left for eight or twelve years. After twelve years the improvement is slight and after twenty years it deteriorates. It does not improve in bottle. A large proportion of Scotch whisky is exported to the U.S.A., on an average of a hundred and eighty million bottles yearly; only about sixty million bottles being sold in the U.K.

There are six different whiskies. In England Scotch whisky is spelt 'ky'—'key' is the spelling for Irish and American whiskey.

1. Scotch malt whisky distilled in a simple pot still from a mash consisting of malted barley.

2. Scotch grain whisky distilled in a patent still from a mixed mash of cereal grain, preferably maize; malted barley converting the unmalted grain.

3. Blended Scotch—a mixture of malt and grain whisky.

4. Irish whiskey—a mixture of malt and grain. Three distillations are used, as opposed to two in Scotland. There is a wider range of cereals and it takes longer to mature in wood. Its taste resembles that of rye whiskey.

5. American bourbon, a mash of mixed cereal grain, fifty-one per cent corn.

6. American rye, a mash of mixed cereal grain, fifty-one per cent rye.

Men will argue endlessly as to the correct way of drinking whisky. Scots maintain that it is a crime to put soda water onto Scotch, and when Scotch is twelve years old there is much to be said for drinking it straight with a glass of water as a chaser. But I have personally always found that Scotch needs soda water to bring out its flavor; bourbon, on the other hand, is in my opinion best taken neat on ice cubes (on the rocks), and is not the first sip of an "Old-fashioned" the best before the ice has begun to melt? But these are matters of individual taste. I enjoy the manhattan cocktail, but there are those who think it criminal to dilute bourbon with Italian vermouth. Peter Arno had a cartoon in *The New Yorker* of a Southern colonel fainting on being offered Seven-Up with bourbon, but personally I like rye and ginger ale.

There are other beverages that in various parts of the world are described as whiskies. Perhaps they would be more palatable if they were given a different appellation. In Bangkok recently, at the end of an excellent dinner, I was offered, as a curiosity, a Siamese whiskey, Mekong. "You need not finish it," my host said. It smelled like hair oil, and one sip sufficed. Two days later, after I had been lecturing at Chula University in the afternoon, after an unalcoholic lunch, one of the English professors suggested that instead of having tea, we should go to a small Vietnam restaurant for hot *hors d'oeuvres* and Mekong. He did not call Mekong whiskey. "It's made of molasses," he said. "It has only twenty per cent alcohol. It isn't at all bad, if you squeeze lime over it." It was extremely good and the three of us had an ample meal, with two glasses each of Mekong, for a dollar fifty.

In Japan you can buy local gin, whiskey and champagne. The bottles are labeled like French and English bottles. The champagne which I drank was very sweet but it was palatable and refreshing. The whiskey could not be mistaken for Scotch, but it was pleasant to taste; it was enlivening and had no after-effects. It was by no means cheap; the best Santoy cost four dollars.

## 4. Rum

"Rum, Jamaica rum, 'Tis the one commodity that reconciles me to these barbarous places." Thus begins John Gay's opera *Polly Peachum*, the successor to *The Beggars' Opera*, written in the early eighteenth century. How many other exiles, wanderers and victims of mischance have not been consoled and fortified by this noble spirit. It was the pirates' drink.

> *Fifteen men on a dead man's chest,*
> *Yo-ho-ho, and a bottle of rum.*
> *Drink and the devil have done for the rest.*

It is the soldier's drink. How many men have not tasted spirits for the first time on the eve of battle, in their tot of rum. It is the sailor's drink. Christopher Hassall gave me the origin of the word "grog." His own second name is Vernon, taken from an eighteenth-century ancestor, Admiral Vernon, the victor of Porto Bello; Vernon was nicknamed "Old Grog" because he wore a weather-worn cloak made out of grogram; he insisted that his men should take a daily dose of rum and water as a cure against scurvy; the dose was known as "grog."

Rum is one of the most wholesome of all spirits. It is made from sugar cane. It is one of the simplest to make. The canes are crushed and mangled between rollers; when the sugar has been extracted from the resultant syrup, what remains of the molasses is taken to the rum factory, to be fermented and distilled. Rum is universally connected with the West Indies. Sugar cane, originally brought into Europe from the Far East during the third century, was cultivated in Cyprus, Sicily, Spain, Madeira; it was one of the first crops that the Spaniards introduced into their new possessions.

It was admirably suited to the West Indian climate and it was admirably suited to the conditions of slave labor. Its cultivation required no skill, merely strength and a capacity to resist the tropical sun. The canes are harvested with a heavy cutlass (the *machete,* with which the many victims of revolutions and slave risings in the area have been hacked to pieces); the stalks are trimmed of leaves and are then carted to the sugar mills.

In the eighteenth century, in the great days of sugar, when the phrase "rich as a Creole" was in common use, when the islands were so much the focus of British foreign policy that the British in 1763 nearly handed Canada back to France in return for Guadeloupe, each estate had its own mill. St. Croix, Antigua and Barbados are dotted with tapering ruins, and early prints show how picturesque those windmills made the landscape. Today the manufacture of rum and sugar is conducted in large co-operatives, and visitors to the West Indies by ship who make their first stop at Barbados are disappointed by the untropical appearance of the island. Much of it is very flat and when the visitor drives across it, he cannot see above the cane crop. But in the hilly sections of Barbados, and in the gently rolling countryside of Antigua, there is a genuine pastoral beauty about the tall spears swaying in the wind; there is always a wind in the West Indies.

There are two kinds of rum, dark and light. The light rum comes mainly from Cuba and Puerto Rico—Bacardi and Don Q—and is drunk more in the United States than it

is in Europe, largely because of the close political links between those islands and Washington, but also because light
rum is better suited to the cocktails and cold long drinks in
which Americans specialize. The rum drinks of the Century
Club reconcile me to the "barbarity" of a New York summer.

Dark heavy rums are more suitable as an antidote to
the cold clammy English climate and hot rum drinks have
always been popular. Jamaican rum, Myers' and Lemon
Hart, are the best known. Recently, Trinidad's Vat 19, a
Fernandez product and a lighter rum, has proved popular.
Barbadian rum is superb but it seems to be drunk mainly
in the Caribbean. All rum is good, the preference for one
rather than for another being a question of personal taste. Myself, I prefer that of Martinique; St. James in particular.
But perhaps that is because it was the first real rum I ever
tasted. I traveled to the West Indies in a French Line ship
and Martinique was my first West Indian island. I took a
bungalow in the country for six weeks. All the time there I
drank the wine of the country.

Martinique rum is heavy; it is rather sweet. I fancy
that it is purer than other rums, since it needs less building
up. It is drunk without accessories. The rum that is shipped
to Europe is dark, but in Martinique unless you ask for an
old rum, you will be served with a white one. It is worth
asking for an old rum. You mix your rum punch yourself.
The bottle is put on the table and you take as much as you
need. You are also given a lime, an earthenware carafe of
water—the kind of porous carafe in which the water is
cooled by evaporation—a bottle of syrup and some ice. The
punch is mixed on the classic formula—one of sour, two of
sweet, three of strong and four of weak—the lime being the
sour and the syrup providing the sweet. In a French Line

ship, if you order a rum punch, grated nutmeg may be sprinkled on the surface. But in Martinique cafés a punch is always prepared in that simple fashion; surely a tribute to its quality. Barbados rum is the only other rum that tastes better neat than after it has been sophisticated.

In British islands punches are nearly always flavored with nutmeg and Angostura bitters, mainly I suppose because Grenada has been nicknamed the Spice Island and produces nutmegs and because Trinidad is the home of Angostura bitters. The history of these bitters is interesting. Early in the nineteenth century a Dr. Siegert, a South American doctor, produced it as a medicine for circulation among his friends and patients, under the name of aromatic bitters, and though its contents are in large measure alcoholic it is registered as a medicine on the tariff of the United States and was imported freely during Prohibition. It proved so popular that he decided to put it on the market, and called it Angostura after the town where he was quartered. The unsettled state of Venezuelan politics forced him to move his factory to Trinidad. It was there realized how excellent a flavoring it was for rum, and the domestic concoction that was devised as a cure for diarrhea is now an essential contribution to the enjoyment of ninety per cent of the world's rum drinks.

The secret of its ingredients has never been divulged. Chemists are unable to analyze its constituent parts. The Siegerts are part of the island's aristocracy and a visit to their factory is a "must" for the visitor to Port-of-Spain.

Punch is a noontide drink, to be sipped before lunch in your own home or taken to the beach in a thermos flask. There are many recipes and a cherry is often added; when the punch is made out of light rum, pineapple improves its flavor. The barmen at the airports of Trinidad and Puerto Rico are experts in producing, in tall wide glasses, infi-

nitely refreshing fruit-flavored punches. But the formula of
"one of sour . . ." remains the basis of all punches.

In the evening, swizzles are preferred to punches. The
swizzle-stick is a foot long, with three or four short branch-
ing fingers; rotated swiftly between the palms, it fulfills the
function of an electric mixer and lashes into a froth a jug
filled with a mixture of rum and ice. Swizzles are sweet or
sour. A sour swizzle is deceptive in appearance. I remember
the first one I drank, in Dominica. It was pale pink; I expected it to taste like sherbet. But it had been compounded
of white rum and Angostura bitters. My first instinct when
I sipped it was to spit it out. A sour swizzle has to be tossed
back in a single swallow.

Rum is cheap in the West Indies. The visitor is always wise to concentrate upon indigenous products, and
since rum can be drunk in so many different ways, as a long
drink or a short one, as an iced one or as a hot toddy, he is
unwise to worry about gin and whisky when he is in those
enchanted islands.

## 5. *Gin*

Reference was made in an earlier chapter to how William
of Orange introduced gin into England and its popularity
at Court encouraged London distillers to provide a gin of
their own.

The type which they eventually evolved and which is
known today as London Gin is very different in taste from
the original geneva. It is produced by distilling in a pot-still
highly rectified spirits together with various "botanicals."
Juniper berry and coriander seed are common to all brands
of London Gin and give it its basic flavor. The additional

botanicals which give to each separate brand its final and distinctive flavor are kept a carefully guarded secret by each distiller.

Today the name "London Gin" refers to a type of gin rather than a place of origin (unlike "Plymouth Gin" which is still a geographical as well as a descriptive name), since the pressure of customs duties has forced London distillers to manufacture their gin in countries to which they used to ship it.

From 1690 onwards, London Gin was so cheap in England that it was within everyone's reach and it was even given to workpeople as part of their wages. The evil reputation that it acquired in those days lasted for a century and a half.

Hazlitt was upbraided for his addiction to it; one of Trollope's characters was horrified when her father, for reasons of economy, adopted it; and Saintsbury writing as late as 1920 admits to having been always sorry for gin, "that humble and much reviled liquid which is the most specially English of all spirits."

Its cheapness as much as anything was responsible for its low reputation. In 1914 its price was half-a-crown a bottle. I realized this fact during Prohibition in New York. As long as I had been of an age to buy spirits in London, whisky and gin had cost about the same amount. When I entertained, I offered my guests after dinner a choice between whisky and soda, and gin and ginger-beer or lime-juice. Myself, I took gin, lime juice and soda, because I preferred the taste. In New York if I had gin and ginger-ale to offer my friends it did not worry me when I ran out of whisky; when I went out for the evening I filled my flask with gin, because it was what I preferred. But I did gradually detect a certain coolness toward my gin and gingers. I made inquiries. An honest friend told me that she always thought of gin as a "mean" drink. The adjective "mean" has a different significance in New York from what it has in London. I pressed her to be more explicit. She shrugged. "Oh, you know, mean in every way!" I saw her point. It was something you made in a bathtub. It cost two dollars a quart and much of the gin that one bought in America in those days was very bad.

It was the staple drink in California in 1928. After three weeks there as a house guest my tongue felt as though it had sprouted a self-protective varnish. I could scarcely tell what I was eating. I could not distinguish between one flavor and the next.

Those days are over now. Gin needs no defense. It is the basis of many cocktails and is an essential ingredient in the best long summer drinks—gin and tonic, gin and ginger beer, and the Tom Collins.

It is moreover a very healthy drink. It began life as a medicine, and is a real specific for certain maladies. It has genuine diuretic properties and it is sometimes recommended to diabetics.

## 6. *Some Minor Items*

There is for each of us a special minor wine, *apéritif*, or cordial for which we have a particular fancy which we do not expect our friends to share but which we rely on them not to deplore. I have, for instance, a friend who prefers at the end of dinner a Crème-de-Menthe frappé to a cognac. Most of us have also a surprising minor addiction to something of which we do not really like the taste. I like vodka in that way, and pernod.

The vodka which I drank between the wars was very

different from the Smirnoff which is enjoying such a contemporary vogue. Prewar vodka came from Poland, it was
distilled from potato mash; Smirnoff—the English variety
at least—is brewed in Camden Town. I do not disparage
Smirnoff; it is excellent with tomato juice as a Bloody
Mary; it is good as a substitute for gin with tonic water;
some like it in a dry Martini. It goes with practically anything. It is wholesome, odorless and almost tasteless. A man
after two vodka Martinis can return to his home or office,
and his wife or secretary will think that he has been in a
coffee shop. Vodka, an essentially Russian drink, was introduced into Europe during the nineteenth century by Pierre
Smirnoff. His family after 1917 settled in Paris and later
moved to London. It was on their recipe that the distilling
in Camden Town was set in motion.

Gilbey's launched their brand in the Coronation summer of 1953, to balalaika music with a party at Oval
Road attended by a thousand guests. Few had previously
realized to how many uses vodka could be put.

The Polish vodka that I had drunk in the 1930's, the
Russian vodka that I drank in Moscow in 1935 and the Persian vodka that I drank again in Baghdad in 1942—it
came from Teheran and since Russian forces were stationed
there was probably the real McCoy—was an *apéritif* and
nothing else. You did not sip it. You shot back a glassful or
half-glassful in a sudden gulp as an accompaniment to
smoked fish, anchovied eggs or caviar. It was oily, it had a
sickly taste. I could not have borne to sip it. But it managed
to go well with those high-flavored *hors d'oeuvres*, or perhaps it would be more correct to say that they tasted excellent after it. It also sent a warm glow through one's veins.
Nor did it spoil one's palate. It led up to wine, in contrast
to the Danish *Aquavit* of which I enjoyed the taste, but which
seemed best as a preliminary to beer.

Smirnoff's Camden Town vodka is an altogether different thing. I do not say a word against it. I always have it in my cellar. It is different, that is all there is to it. When shall I again drink Russian vodka? Maybe never.

The other drink that I enjoy but of which I dislike the taste is Pernod, and its various cousins. The pervading flavor is of aniseed. As Pernod it is green, as *pastis* yellow, as *ouzo*—in Greece—white. You add ice, then pour cold water and the clear liquid clouds. It needs to be drunk slowly. It is an economical, as well as a refreshing drink, in the south of France, since it takes as long to drink as two vermouth cassis, and also because it is everywhere of local origin and therefore cheap.

Aniseed is an acquired taste. The first time I tasted *ouzo* —in 1926—I could not finish it. I learned to enjoy it in 1941 when I was stationed in Beirut. The Lebanese arrack is made from grapes. A dangerous liquid, it was forbidden to troops. The Bedouins used to sell them "hard oranges" which had been spiked with arrack. You have to eat while you are drinking it. It leaves a residue inside the lining of the stomach and if in the morning after drinking arrack, you drink a glass of water before you have had breakfast you may find yourself half-drunk.

You sip it slowly and between sips you eat. In cafés when you order it as an *apéritif* they serve *messe* with it— small *hors d'oeuvres*, side-dishes of cheese and nuts and radishes. If you do not eat while you are sipping, you will be drunk in a few minutes. Sometimes if you are talking, forget to eat and treat arrack as though it were a whisky and soda, you will feel the room swaying around you, but a couple of quick mouthfuls will set you straight.

I went once to a Lebanese arrack party. Five of us sat at a small table. There were twenty dishes, cold or nearly cold. There were sliced hard-boiled eggs, pistachios, *kibbe* which is minced meat pounded up with corn into a cake, *tabouli*—a cool-tasting salad, gherkins, cheese, olives, various garlic salads. We ate with our fingers. Every so often the host prepared a particularly good mouthful and fed a friend with it. A hot dish of small birds was brought. We first mopped up the gravy with our bread. We ate very slowly. The meal lasted three hours. We did not drink more than four small glasses of arrack in the evening. Eventually we turned on the radio and danced.

Pernod is an emasculated cousin of an *apéritif* which the contemporary traveler will seek in vain for, the absinthe which was so renowned during the nineties as to become the symbol of the nineties; the cocktail hour was then known as *"l'Heure Verte."*

It was suppressed in France at the start of the First World War as a temporary war measure, and like the majority of such measures was not repealed. Not so many people alive today have drunk it. I did in the Domino Room at the Café Royal. I took it with appropriate reverence, in memory of Dowson and Arthur Symons, Verlaine, Toulouse-Lautrec and the Nouvelle Athènes. I watched with awe the ritual of its preparation, the green liquid in the tall glass, the silver filter across its top with the lump of sugar laid on it; the water poured slowly onto the sugar and dripping through to cloud the liquid in the glass below.

I only drank it once, for I loathed the taste of it. In those days when you ordered a dry Martini "with a dash," a dry Martini was half gin and half French vermouth and a dash was not Angostura bitters but absinthe. Even thus diluted I thought it ruined the cocktail. But I daresay I should like it now. Whereas I hated my first taste of the Greek *ouzo*, with its overpowering flavor of aniseed, I have come to like Lebanese arrack, Pernod and the *pastis* of the Mediterranean. Absinthe contained the herb wormwood—*artemesia absinthium*—a fact which alone would have endeared it to the decadents. It had curious properties, every drink taken after it being doubled in intoxicating power. It was supposed to be a wonderful pick-me-up after a Channel crossing, but Channel crossings have lost their terror in days of large ships and dramamine. There seems little doubt that it damaged the health of those who were addicted to it, but it is very possible that in the mood they were in, in tune with the temper of the time, cognac would have done their work for them just as well.

It is in this section, I think, that I should pay tribute to a wine that I have only drunk once and cannot expect to drink again, Imperial Tokay. I drank it at a very small dinner party given in the spring of 1938 by Desmond Flower at the Écu de France in London. I have particularly happy memories of that dinner because Cyril Lakin of the *Sunday Times* was one of the guests and by the end of the evening I had been commissioned to report the Test matches for his paper.

Tokay exists no more. It was, I suppose, scarcely a wine at all: it was really a liqueur. The grapes shriveled on the vines. After being picked they were left to dry for a day longer in the sun. They were placed in vats and their essence was allowed to ooze through a hole in the bottom without any pressure other than the grapes' own weight. Many grapes were required. Its manufacture was only possible in a good year. Each bottle was numbered and distributed by the Austrian Emperor. It never reached the market. The bottle that I drank had come from the Imperial cellars. It was long past its prime but its bouquet was astonishing.

An Hungarian once said to Mrs. Vyvyan Holland, "Think of the most beautiful picture you have ever seen, the most wonderful symphony you have ever heard, the most beautiful sunset on earth, the fragrance of the most exquisite perfume in the Rue de la Paix and the company of the person you love most in the world. Add a touch of original sin, and there you have Tokay!"

┌─────────────────────────────────────────┐
│  ✣                                    ✣  │
│                                           │
│      # THE FORTIFIED WINES                │
│                                           │
│           *1. Sherry*                     │
│                                           │
│  ✣                                    ✣  │
└─────────────────────────────────────────┘

## 1

IF Spanish Apes ate all the grapes what should we do for sack?"

Dr. Abernethy, when asked what was the best time to drink a glass of brown sherry, replied, "Whenever you can get it, Madam."

If you omit the adjective "brown," no one would quarrel with that answer. There is always a right moment for a glass of sherry.

Sherry is a fortified wine made from grapes grown in the triangle formed by three Spanish towns that lie west of Cádiz—Jerez de la Frontera, Sanlúcar de Barrameda and Puerto de Santa Maria. There are many imitations of this wine: Australian, Californian, South African. They are wholesome and palatable but they are no more sherry than a red wine made from pinot or gamay grapes in California is Burgundy. It is a great pity that the Spanish wine merchants are not allowed a monopoly in the name of sherry as the Portuguese are in regard to port. As port derives from Oporto, so does sherry from Jerez which was originally called Xeres. Sherry is the product of a defined geographical area.

There are several different kinds of sherry. It can be straw-colored, pale yellow or dark brown. It can be dry or sweet, light or heavy. That is why there is always a right moment for a glass of sherry. In Victorian days the morning visitor was invariably offered it with a dry biscuit. It is a sound *apéritif*. It goes well with soup. A sweet, rich sherry rounds off a meal as happily as a glass of port; and it has this advantage over port that its flavor is not damaged by cigarette smoke.

There are two main types of sherry, *fino* and *oloroso*. They are quite different in character, the *fino* being much lighter in body, color and alcoholic strength. The two types are subdivided, the one into *finos* and *amontillados*, the other into *olorosos* and *rayas*. *Finos* are pale, straw-colored and very dry; the *amontillados* darken as they age, acquiring an amber hue. They have a nutty flavor and have more body than the *finos*. The *olorosos* are completely dry but because of their greater vinosity on the palate, they appear to leave a trace of sweetness. *Rayas* have less refinement than *olorosos* and lack their delicate aroma and clean bouquet; they often contain a vestige of grape sugar through incomplete fermentation.

There are two other wines about which there is some confusion, manzanilla and montilla. Certain purists insist that neither should be described as sherry. Manzanilla comes from Sanlúcar de Barrameda and is the child of the fresh sea breezes. It is lighter, paler and drier than the Jerez *finos*. Since the grapes from which it is made are grown within the triangle, it would appear captious to deny it the name of sherry. Montilla, however, is in a different category. Its grapes are grown outside the triangle, and it has three production centers: Montilla, Los Moriles and Aguilar de la Frontera. In 1944 its makers obtained from the Spanish Ministry of Agriculture the right to describe their product as Montilla-Moriles. Its alcoholic content is light. I have even seen bottles that are labeled "unfortified." It is pale and dry. It is very popular in southern Spain. It tastes like a mild *fino* and in Edwardian menus it was accepted unquestioningly as a sherry.

England, with its damp, clammy climate, has always welcomed the antidote of rich, fortified wines and sherry was the first such wine to reach it. The Spaniards had a long start on their European competitors. The Moors, who occupied Southern Spain until the middle of the fifteenth century, may have been prohibited the use of wine, but they were good husbandmen. Andalusia is rich in fruits and metals. The Moors made one very great mistake; they felled the trees and thus changed the country's climate, but much stands to their credit; they restored agriculture, irrigated the countryside, planted vines, built palaces. They also brought with them from Damascus the art of distillation. When Jerez was recaptured by Alfonso the Wise, two hundred years before the kingdom of Granada fell, Cádiz was admirably situated to take its place as one of the chief wine ports of the world.

That was in 1264, but it appears that sherry was being shipped to England during the Arab occupation. Señor Manuel Gonzalez Gordon in his authoritative work *Jerez-Xerez-Scheris*, which is in process of being translated into English, produces documentary proof that shipments of sherry were being made to the British Isles in the twelfth century. This must have been a "bootleg" operation and it was in English bottoms that the wine was carried. It was presumably for this reason that a precedent was established for reversing the usual procedure of trade, the English coming to fetch a wine instead of the Jerez merchants transporting it to England.

By the sixteenth century, sherry was firmly established as the Englishman's favorite drink. Sir Francis Drake, when he "singed the King of Spain's beard" in 1587, stayed an extra three days in Cádiz, at great personal risk, so that he could take on a cargo of sherry.

Into Falstaff's mouth Shakespeare put the most quoted tribute to wine in literature.

"Good faith," said the knight. "This same young sober-blooded boy doth not love me; nor a man cannot make him laugh; but that's no marvel, he drinks no wine. There's none of these demure boys come to any proof; for thin drink doth so overcool their blood, and making many fish meals, that they fall into a kind of male green sickness; and then when they marry, they get wenches; they are generally fools and cowards; which some of us should be too but for inflammation. A good sherris-sack hath a twofold operation in it; it ascends me into the brains; dries me there all the foolish, and dull and crudy vapors which environ it, make it apprehensive, quick, inventive, full of nimble, fiery and delectable shape, which delivered o'er to the tongue which is the birth, becomes excellent wit. The second property of your excellent sherris is the warming of the blood, which before cold and settled left the liver white and pale, which is the badge of pusillanimity and cowardice, but the sherris warms it and makes it course from the inwards to the parts extreme. It illuminateth the face, which as a beacon, gives warning to all the rest of this little kingdom, man, to arm, and then the vital commoners and inland petty spirits muster me all to their captain, the heart; who, great and puffed up with this retinue, doth any deed of courage, and this valor comes of sherris; so that skill in the weapon is nothing without sack, for that sets it a-work; and learning a mere hord of gold kept by a devil, till sack commences it and sets it in active use. . . . If I had a thousand sons, the first human principle I would teach them should be, to forswear thin potations and to addict themselves to sack!"

How many subsequent tributes to wine have done little more than paraphrase that speech.

It was originally believed that the word "sack" came from the Spanish word *seco,* meaning dry. But it is now held that the word comes from the verb *sacar,* to take out, *Vinos de Saca* being the technical word for the wines made at Jerez for export. This seems more likely in view of the English preference for strong sweet wines. Geoffrey Harrison quotes a sentence from the Town Clerk of Bristol in 1577, "came from Andaluzia such sweete and pleasant sacks in general as by repute the like was never known." An Act of Henry VIII in 1531, the first reference to sack in England, controls the price of "Malmseys, Romaneys, Sakkes and other sweet wines."

We know the Elizabethans mulled their wine. "I'll go burn some sack," said Falstaff. We also know that they doctored their wine, sprinkling it with lime to keep it from going bad. We may presume that it was an *oloroso* that Shakespeare loved. Certainly it was *oloroso* that was drunk mostly at the start of the nineteenth century. It was not till 1860 that dry sherry was shipped to England. This wine was not universally popular at first. The contemporary Earl of Derby, who was suffering from gout, was advised to try manzanilla, but after sampling it he decided that he preferred gout. A taste for dry sherry was, however, soon developed; to such an extent indeed that Edward VII on his accession in 1901 sold five thousand bottles of sherry from the royal cellars. This greatly damaged sherry's reputation at the time, but it was *oloroso* that he sold and in retrospect the sale can be seen as a sign that sherry was passing through a transition period, that it was ceasing to be an after-dinner wine and becoming an *apéritif.*

## 2

I have drunk a great deal of sherry in my time and I have read most of what has been written about it. In particular I am indebted to the excellent book *Sherry* by my friend Rupert Croft-Cooke, but I find it difficult to visualize a place from descriptions. To write of sherry I needed to see the vineyards where the grapes are grown, the bodegas where the wine is housed and the soleras in which it matures; so in the early spring of 1958, I set out, with a congenial companion, for Jerez de la Frontera. There is a good deal that is unusual about the making of sherry and I wanted to see it for myself.

Jerez is only a few miles inland from Cádiz, and a study of the map would suggest that it was an easy place to reach, but in Spain every journey has its individual complications. Many of the roads are poor, the best roads radiate from Madrid, trains are slow and public transport is, in terms of time, capricious. Cross-country journeys would be penitential were it not for the unfailing good manners and helpfulness of the Spanish people. If you enter a country inn where a man is eating, he will invite you to sit at his table and share his meal. You will, of course, refuse, but the gesture is symbolic. The stranger is always welcomed and helped.

I was coming from New York, and indirect though the route may seem, the easiest way of reaching Jerez was by flying to Tangier via Lisbon, and taking the ferry to Algeciras whence an afternoon bus ran straight to Jerez. I should by that route have an opportunity of seeing the Spanish countryside. This trip happened, however, to be one on which every pre-arranged detail went slightly wrong, yet in its general sum proved infinitely more enjoyable than I had dared to hope, and the day before we were due to leave Tangier, that powerful wind, the *Levante,* which is the one considerable snag to a residence in Tangier, roared so fiercely through the straits that the ferry could not leave Algeciras. We were forced, therefore, to take the British ferry which did not dock in Gibraltar till six o'clock, so that our motor drive to Jerez was made for the most part in darkness. It was a disappointment at the time, but in retrospect, its effect was negligible.

I was traveling to Jerez under the best auspices, on the invitation of the firm of Gonzalez Byass, whose family and business links with the house of Gilbey are very close. I had already met in Oporto one of the younger members of the family, Gabriel Gonzalez, and his uncle Manuel Gonzalez Gordon had made himself responsible for my visit. I spent three days at Jerez at the Hotel Los Cienes; days as happy as any that I have ever known, which have left me with an even warmer feeling than I had before for the wines of that pleasant city.

It is indeed a very pleasant city with a long past. It acquired its name "de la Frontera" because after it had been captured by Alfonso the Wise, it stood for two centuries on the fringe of the Moorish kingdom of Granada, with immense strategic importance as the principle fortress of the region.

For five centuries it had been under Moorish rule. Architecturally, the influence of the Moors is very marked; there are traces of the Roman occupation, but though in the fourth century B.C. Theopompus referred to it as Xera, a name which was changed to Ceret by the Romans and to Serit by the Visigoths, its real history does not begin till it

was captured by the Moors in A.D. 711 and renamed Sher-
ish or Saris. Its ancient walls are of Arabic origin, with the
turreted Alcazar one of its most charming features. It is a
city of gracious squares, of white houses with ironwork bal-
conies, with unexpected anglings of light, and sudden long
vistas down narrow streets; with a church spire at the end
above the roofs. It is a city where the visitor can profitably
and enjoyably spend two days of sightseeing.

The prosperity of the town depends upon the sale of
wine; and Jerez has an air of broad-based, deep-rooted security, of wealth that has been accumulated slowly; it has
enriched itself like the wine that has matured in its bodegas,
acquiring greater merit year by year. There is an atmosphere of calm and leisure, admirably suited to the Spanish
temperament, to men who reach their offices at half-past
ten and lunch at three. The bodega of Gonzalez Byass—I
suppose the translation into the language of the estate agent
would be business premises and warehouse—is a low building in that it is one-storied, but the office rooms and the
warehouses are long and high. Rupert Croft-Cooke compared the warehouses, with their veiled lights and the rows
of casks laid one on top of the other, three or four high, to
the nave of a cathedral, "with the same vaulted roofs and
rows of columns . . . Indeed," he added, "it sometimes
seems almost surprising that there are no stained glass windows but instead small barred windows usually covered
with matting. There is the same coolness here after the blind-
ing sunlight of the street, the same dim distance down the
aisles."

When I was shown on my arrival into Manuel Gonzalez' office I had somewhat the same feeling that I had had
over a quarter of a century ago when I first called at my publisher's—Cassell's in La Belle Sauvage—to see Newman
Flower. That had been on a winter's day and a large fire

was blazing in the hearth; this was a warm spring morning but on both occasions I had found myself in an atmosphere of old furniture and family portraits. I felt myself to be a guest in a country house. In the days when a social distinction existed between a trade and a profession, it was this atmosphere that was underlined.

As I have already said, there is much that is unusual about the making of sherry. It is, like port, a fortified and a blended wine. As in the case of port, the fermentation is checked with brandy before all the sugar in the grape juice has been converted into alcohol. Like tawny port it matures in wood and like tawny port it is eventually blended so that the shipper can maintain a uniformity of look and flavor, but there the resemblance between the two wines ends.

In Jerez, the grapes, after they have been picked, are laid on rush mats outside the *lagar* for twenty-four hours so that some of their moisture may evaporate; they are then trodden, but not by the bare foot as in Portugal. The workers wear leather nail-studded shoes. In some *lagares* machine presses have been introduced and for the second pressing hydraulic force is used, but there is a general belief that the touch of iron damages first-grade sherry. Gypsum is added to increase acidity. At one time purists objected to this "plastering" of the wine, but gypsum is after all only the calcinized essence of the white soil in which the grapes are grown. The Romans practiced "plastering"; it is surprising how often by guesswork, by trial and error, the ancients discovered the solutions which we have reached by scientific experiment. The wine is then left to ferment in casks, which have not been wholly filled and which have been left open to the air. That is one of the chief distinctions in the making of sherry. It needs air and ventilation for its development and the bodegas in Jerez are built at ground level and in the highest and airiest sections of the city.

The fermentation is slow and lasts for about three months. Till the fermentation is complete the vintner cannot tell what kind of wine is being produced. That is the mystery of sherry. The contents of one cask may be quite different from that of another which has been filled with wine produced from the same vineyard on the same day. When the casks are filled from the *lagares* the vintner has no idea whether his wine will prove to be a *fino* or an *oloroso*.

The first racking takes place in December and then a curious phenomenon occurs: a white film known as *flor* (flower) appears on the surface of the wine. Tovey describes it as, "Something I can only compare to small native oysters taking a swim without their shells, but which I know at once is fungus, showing more or less a progress to decay." This flower was known to the ancients and approved by Pliny. The Romans considered a clean white flower the proof of a good wine.

The wines of the Jura also throw a "flower" and it was here that Pasteur, a native of Arbois, made his experiments. It is interesting in this connection to remember that Arbois was Spanish until the end of the seventeenth century and Château Chalon, its best wine, has a taste of sherry.

It is not till this point that the vintner is able to judge the quality of his wine. He marks the barrels with white chalk, one stroke (*raya*) for the best, three for the worst. Some wines do not even receive three strokes and are turned into vinegar.

After the first racking the wine is fortified with brandy. The vintner is by then able to decide whether his wine will be a *fino* or an *oloroso*. More brandy is put into an *oloroso* than into a *fino*. The extra quantity of brandy in the *oloroso* kills the *flor*. The flowering of a *fino* lasts eighteen months.

In Oporto ruby and tawny port mature in the same cask into which they have been consigned on their arrival, though the cask is replenished to meet the demands of evaporation. In Jerez a different method is followed; the solera system in which a series of casks are replenished from each other. A solera consists of three to ten casks, the youngest wine is in the first cask, the oldest in the last. There can be no dating of sherry; the evaporation is too great and the replenishment too constant. The visitor to the Gonzalez Byass bodega is shown a cask with a glass flank which has not been replenished and whose markings on the side show how the level of the wine has sunk year by year.

You may hear a wine merchant say, "This solera was begun in 1912," but that does not mean that any of the wine that was trodden in 1912 remains in it. It is worth noting that sherry gains in alcoholic content during its time in wood, whereas port loses.

One of the things that I was most anxious to see in Jerez was the solera system in operation. I wanted to see how the casks were stacked one on top of the other. Usually the rows were three casks high, on occasions they were four. I also wanted to see the flower that covers the surface of a *fino*. It was quite easy to see this. The barrels are not filled to the brim. The two bungholes are not stopped. They merely have a light, loosely fitting wooden cover. If the guide lifts one cover and flashes a torch on the surface, you can see the "flower" through the other hole. It did not seem to me to look like "oysters without their shells." It looked like the scum you see on a brackish pool.

When I read Rupert Croft-Cooke's *Sherry* for the first time I had not particularly noted his comparison between the atmosphere of a cathedral and a bodega but I realized how apposite it was when I walked between the long rows of casks; it was twilit and calm; everything was clear and quiet and the air was rich with the scent of wine instead of incense.

It is this kind of experience that convinces me of the necessity of going to see for myself. Other people's descriptions do not tell me enough. You have to be inside a building to appreciate the quality and colors of a stained-glass window. A great deal of what I was shown in the Gonzalez Byass bodega I knew already. I knew, for instance, that sherry was shipped in casks made out of American oak from New Orleans, and that owing to the shortage of that oak it was necessary for the foreign merchants to return the empty casks; but I had not really visualized the transaction till I saw in the cooperage workshop the wine-soaked strips of oak being reassembled. I knew that in the soleras one cask was replenished from another, but I could not picture how it was done till I had watched workmen filling large wooden jars and pouring from them into the lower casks. To get "the feel" of a place I have to see it.

There was one thing, however, which I had not expected to see, of which I had never read. I had not expected to see at floor level by one of the casks a grill work to which were attached pieces of dry toast. These, I was informed, were for the mice. Mice were encouraged, and cats kept off the premises. I saw a number of mice who were appreciating the care that had been taken for their safety and their comfort. They were extremely small. It seemed to me that it would be very easy for them to push aside the light covering of the bungholes. I remembered being told years ago that at one time rabbits were put into sherry casks, that the alcohol in the wine fed on them and was enriched. I wondered, watching those midget mice, but I decided it was more prudent not to be inquisitive.

Sherry is a blended wine. Much remains to be done to it after it has been drawn from the final cask. It is completely dry and it needs to be fined with eggs and in many cases sweetened with white wine. This wine is made out of

*Pedro Ximenez* and *Muscatel* grapes which are treated in rather the same way as Sauternes; being left to dry on rush mats till they have achieved a *pourriture noble*. *Pedro Ximenez* wine has over twenty degrees of sweetness. The wines of fifteen soleras may be requisitioned before the merchant is satisfied with his blend.

Every day the bodegas are visited by tourists who are given a chance of tasting the local products. They are first given a glass of brandy, for though Spanish brandy is little known in Britain and the United States, it has a large sale in South America and is very good. After the tour they are taken into a long room decorated with bullfighting posters, at the end of which stand butts of sherry, whence they may taste the wines that they have seen maturing in the solera. The wine is drawn off from the casks in a long springy wand-like whalebone instrument with an inverted silver container, and is poured into the glass in a cascade from a distance of eighteen inches with a flourish that is Andalusia's speciality.

Each shipper has his own brand names, and the names which are familiar in Spain will not be met, with one or two exceptions, in England. Sherry is shipped to England in cask and bottled there; more sherry is bottled in England than in Spain and much of the sherry that is drunk in America has been bottled in Bristol by Harvey and by Avery. You would look in vain on an English wine list for Gonzalez Byass' Rosa, Nectar and Solera 1847. There is one wine, however, from their bodega that you will find on every good wine list in the world, Tio Pepe, and that wine has a curious story.

It is the most famous of all *finos*, it is the driest, the palest and most delicate. It should be served cold, as all *finos* should. For some palates it is too dry, but it is supreme as an *apéritif*. *Tio* is the Spanish for uncle and *Pepe* is an abbreviated Christian name—the equivalent, let us say, of

Joe. Nobody seems to remember very much about this Gonzalez, who was known as Tio Pepe: it all happened in distant days. He greatly enjoyed manzanilla and he asked the father of the present Manuel Gonzalez if he could not produce a similar *fino* for him. "And so," I here quote from Rupert Croft-Cooke, "a little solera was started in a cellar-like adjunct of the bodega specially for Tio Pepe and there the old gentleman would entertain his friends with his dry wine and slices cut from a ham hung overhead, for ham becomes exquisitely seasoned in the sherrified air. It was Tio Pepe's solera and in time its wine was named after him." Tio Pepe—it is a name that catches the attention and lingers in the memory. It has been advertised very cleverly. The owners of other bodegas are often disconcerted by being asked by guests who do not know the history of the wine if they may have a Tio Pepe.

On my second day in Jerez, a bitterly cold wind blew from the Atlantic. It was so cold that snow fell in Madrid and I could appreciate Manuel Gonzalez' complaint that that the Moors had spoiled the Andalusian climate by cutting down the trees; it was so cold that we had to modify the sightseeing program that had been prepared for us under the guidance of that fine scholar José de Soto, who, out of Manuel Gonzalez' monumental work on sherry, had condensed for the benefit of those who do not speak Spanish, the attractive and useful brochure that is offered to visitors to the bodegas. We drove out to the El Bosque restaurant and we saw in its grounds the statue to Shakespeare which bore on its pedestal Falstaff's dictum, "If I had a thousand sons . . ." but we could not, as we had hoped, sip our pre-lunch sherries out of doors.

This was, however, as I have said, a trip in which everything went slightly wrong to start with yet turned out for the better in the end, and had the sky been blue that Sun-

day we should not have concentrated so thoroughly on the
choosing of our lunch; we felt we had to compensate for the
uncharitableness of the weather; and the cuisine at the El
Bosque is one of the best in Andalusia; it well rewarded our
attention.

We each took separate dishes and sampled each other's choices. I had not believed that cod could be so palatable. I had never eaten a more savory *paella*. We enjoyed
that lunch more because the wind howled outside; and very
likely if it had not howled Señor de Soto would not have
suggested that after our visit to the cathedral, we should
pause in his flat for a glass of sherry. Our half-hour there
was one of the most stimulating experiences of the trip. One's
flat or house is a mirror that reflects one's life, and I have
not seen a house dedicated so utterly to scholarship.

Señor de Soto is a bachelor in his middle sixties who
has recently moved into a modern flat. At no point on its
walls was there a six-inch gap between its pictures. They
were old pictures, many of them Madonnas, many of them
prints of Jerez. It was clear that he had made a recent move
from an old family house; but it was the library more than
the pictures that was revealing. Not only were the walls
lined with books from floor to ceiling but the room had been
partitioned by narrow walls of shelves, and a long working
table was covered a foot high with papers, manuscripts,
magazines, original documents with rubber bands, in whose
midst a large amber-colored Persian cat slept contentedly.

I was reminded of a poem called *Books* which my father used to read to me when I was a schoolboy, about a re-
cluse whose floors and tables and window-seats were covered
with books. It was a Victorian poem, and like a Victorian
picture "told a story"; it was addressed to a wife who had
deserted him in favor of a suitor with less sedentary tastes.
I have forgotten the author's name and should not now know

where to look for the poem, but I remember the line, "You don't find railway novels where you left your Elzevirs," and the final punch line of how he lived with the memory "of what you know, my dear, you never were."

The picture which that poem built for me had anticipated Señor de Soto's study. I asked him about the books which he himself had written. He shook his head; he was not interested in writing books himself. It was research that he enjoyed. He liked to collaborate with other men, "putting them on" to the documents and sources of information that they needed. He was content to remain anonymous: a dedicated man.

The cold weather persisted the next day but the sky was blue and the sun was shining. Gabriel Gonzalez motored us out to the house of his uncle Fernando, which was set among the vineyards, attached to a *lagar*. The vines were low in the chalky soil and there was a sense of suspended animation in the fields. April is a quiet time. February and March are the period of *Cava-Bien*, the light tilling of the soil to a depth of eight or so inches; in May comes the *Golpe-Veno*, the digging up of the soil and the killing off of weeds. April is the period of casual odd jobs. The gently rolling fields seemed to be waiting their time in the mild misty sunlight like the great wine presses in the *lagar*. I saw here for the first time the special screw that is used to press the *marc* after the first wine has been drawn off. It stands six foot high and has a heavy wooden block. The *marc* is packed around it with wooden spades and held in place with strips of grass matting.

We had been invited to lunch by Manuel Gonzalez in the bodega, in the partners' dining room, a long high room looking out upon a formal orchard set with orange trees, flanked with eucalyptus, cooled by a fountain, with rose bushes in flower. It all looked very summery seen through

glass, but I was grateful for the large log fire that was blazing in an open grate.

It was the first time that I had been the guest of Spaniards. I do not know if it was a typically Spanish lunch. It
was a most congenial one. There were nine of us in all. It
was very much a family party, and through my association
with the House of Gilbey, I have come to think of myself as
an adopted member of that family. Gordon Gilbey is a good
friend of mine. As I have already told, I was his guest at
Château Loudenne and on the Douro. His sister, the wife of a
Spaniard, was there, and also a niece of Sebastian Gilbey, who had once been my neighbor in Silchester. We had
been invited for half-past two, which is a little early for a
lunch in Spain. Two tables had been laid. At the smaller one
*hors d'oeuvres, entremeses,* were set out, cheese and shrimps
and olives and three bottles of sherry—a very pale *fino,* a
dark *oloroso* and an *amontillado.* It was after three when
we moved to the larger table. My friend and I were catching
a seven o'clock train to Seville for the fiesta. We made it,
just.

I cannot remember exactly what dishes we were served.
There is a resemblance between Spanish dishes. It is an oily
cuisine; it is heavily seasoned, but it is not hot in the way
that an Indian curry is. There is a good deal of rice; there
is usually olive oil, certainly there will be olives. The cheese
is dry and hard and excellent, with a bite like that of cheddar. I remember the wines better than the food. There was an
excellent *rioja,* a Marqués de Murrieta that had the body
and flavor of a St. Émilion.

I do not think that in England and the U.S.A. we appreciate the qualities of Spanish wines. Perhaps it is the fault
of the Spaniards themselves. They have not bothered to develop their export markets. They have concentrated upon
their sherries, and their table wines that reach England and

America are rough; moreover, in England for some time now the preferential tariff that French wine receives makes it a "better buy." But in Spain itself you drink better wines in an average restaurant than you do in its equivalent in France. The date of a wine means nothing in Spain, but in Tangier, Torremolinos and now on this recent trip, I have drunk some excellent red wines: Imperiale, Marqués de Riscal and Marqués de Murrieta. There is also Mónopole, a clean white wine, and for those who enjoy a sweet wine at the end of a meal, there is Diamante.

At the beginning of this trip, I had bought a small house in Tangier, which means that the Costa del Sol will be within easy reach of me. I fancy that during the next decade, I shall drink more casual Spanish wine than French. I do not feel that it is "a fate worse than death."

## 1

**B**ORROW in *Lavengro* writing of the year 1820, describes how as a very young man he was asked by a Justice of the Peace what he would like to drink; he chose Madeira. "Did you ever taste better Madeira?" his host asked him ten minutes later.

"I never before tasted Madeira."

"Then you ask for a wine without knowing what it is."

"I ask for it, sir, that I may know what it is."

It was in that spirit of curiosity that I sailed from Southampton on a chill May morning in 1958 for the island of Madeira.

I knew certainly rather more about Madeira than Borrow had. I knew what it tasted like, and I had drunk quite a

little of it, during the 1920's and lately during my stay in
Denmark. Shortly before the second war I had drunk at the
Saintsbury Club a Napoleon Madeira. The story of its provenance is this. When the ship that was carrying Napoleon
to St. Helena called at Madeira, the British Consul, Henry
Veitch, came on board, tactfully called the emperor "Your
Majesty," in spite of Whitehall's contrary instructions that
he was to be addressed as "General," and persuaded him to
take on board a cask of the local 1792 vintage. Napoleon
never broached it, under his doctor's orders, and after his
death Veitch petitioned for its return, on the grounds, so it
was alleged, that it had never been paid for. Doubts have
since been cast on the accuracy of this story. There are those
who assert that the wine was paid for with gold louis, some
of which were included in the foundation deposit of the English church. The source of the legend has been attributed to
the imaginative garrulity of the Blandy family who inspired the limerick starting,

> "There was an old man of Maderia,
>   Whose stories grew queerer and queerer."

But the legend has been given general credence and in 1941
a bottle of this wine fetched a high price at a Red Cross sale.
It had been bottled in 1840 and the label bore the inscription "Blandy 1792-1840." At the Saintsbury Club dinner it
was served with a turtle soup, out of deference to Sir Stephen Gaselee's predilection for it. Many of us thought this
was a mistake. The Madeira was so rich and sweet that it
killed the light Bâtard-Montrachet that succeeded it. It
should have come at the end, but it is a tradition of the club
to finish with vintage port. We could scarcely have had both
and cognac. Still, it was a rare experience. It was astonishing that so old a wine could be so full of vigor. There are
certain Madeiras that could be mistaken for East India

sherries, but this one could have been nothing but Madeira.

Longevity is the best known characteristic of Madeira, and a bottle that has been decanted will stay good for half a year. It has other features too with which most amateurs of wine are familiar. It is a blended fortified wine and in the days of sailing ships it was found to be improved by the heat and shaking engendered during a journey to the tropics; for the last century and a half therefore it has been rocked and heated in the lodges of Funchal. That much I did know but I knew little more when the *Arundel Castle* sailed up the Solent.

I had, however, provided myself with two books from the London Library—A. E. W. Marsh's *Holiday Wanderings in Madeira* published in 1892 and W. H. Koebel's *Madeira Old and New* published in 1909.

Madeira, I learned from them, is a lucky island. lucky in its location, lucky in its history. It is the chief of a group of islands that lie in the path of the Gulf Stream six hundred miles north of Capricorn, three hundred and fifty miles west of Africa, level with Casablanca. It has no winter; its summer is mild. The temperature of Funchal, its capital, has a range in difference of less than twelve degrees. It is mountainous and the soil is fertile. There is no lack of water. It was uninhabited when the Portuguese discovered it early in the fifteenth century, though there are those who maintain that the ancients knew of it, that it had given rise to the legend of Atlantis and that these were in fact the Fortunate Islands of which Pliny wrote.

I repeat it is a lucky island. Its greatest piece of luck came when it was not included in Catherine of Braganza's wedding dowry to Charles II of England. The Infanta was extremely anxious for the wedding to take place. She offered Bombay, Tangier and a sum of money. Madeira was the card she kept up her sleeve. The agreement to include it had been drawn up, awaiting signature, if Charles was hesitant. But Bombay, Tangier and the money proved sufficient. It was lucky for Madeira that they were. Otherwise it might have become a second Cyprus: an island in this case predominantly Portuguese under the British flag.

As it was, it got the full advantage of Charles' attachment to Portugal. He gave the island special privileges. At that time no goods could be shipped in British ships to the West Indies and the American colonies except from British ports, but an exception was made in favor of Madeira. This meant that Madeira had a monopoly of the wine trade. It lay in the direct path of the slavers. There was no cold storage then and it was invaluable as a port of call for the ships bound both for the Thirteen Colonies and for India. At the time of Charles II's marriage, fruit, sugar-cane and wine were the chief products of the island but the demand for Madeira's wines soon became so great that the vine supplanted the sugar cane.

Portugal has always been the hereditary friend of Britain. Prince Henry the Navigator was the grandson of John of Gaunt and, owing to the special concessions that Madeira received, British firms settled there as confidently as they did in Oporto. At first the wines that they shipped were unfortified, but by the middle of the eighteenth century fortification had begun.

Madeira was known in America under the names of the families who imported it—the Pinckneys and the Rutledges in Charleston, Aspinall and Howland in New York, Cadwallader in Philadelphia. Being Portuguese, the island enjoyed the immunity of neutrality during most of the wars of the eighteenth century. When the French ports were closed, as they often were, its business flourished. After the Jacobite rebellions of 1715 and 1745 a number of Scots settled there. When Napoleon invaded Portugal, the British took

Madeira under their protection. There was some talk in 1815 of Britain acquiring the island, as part of a general re-deal at the Treaty of Vienna, but luckily it was only talk and the island remained Portuguese, although in the small town of Funchal thirteen British wine firms were by then established.

George IV as Prince of Wales laid down what he described as "Royal Madeiras" and in 1795 Dr. Wright was recommending that "Madeira when good though too potent for common use is one of the most useful and best for elderly persons in gouty habits when the functions of life have begun to fail."

In five hundred years Madeira has only had two setbacks; oidium, a fungus disease that attacked the vines in 1852 and the phylloxera insect that struck in 1873. Both these disasters were eventually overcome by British enterprise, the Leacock family re-establishing the vines and the Blandys the island's commerce.

I went to Madeira for a week's stay under the pleasantest conditions as the guest of Graham and Mildred Blandy; they lodged me in Reid's Hotel, which is part of the Blandy empire. I also went there at what I fancy will be seen by history as the time when the island had most to offer. It has at the time of writing all the conveniences of the mid-twentieth century, but it is still hard to reach and is not crowded by tourists. It has not yet got an airstrip, though it will have one in a few years' time. As soon as it has, it will be a stopping-off place on transatlantic flights. At the moment it is connected with England and Lisbon by a seaplane that makes one trip a week; very often the sea is too rough for the machine to land, and winter visitors have been stranded for two weeks at a time. There are sailings to Lisbon but they are uncertain. The only sailings on which you can rely are the Norwegian ship that does a weekly shuttle service from Southampton and the fortnightly sailings of the Union-Castle Line on its way to and from South Africa. There are indeed fewer ships calling at Madeira now than there were fifty years ago when it was important as a coaling station and the women carried the baskets of coal upon their heads, as they did in the West Indies when I went there first, at so much a basket.

But though the island is less accessible than it was at the turn of the century, its amenities have been vastly increased. The motor car has made an immense difference. When you land at the pier you will see a curious form of sledge attached to a couple of oxen, attended by two men wearing straw hats, bound with wide light blue ribbon, rather like a Venetian gondolier's. Before the arrival of motor cars, this sledge—*caro* was the word for it—was the only form of transport; the roads were too steep for wheels. The sledge was iron-shod. It had an awning and curtains as a protection against the sun. It could seat four passengers. One driver—often a boy—would lead the oxen by tugging on a piece of stout cord that was attached to their horns. The other driver walked behind, prodding the oxen with a long pike and exhorting them with yells. The pace of this contraption was a mile and a half an hour.

You may also see at the pier the other Victorian form of transportation—a canvas hammock, covered with bright cloths, fitted with a hood and slung on a long pole that two bearers can carry on their shoulders. They could cover upwards of thirty miles a day, but they were careful not to allow a passenger to fall asleep and become a dead weight—as they think that people get heavier when they sleep. The steepness of the roads made any other form of movement impossible before the motor car arrived; though there was for downhill journeys a form of toboggan—a *carinhos* —a wicker basket set on runners that could hold two persons; the conductor steered it from the back, giving it a push, then jumping onto a narrow ledge. A railway used to run up the hill behind Funchal and the return journey into the town could be made in the *carinhos* in five minutes. On boat days this expedition is a big tourist attraction.

I venture to prophesy that as soon as the airstrip is completed Madeira will become one of the most popular of tourist islands. It has much to offer. It has excellent hotels and it is very beautiful. I have never seen such a profusion of flowers. The jacaranda was in bloom during my visit. Reid's Hotel is built upon a cliff. Its bar and dining room are walled with glass: they face the town. I never grew tired of looking across the sea and the dividing valley, at the cypresses, the banana plants, their greens embellished by the pale mauve bloom of the jacaranda and the pink of the geraniums. The weather was not particularly clement. It rained very little but the sky was overcast. Yet there was such a blaze of color from trees and flowers that I did not miss the sunlight.

The garden of the Quinta da Palheiro—the home of Graham Blandy—is thrown open to the public once a week. Experts like Lanning Roper hold it to be unique. It covers an area of thirty acres. The soil, since it is volcanic in origin, is shallow, but it is rich. Its camellias are phenomenal. Great care is taken over them. Fallen flowers are not swept away and this soil blanket protects the roots and retains moisture. The tidy Portuguese gardeners have to be watched carefully or they will sweep the leaves away. Camellias flower from early December into May. At that time magnolias are in blossom also. There is no month which has not its special beauty.

There is little to be said against the island. There is a hot breeze from Africa—the *Pesta*—which is tiresome, when a hot haze, full of particles of desert dust, hangs over the sea, bringing the locust with it, but it does not come often and its stay is brief, three days at the most. It is not a rich island but it is prosperous and its people are contented. They grow vines, sugar cane and bananas. They convert their many willow trees into excellent wicker baskets. In the eighteen-fifties an English spinster introduced the technique of embroidery and exquisite embroidered blouses, table-cloths and handkerchiefs have become one of the chief exports. The womenfolk are never idle.

W. H. Koebel wrote in 1909, "The amusements of the Madeira populace are of a simple order. They consist mainly of kite-flying in infancy; courtship, the playing of the *machete* (a species of guitar) and the explosion of fire-works in adult years; gossip and basking in the sun when old and expectoration at all ages." I did not see any kites in the air myself, but I was very conscious of the general atmosphere of contentment.

## 2

On my first morning I was driven through the vineyards. The vine is cultivated here in a manner that I have seen nowhere else. It is arranged on pergolas, six feet high, so that another crop, the potato, can be grown beneath it. The potato is planted in October, after the harvest when the branches are leafless, and pulled up in April when the leaves have begun to bud. The soil is so scarce that it cannot be wasted. These pergolas in late May gave the impression that the hillside was covered with the awnings of bright green tents.

The hills are very steep and tightly terraced, so that the winter rains will not wash away the precious soil; they are irrigated by *levadas,* narrow, stone-built water channels. The ground is owned for the most part by small peasant proprietors. This presents a certain problem to the wine trade since some proprietors find it is more profitable to raise sugar cane than vines. The grapes are trodden in the hills by these proprietors; the juice—the *mosto*—is brought down to Funchal in goatskins which runners—*borracheiros*—sling over their shoulders and which contain twelve gallons each. The juice does its fermenting in the lodges and is known as *vinho claro;* it is then exposed to heat—the equivalent of the eighteenth-century trip to India—at a temperature of one hundred to one hundred thirty degrees, when it is known as *vinho estufado.* It is racked and becomes *vinho trasfugado,* finally it is fortified with ten per cent of alcohol. It is then *vinho generoso* and time is left to do its work.

Not all the wine is submitted to this elaborate treatment. The people of Madeira have recently developed a taste for their own products. At one time most of the grape wine was available for export because the Madeirenes themselves drank a powerful spirit made from cane. This was found to be having such a bad effect upon their health —TB was increasing at an alarming rate—that the government intervened and imposed such a heavy tax upon cane spirit that few could afford to drink it. The Madeirenes drank their own wines instead, not the fortified *vinho generoso,* but the young *vinho claro.* Of the nine million litres of wine that are produced each year, six million are consumed in the island.

Sixty passengers got off the *Arundel Castle* at Madeira and Graham Blandy had come out by the launch to meet us. Blandy is one of the big names of the island. The Blandys have been there for four generations. In addition to their wine interests and Reid's Hotel, they own a bank and are agents for every shipping line that makes a call there. The first question that the visitor to the island is asked on his return is, "Which of the Blandys did you meet?" There are other names of course. The Leacocks and the Cossarts have been there longer, and Cecil Miles, the author of *A Glimpse of Madeira*, has one of the most beautiful old houses in Funchal. But by and large, Blandy is the first name that is known outside the island.

When I met Graham Blandy in the ship, I told him that I also had a letter to Cossart, Gordon & Co. I had asked Gilbey's advice before I started and Cossart, Gordon are their correspondents there. Blandy smiled. "You'll find that we're all very much one family."

By that he meant, so I found out next day, that for the last thirty years the chief wines of the island have been marketed abroad through the Madeira Wine Association, that the same lodge in Funchal treats the wines of the six chief shippers, Portuguese and British, and that though the wines of these shippers are handled in different countries by different agencies, there is no such rivalry between the firms as there is in Oporto between Croft and Graham, Sandeman and Cockburn. The wines that appear to be in competition with one another have been in fact blended in the same casks at the same time: and I think I am safe in saying that no amateur purchaser of wine would say to his London or New York wine merchant, "I'd like a Blandy" or "a Leacock wine," in the way that he would say of sherry, "I like the Gonzalez Byass wines," or of port, "I'd prefer one that was shipped by Croft."

Madeira is known and ordered by its four different styles or rather by three of its four different styles, because *verdeilho*—a rich golden wine that can be drunk as an *apéritif* or with soup—is not generally well known because the name is hard to remember and because it is produced in smaller quantities than the other three: *sercial, bual* and *malmsey*.

The different wines come from different kinds of grape, both white and red, not from the locality where they are grown. The vines were originally brought from Crete, by the Portuguese. *Sercial,* a newcomer, is rather different. It came from the Rhine, and is still known as the Riesling wine. It is far more dry than the others and it makes a good *apéritif.* *Bual* is produced in greater quantities than the other three. It is essentially a dessert wine and is considered the best balanced. *Malmsey* is a much bigger wine. As it ages it acquires the characteristics of a liqueur. Its grapes—the *malvasia* —are gathered late, like a Sauternes', and are only cultivated on the sunny southern shores. The greater care that is required for its production makes it the most expensive wine. To my taste, it is easily the finest, because it fulfills so admirably its function of rounding off a meal. I would, as a variety, now and again prefer it to a vintage port, but excellent though *sercial* is, I would only take it with soup when I could not get a good *amontillado.*

On my return from my drive around the vineyards, I was taken into the lodge of the Madeira Wine Association to be shown what big differences there are between the production of sherry and Madeira. In the first place, there is no bung in the trough where the grapes are trodden. The juice pours straight into containers, and in consequence does not acquire the color of the grape.

The harvest had been finished several months earlier so that I could not see the must fermenting. It had by now reached the heated chambers—the *estufa*—which takes the place of the old six months' sea journey with four crossings of the equator. I was shown the thermometer which has a seal set at 130 degrees by the government. If this seal is broken by intentional or accidental overheating, the wine is confiscated by the government, because overheated wine appears older than it is. The Portuguese government is as jealous of the reputation of its Madeira as of its Port.

I was then shown the soleras; there is a very real dif-

ference between the Portuguese and Spanish solera systems.
You will often see in a Portuguese wine list the word "solera" followed by a date; and this date has a considerably
more definite guarantee of longevity than it would have on
a Spanish wine list—though in actual fact you would never
see the date on a Spanish wine list.

There are, in fact, three things that you can see on a
Portuguese wine list. You can see *sercial* vintage 1835, or
*malmsey* solera 1910 or *bual, tout court*. These definitions
mean three quite different things. In early days there was
such a thing as a vintage Madeira. It was wine of a special
year that had matured in cask and had been bottled after
an unspecified number of years. Sometimes a vintage Madeira was shipped in cask or in a demijohn. When the phylloxera struck the vines, owing to the longevity of Madeira,
there was a great deal of vintage Madeira in the lodges—
the greater part of which Graham Blandy's grandfather
had the prescience to buy up. Great wine was so scarce that
it was decided to use this for blending, but blending in a
special way, on the solera system.

Let us say that a cask of *malmsey* 1860 was set aside,
a cask of 1880 set beside it, a cask of 1890 set later on the
far side of them. Wine would be drawn and bottled from the
1860 cask, that cask would be refilled from the 1880 cask
which in its turn would be replenished with wine taken from
the 1890 cask. The wine in each case would be siphoned
from the top. It resembles the Jerez system but is not quite
the same. Madeira is not exposed to the air, evaporation is
much slower. There is no subsequent blending. The wine
drawn from the first cask is bottled straightaway. Solera
wines are only sold in bottles: and in the original cask there
is always a residue of the original wine. The date after the
word solera is a guarantee of longevity. Practically no vintage wines have been put on the market since phylloxera,

though the wine shippers have certain special wines in their own cellars.

Blended Madeiras are in a different category. They are standardized in the same way that sherries and wood ports are. They are twelve to eighteen years old, and they are usually shipped in casks or demijohns. Blended wines are naturally a good deal cheaper than solera wines.

I drank much good Madeira during my visit—in particular at the Blandys' a vintage *malmsey* of 1795, and with Tom Mullins, the president of the Association, a *sercial* 1802. I also ate peacock, a dish that I had not met before and that I do not expect to meet again. Its appearance rather than its taste surprised me. I did not associate it with any particular flavor. It was perhaps rather tasteless, or maybe I was too concerned with a Cos d'Estournel of 1952 to give it my full attention; it was served in thin round slices and the flesh was pale.

I was given fortunate opportunities of studying the old records of the Blandy and the Leacock families. The present head of the family, Edmund Leacock, is a cousin of Stephen Leacock and his papers contain a letter in which the humorist says, "I enclose a recent picture of myself. I forget just how old—not very. It will show you that the years have used me fairly well, though in return I have to treat them pretty carefully."

The founder of the Madeira branch of the family— the spelling was Laycock then—came out to the island as a sixteen-year-old apprentice in 1741. His contract makes curious reading. In return for seven years' food, lodging and clothing he promised not to commit fornication or contract marriage. "He shall not play at cards, dice, tables or any other unlawful games by which his said master may have any loss with his own goods or others . . . He shall not haunt taverns or playhouses."

It was not long before Leacock found his feet. He had a brother in the West Indies, in Antigua, and their correspondence throws interesting sidelights on the closeness of the trade relations at that time. There are several references to the slave trade. "Negroes may be imported here and pay a duty of ten per cent. A few, about 50 to 100, may be disposed of here, the oldest not to exceed thirty years . . . Slavers may touch for refreshment without paying duty."

Leacock certainly had a great deal of trouble with a Negro wench Amelia whom he bought in London for three pipes of rum but who liked the wines of the country more than work and was eventually shipped to Grenada on a bill of lading. There are, however, no signs of African parentage in the present-day population—Moorish perhaps, but not African.

There are sidelights, too, on the problems that arose through wars and it is encouraging to reflect on how trivial these problems were eventually to prove. A letter, for instance, from London written in 1757 refers to the plague in Lisbon. "When you reflect on the many surprising and unfortunate accidents that have happened to Portugal and these kingdoms since we first agreed to adventure together you may easily account for the little success I have met with. Our factory in Lisbon have only just been able to keep themselves up from sinking since the earthquake and now the plague will I fear ruin them entirely and here in England people know not what to do, our public affairs being in a most miserable condition." Who thinks of that plague now?

There is a letter from Madeira written in 1756. "We wish public matters were in a settled state either as peace or war, the latter would certainly have a very good effect on our trade in general, which would render it no disagreeable event to us, but as a British spirit we wish it only as it may redound to the honour of the nation."

From 1796 there is a note. "We are here in a most critical situation and we much fear in the negotiations between France and Portugal that the British subjects residing in the Dominions of Portugal will be entirely excluded." How smoothly these problems were arranged.

But for the oenophil the most interesting sections in the Leacock letters are those that deal with the wine itself. There is for instance a reference to *malmsey*, "The whole island only produces about 50 pipes annually and they are the sole property of one gentleman."

It was in the middle of the eighteenth century that Madeira was first fortified and a letter of July 1756 says, "If a couple of gallons of fine clean brandy was put into each pipe of our best wines 'twill improve them greatly. . . . I observe that the Madeira drunk here in Gentlemen's houses are fine pale amber colour nothing tending to a reddish."

There is a satisfactory consensus of opinion that the wine must be good, "bad wines will not sell at any price and we would choose to have them of a pale colour and good body." There is another reference to "a fine pale colour such as is much esteemed nowadays."

This was the period of experiment. There was apparently an attempt to imitate the Jerez method. "Take the quantity of a quarter cask out of each butt and let the bung be but lightly put in so as not totally to exclude the air and you'll find that method of treatment the readiest to ripen them."

It would seem that one of the shippers' difficulties was that they did not always taste the wine they sold. They would dispatch a cargo via India and not know how it would appear in London. A letter of 1789 says, "In the course of eight or nine months' continual agitation on board a vessel, the extra fire and spirit of the brandy must be much exhausted and softened and the wine receive the strength which is quite different when the wines remain quiet and undisturbed in our stores, where the additional dose of brandy takes away the flavour and pleasantness of the wine and is apt to give it a disagreeable harsh twang."

It was not till the very end of the century, during the Napoleonic wars, that the wines were rocked and heated in the lodges themselves, though it is not clear whether this procedure was adopted as a wartime precaution. A note of 1799 records that "It is now become a general practice to put wine into dung that it may improve by the heat. . . . We do not like the taste of the wine at present, but it has a fine smell and looks very pretty having lost all its colour and harshness."

Within a year, however, the *estufado* had been discovered. At first it would seem the wine was boiled and there was some question as to how long it should be boiled, for six months or three. The wine merchants were apparently dubious about this innovation. "We don't think," they wrote, "that the deception can be easily discovered, however the secret will soon be known abroad and may perhaps prejudice the character of Madeira wine." The proof of the pudding lay, however, in the eating and the new heated wines were appreciated in England and the United States as warmly as the traveled wines had been.

Graham Blandy's library contained nearly everything that has been written about Madeira in English. I was particularly fascinated by a curious little book three inches tall, a hundred pages long, illustrated, elegantly printed and published by the Century Company of New York in 1896, which cast an interesting light on the social customs of the day. It was called *A Madeira Party* and described a dinner in New York in the 1850's. It was a masculine occasion for some four guests: the meal was slight, a terrapin and the breast of canvasback duck; no wine was served with it. When the table had been cleared, in its center was set "a silver bowl of water. The notches in the rim received each the stem of an inverted glass. Before each guest a glass bowl, much like a modern fingerbowl, held also two wineglasses. Thus there was to be a glass for each wine, or at needs the means for rinsing a glass. Each guest was given a crust of bread to clean the palate."

The wine was discussed in the same way that port would have been in England, and it is very clear from this book that Madeira was attended in America with the same ritual as port. Each class at Harvard, we learn, imported a tun of wine which was bottled and distributed among the graduates. There is much talk about the mistake of bottling Madeira. "It improves in its own company as greatness is apt to do," says one of them. There is powerful contempt for the host who served Madeira in half-quart decanters. It should be stored in nothing smaller than a five-gallon demijohn, and, always during the decline of the moon, "a gentleman fined his own wine with eggshell, white of egg or milk." They do not appear to have had the same faith as we do in the longevity of the wine. "I never drank a wine over seventy years old that had not something to regret, like ourselves, eh, Wilmington?"

There is a strange assertion that wine should always go the way of the clock because "it soured if towards the right."

It is a curious little book, not a good one, but more interesting than many which are, and it makes one wish that Madeira were still honored as highly as it deserves.

# WINE BETWEEN
# THE WARS—
## *and After*

1

**T**HERE IS MORE to be said for being sixty than I had thought there would be when I was twenty. I visualized the age of sixty in terms of repose, contemplation and arms laid upon the shelf. I dreaded the day when I should have to give up cricket. It has not turned out that way. I gave up cricket without a qualm when I found that I was missing more catches than I held, was turning full pitches into Yorkers and more often than not returning at the end of the day dissatisfied. Certain other doors are no doubt soon to close for me. It has been like that in certain other ways. But life is an adventure still; I have not lost the sense of the unexpected being "just round the corner," though there is a smaller variety of things that I can find there. On the credit side, morever, there stands a compensating sense of distance, of being able to look back and make comparisons, of seeing how various equations have worked out. In the world of wine this is a very great advantage. Working in terms of Ford Madox Ford's formula from the known to the unknown, I wonder whether so many changes can possibly have taken place as rapidly in the nineteenth and eighteenth centuries. To those of us who had no adult life before 1914, it seems in retrospect that those twenty years between the wars were marked by a succession of changes in the drinking habits of Britain and the U.S.A.

Three events stand out as the chief causes of those changes: Prohibition in the U.S.A.; the financial crisis of 1929 which was followed by three bad harvests in 1930, '31 and '32; finally, there came repeal in 1934.

Prohibition, during its fourteen years' occupation, practically killed wine-drinking in the U.S.A., but it increased the amount of spirit-drinking. There was homemade "bath-tub" gin, there was illicitly brewed rye and bourbon, Canadian whiskey was run over the frontier. English firms were besieged by mysterious visitors carrying large sums in cash, anxious to pay in advance, with very particular requirements as to the packaging of their goods, but understandably vague as to their final destination. The principal bases of supply for the "bootleg" trade were Vancouver, which worked the West Coast; Nassau, which supplied Florida and the Southeast; and St. Pierre et Miquelon, where large warehouses sprang up as a base for the East Coast. Some importers wanted their cases made up in lots of six bottles each, in hessian bags; others asked for wire handles. In the late nineteen-twenties and early nineteen-thirties the export warehouse of most London houses employed rows of women sewing hessian bags to complete these orders. Shipment was made either to Hamburg or Antwerp, to avert suspicion, and there the bootleggers took over. At St. Pierre, the wooden cases were hacked open and discarded (causing a serious disposal problem) and the bags and bottles were loaded in shallow-draught vessels which dumped their cargoes in shallow water, to be collected later by land-based operators.

The cocktail and the highball were then the chief sources of conviviality in the U.S.A. During meals you drank coffee or iced water. Repercussions of this new fashion came to Europe, and by the end of the 1920's, the cocktail party had replaced the after-dinner party in London life.

The fashion came very quickly. By 1927 it was established. In 1925 it was an innovation. Guests were tending then to drop in for a cocktail at six, rather than for a "dish of tea" at half-past four; but in 1924 it was relatively unknown. There is no reference to a cocktail party in either *Antic Hay* or *The Green Hat*. I recall, in April 1924, discussing with C. R. W. Nevinson, the painter, and his wife, the difficulty of finding anything to do in London in the winter between tea and dinner. The Nevinsons decided that it might be a good time at which to give a party and sent out an announcement that they were emerging from their winter retirement and would be at home on the last Saturday in April between five and seven. Questioned, years afterwards, they were vague as to the number of invitations they sent out; but some thirty glasses were arranged beside a large earthenware jug containing a yellow, coolish but not cold mixture, in which rum was the chief ingredient. Only two guests arrived. The Londoners of the Nevinsons' acquaintance—and the Nevinsons touched life at very many points—were puzzled by the novelty of the invitation. Londoners tend socially to avoid what puzzles them.

Remembering the experience of the Nevinsons, I took the precaution in October, 1925, of inviting my friends to tea at half-past five. I served a rum swizzle, mixed by a New York friend. It was sweet, cold and strong, and Sheila Kaye-Smith who, because it was cold and sweet, mistook it for a kind of sherbet, failed to achieve her subsequent dinner date. Within eighteen months the cocktail party was an established form of entertainment. For a quarter of a century it has retained its popularity, though it yielded momentarily, in the early 1930's, to the sherry party. It has grown more elaborate as time has passed; substantial food is now provided and hostesses have come to realize that unless they specifically state "6 P.M.—8 P.M." on their invitation, or unless, in winter time, they start opening windows and stop serving drinks, they must be prepared to have at least a quarter of their guests stay on to supper.

## 2

The Eighteenth Amendment was repealed in January 1934, a date which marks the turning of the tide not only in America but in world affairs. The slump was ending, the prewar period was beginning, and in the world of wine, the height of the slump had coincided with three disastrous vintage years in France, '30, '31 and '32. Whether it was the outcome of the economic crisis, of these three bad vintage years or whether it was the prospect of new markets opening across the Atlantic—at any rate it was at this point that the French wine trade decided to put its house in order, to ensure that the customer was not cheated with faked commodities by insisting that reputable wine merchants should give a guarantee of the soundness of their wares, and should not sell as Beaujolais blends of Algerian and Languedoc vineyards. The system of *Appellation Controlée* was devised, and it was established in 1936 by the law that is known as *Appellation d'Origine*.

In its details the law is complicated; because different regulations exist for different wines and different areas; the words *appellation controlée* on a label do not mean that the wine is first class, they merely mean that it is what it says it is; the law defines the area of certain vineyards. If a bottle is labeled Médoc it means that the wine has been grown from vineyards approved by the authorities and with the vines that are prescribed. The rules as regards grapes are much stricter in Burgundy than in Bordeaux. In Burgundy the *gamay* grape produces a great volume of wine of secondary quality, the *pinot* grape a small quantity of high quality. Laws define in what proportion the produce of the *gamay* may be used with that of the *pinot*. The laws are stricter for a district than a commune; for a bottle of Chambertin than for one of Gevrey-Chambertin. The customer does not need to know the details of the law, he asks to be protected. The phrase *appellation controlée* gives him this protection; though there are certain tricks against which he has to be on his guard.

The statement on a Burgundy label *Mis en bouteilles dans mes caves* means nothing at all. All wines are bottled in cellars. The same applies to *Mis en bouteilles au Château X*, which merely means that the bottler has hired a cellar in a large country house in which to carry out his bottling.

These are devices to trick the customer into paying a higher price; but if the bottle is sold as Mâcon and bears in addition to a pretentious and meaningless designation, the words *appellation controlée*, the customer knows that he is buying wine from Mâcon which has satisfied the regulations.

The words *appellation controlée* only hold good in France, and for wines drunk abroad that have been bottled in France. With wines that have been bottled in Britain you have no guarantee other than the wine-shipper's name. But a

French shipper has to satisfy his own authorities that the wine he is exporting satisfies the *Appellation d'Origine* instructions.

On certain bottles there appears a very small label, lettered V.D.Q.S. (*Vins Délimités de Qualité Supérieure*). This means that the wine is rather better than the large label suggests. If a shipper has more wine of a good quality than he can find a market for, he bottles what is left under a simpler banner. A V.D.Q.S. wine is something of a bargain.

In the world of wine many things happened simultaneously in 1934. The Eighteenth Amendment was repealed; the French wine industry put its house in order, there was a revival of interest in wine; and as a corollary to that interest André Simon founded the Wine and Food Society, with its quarterly magazine, to arouse a need for knowledge of the pleasures of the table. The Society issued to its members small ivory cards, showing which wines had quality in which years. Marks ranging from 7 to 0 were allotted to each year and each type of wine. Today shippers and merchants grow a little impatient with the neophytes who, when they are offered a Pauillac 1948, pull out their little cards and shake their heads. "Sorry, '48's aren't any good." Patiently the merchant explains that you can get good wine in a poor year just as you can get poor wine in a good year, and that the Pauillac '48 which he is selling may contain much of the wine from the Château Margaux vineyards. One must not place too great a reliance on those little cards but it is prudent to consult them; they are a very good general guide and they have made the British and American publics vintage conscious.

When one has lived through a period, and that period has become history, one is surprised at the discrepancy between the historian's view and one's own recollections of it. Perhaps our view of the Elizabethans may be equally out of focus. The 1920's are invariably presented as a period of hysterical debauch. As I remember them, they were not at all like that, in England, anyhow, during the early '20's. We were exhausted by the war, we were heavily taxed, few of my friends had much money. We were young, we enjoyed living. We played cricket and football and generally over the weekends "clashed cymbals in Naxos," but we worked hard. In America it was no doubt different. The country had not been in the war so long. Its casualty list was short. Taxes were so low as scarcely to exist. The war had been a stimulant and Prohibition dramatized a trip to Paris. But in England, in my experience, it was not like that. I sometimes wish it had been when I listen to the reminiscences of my New York contemporaries.

It is the same with the 1930's. History is already presenting them as a shamefaced period of cowardice, of time-saving, of responsibilities evaded; and it cannot be denied that it was a period of gathering gloom, of a gradual recognition that a certain account could not be allowed to run on forever, but at the same time I personally did a lot of work and had a great deal of fun. A large proportion of that fun was concerned with wine.

It was the first time that I had been based on England with enough spare money to indulge occasional extravagances. My wife's Australian income took care of her house in the country and of our children. American magazines were proving hospitable to my short stories. I was able to fill my wife's cellar with good wines and in London make an adequate contribution to the general gaiety. It may seem to some people to have been a trivial, rather unworthy fiddling while the faggots were being stacked outside the citadels, but to me it has always seemed wise to enjoy the sunlight, to take a short view, having once given the far horizon a steady look. In retrospect I am glad it was the way it was. It will not come again.

It was a halcyon period for the wine lover. Wines were not too expensive. There were many good wines to drink; thanks largely to the Wine and Food Society there were many interested in drinking them, and there were many congenial opportunities of doing so.

Much of it in England centered around certain London clubs: the Savile, the Saintsbury and the Odd Volumes. I have already spoken of the Odd Volumes, but I have not referred to the small private dinner parties at which the business of the Sette was conducted. At our monthly dinners we each brought guests and in consequence saw little of one another. But there were frequent meetings of the Odd Council and of small groups of officers to discuss the future of the club and the candidates who had been proposed for membership. Guests may have found our dinners rather dull, particularly on inauguration nights when there was a great deal of ritual. But for the Brethren of the Sette such evenings were a part of the obligation that we accepted in return for the cozy little dinners and luncheons where we mellowed the temper of our deliberations with fine wines.

The Saintsbury Club is a great deal younger than the Odd Volumes. Founded in 1931 in honor of George Saintsbury, its members are, in the main, wine experts or men of letters. Sometimes they are both. The one essential qualification for a candidate is that he should be a gourmet. André Simon is the cellarer. Vyvyan Holland is secretary. Membership includes or has included, Robert Gibbings, James

Laver, Hilaire Belloc, Compton Mackenzie, Charles Morgan, J. C. Squire, Low. Raemakers and C. B. Cochran, such respected aristocrats of the wine trade as Ronald Avery, Anthony Berry, Ian Campbell, R. W. Byass, Francis Berry, F. A. Cockburn, John Harvey, while Debrett is represented by Devonshire, Portsmouth, Huntingdon and Woolton. The annual subscription is six dollars; the price of dinner is usually seven dollars and fifty cents. The entrance fee is a case of wine. The accepted candidate is unfettered in his choice but his contribution is expected to test his powers of discernment. The cellar is also maintained by unsolicited gifts and legacies.

The membership is limited to fifty, that being the number for whom an Impériale will provide a glass apiece. It dines twice a year in the Vintners' Company's paneled dining room, at a table richly decorated with gold and silver plate.

The dinner, appropriately to such a setting, is attended by a certain ritual. Black ties are worn, but there is a welcome absence of long speeches. There is in fact only one set speech—the Saintsbury Oration which, delivered on each occasion by a different member, lasts about twenty minutes. If the committee decides it is to be so honored, it is subsequently published as a brochure, with the menu, the list of members, and the names of the members and guests who were in attendance. A complete collection of the Saintsbury Orations will be one day a valuable item for the bibliophile.

The Odd Volumes after one lunch during the "phony war" closed down completely in 1940, but the Saintsbury, because it possessed a cellar of its own and through the courtesy of the Vintners' Company a dining room in which to meet, was able to function during the war, substituting lunch for dinner. It was one of the pockets of resistance that maintained alight the lamp of gracious living during a period of austerity and rationing.

Now that that time has passed—and it is barely a decade away—it is hard to remember quite what a strain it imposed on Britain. In practically every country there was a strain of some kind, but in Britain it was more diffused; only a few had access to black-market merchandise and those were mainly people with whom the average citizen was not brought in touch.

After the collapse of France, no wine could be obtained from the Bordeaux merchants; ships could no longer put into Spanish or Portuguese ports; many cellars and warehouses were destroyed by bombing; submarine attacks made the importation of grain extremely difficult; and barley, the raw material of Scotch whisky, had to be diverted from the distilleries to the feeding of livestock.

But on the whole the wine-lover in England fared better than the gourmet. The behavior of the wine trade during these years did credit to a community whose reputation for square dealing has always stood enviably high. No attempt was made to make undue profits out of an exceptional situation. Each firm compared the extent of its stocks with the needs of its customers, the amount it had paid for the wine, the interest that had accrued, the increased cost of living and then estimated a fair price. The quota system was evolved. Each month the customer received a parcel. A new regard grew up for a commodity rather than for a name, and the wine merchant, instead of saying that he had bought a certain consignment, would genially remark, "I think I shall be able to give you a dozen half-bottles of red wine this month."

The Minister of Food at that time was, luckily, a Saintsburian, Lord Woolton, and the chairman of the Wine and

Spirits Association was also a Saintsburian, Colonel Ian
Campbell. Between them they devised the "concession" system, by which as shipping became available—a troopship,
for example, returning empty from the Middle East—im-
ports from various countries were allowed. Some curious
beverages found their way by this system on to British tables: a bottle was a bottle. But for a special occasion you
could usually get something special.

The family that had not dealt with a wine merchant,
but had sent out to the grocery for a bottle of gin or whisky
was at that time in an unfortunate position; so was the
family that moved to a different part of the country and
had no connection with the local wine trade. Those were best
placed who before the war had scattered their custom
among several wine merchants, so that they could draw on
more than one quota. Myself, I had not. I had followed the advice of my solicitor, the late E. S. P. Haynes, whose *Lawyer's
Notebooks* earned such a wide and deserved success. His advice was based on a remark of Dr. Johnson's, "You can dodge
the cannon-balls, but the bullets will get you down." Which
meant that you can stave off a big creditor with post-dated
checks but that a volley of small bills will land you in the
Bankruptcy Courts.

By following this advice I found myself in 1940 with
only one string to my bow. Luckily it did not worry me as
I was posted to the Middle East in the autumn of 1941. A
year later my wife's solicitor informed me that he was safe-
guarding my interests with Saccone and Speed "by main-
taining my quota and credit." I took this to mean that he
was receiving himself my monthly bottle of whisky, an as-
tuteness that made me think I had been wise in recommending his services to my wife.

In the United States the situation was far less difficult.
There were local gins and whiskies. There were Californian

and New York State wines. There was Chilean wine and rum in plenty. When I returned to New York in September, 1945, I found that the best way of getting a bottle of Scotch whisky was by buying a case of rum. The shortage of Scotch whisky was negligible by 1946. In Britain, however, V-J Day did not by any means bring down the curtain on war conditions.

Wine was still a "concession" commodity, and a Labor Party administration was inclined to regard wine as a rich man's privilege. One of the most amusing episodes in the argument maintained between the authorities and the wine trade is the dispute between the Ministry of Food and the House of Harvey, which M. Geoffrey Harrison records in his "Bristol Cream."

It took place in 1949 when the Ministry drew Harvey's attention to Regulation One of the Defense (Sales of Food) Regulations 1943, which makes it an offense to mislead as to the nature, substance and quality of a food or in particular as to its nutritional or dietary value. "In the Ministry's opinion," it continues, "the use of the wording, 'Bristol Milk' might well be held to contravene the said regulations on the ground that this indicates the presence of milk and as such suggests that the wine has certain special nutritive qualities."

The chairman's reply after pointing out that the term "Bristol Milk" had been in use for over three hundred years, remarks that presumably the same objection would apply to "Bristol Cream" and as a result to all shaving creams, hair creams, face creams, boot creams, etc. as suggestive that they have a nutritive value.

What presumably softened the Ministry most was the fact that five hundred thousand dollars a year came from the export trade to U.S.A. of these two sherries.

The Ministry incidentally prevented Gilbey's from in-

cluding in their catalogue "Invalid Port" on the grounds
that it might be mistaken as a medicine. Digestive Biscuits
also left the market.

It was gradually, stage by stage, that relief came to
beleaguered Britain. Much of that time I was abroad, and
always on my return I found that some fresh barrier was
down. One time it was to discover the possibility of buying
champagne by the case, on another that I could get all the
gin I wanted. On my return from the Middle East in 1945, I
had resumed my quota with Hankey Bannister and each
month I received a dozen assorted bottles. I had these delivered to my agent's office, as I could not drink them all
during the few weeks I was in London. I let him take over
what I did not need. In 1950 I received a letter from his
secretary, telling me that I could discontinue this practice
as the store of bottles to be consumed exceeded her employ-
er's capacity. The hour of deliverance had come. I prayed
that never again would wine be rationed.

I ONCE PLANNED a travel book to be called "Out of Season." The opening chapter would explain that with tourism a major industry in every European country, with facilities for travel at nearly everyone's disposal, the pleasantest places of the world had become impossibly crowded during their proper season, and that to appreciate the characteristics that had endeared them to the Edwardians, we had to visit them "out of season."

I mentioned this project when I was spending a winter in Denmark to the British Ambassador, Sir Eric Berthoud. "If you do that," he said, "I hope you will remember that for the Danes themselves, the Copenhagen season is in winter. It is the time of the ballet, the theater and social activities. In the summer the Danes are in the country, swimming and sailing."

That was in January, 1955; I was in Copenhagen during its own season, but it was not the tourist season. I went there, as I have made so many trips, by chance. I had no long-scale travel plans. I had a book to work on. My mother, in her eighty-third year, was in failing health. I needed to be within easy reach of London. In the previous summer at the MacDowell Colony, I had met Virginia Sorensen who was headed for Denmark on a Guggenheim to obtain material for a novel of Mormon life. As a traveler I have always made a point of visiting places where I had one genuine friend. I had never been to Denmark. Why not? I thought.

It was a lucky decision. I have seldom liked any place as much. The Danes are gay and friendly. In London, New York and Nice, the three places that are nearest to my heart, I invariably find myself losing my temper mildly, every other day, over some trivial irritation—a shop assistant has been rude, a waiter offhand, someone has pushed in front of me in a bus queue. But at the end of a month in Copenhagen I realized that I had not lost my temper once. This was in no sense due to any greater measure of self-control on my part, but simply to the amiability of the Danes.

Copenhagen is an enchanting city. It has been admirably interpreted in *Danish Delight* by Monica Redlich, an Englishwoman married to a Dane. She has described its waterways, its canals, its spires, its green copper roofs, and its many individual features: the guard headed by a band that marches through the city every day at noon, the postman red-coated as though he always brought good news, the children's guard in Tivoli in summer. She has pointed out the family closeness of everything in the old city, with its fish market within sight of its chief shopping area, as

though Buckingham Palace, Regent Street and Billingsgate
were within five minutes' walk of one another. She has explained many of the charming formalities of Danish life,
the absolute necessity, for instance, of a guest either arriv-
ing with flowers or sending flowers beforehand to say how
much he is looking forward to his evening entertainment, and
on his next meeting with his hosts saying as soon as possible,
"Thank you for your hospitality." (*"Tak for sist."*) She
has done it all so well that there is no need for me to retread
that ground, and anyhow the purpose of this book is to discuss the pleasures of the table which are admirably catered for
in Denmark.

I made my first journey there by ship from London.
There could be no better introduction. Airplanes are im-
personal. There is little difference between the machines of
one country and another. The seats are the same, the food is
much the same, the hostesses look the same, though they may
speak English with a foreign accent. There is no sense of
nationality. You do not feel that you are in Switzerland
when you travel by Swissair. But the French Line justifiably
advertises itself as "France Afloat" and the moment you
step on board the *Flandre*, though the tall spires of Manhattan tower behind you, you are in France. And as I walked
from the quay at Harwich on to the *Crown Prince Frederick*, I knew myself to be in Denmark.

The sailing was at an appropriate time, shortly before
noon. Lunch was served as soon as the anchor had been
weighed and lunch is the best meal in Denmark. It starts
with an immense cold table, fish and meat and salad, most
of them highly savoured to match the ice-cold *Aquavit* and
the Danish beer. No Dane would drink schnapps until he
had eaten something. It is too powerful to be treated like a
dry Martini. An English novelist at a cold buffet reception
astonished his host by drinking four glasses quickly and

then demanding that they open the double windows with which the Danes prudently keep their room warm in winter, thereby threatening them with pneumonia. *Aquavit* should be taken slowly with the cold dishes of a meal, to be returned to afterwards—if cheese is served as a final course. Three glasses are ample for a lunch. Wine can be served with the hot dishes, but the Danes, in my experience, prefer beer.

There are two breweries in Denmark, Carlsberg and Tuborg, and there are two kinds of beer, the light Pilsener and the stronger, more expensive export brand, which is wrapped in a gold-foiled bottle. It would be difficult to enumerate the charities and public utilities that have benefited from the success of those two firms, and at any public function it is considered a solecism not to serve the products of both firms. It would be impolitic and invidious to distinguish between them, and in fact I do not think there is any real difference in their taste. They rank with the best German and Swedish beers. It was export beer that they served for that first lunch on the *Crown Prince Frederick*. Before the coastline of England was out of sight I knew that in one respect at least I was going to enjoy my winter in Copenhagen.

I had made some preparations before my arrival. I had got in touch with the British Council, offering to be of any assistance to them that I could. The British Council and the British Information Services generally were at this time being constantly attacked by a certain section of the English press. But with the limited means at their disposal, it seems to me that they are doing an excellent job of work in presenting the British way of life to foreigners. I have always found their representatives extremely helpful. They have put me in touch with aspects of a foreign country's life that otherwise I might have missed. I have given a lecture or two at their Institute. After the lecture there has been a party, and through those parties I have met local notables.

I also before going abroad take steps to be presented to the British authorities, consular, diplomatic or gubernatorial, and before leaving London I had looked up the British Ambassador in *Who's Who*. Sir Eric Berthoud was a year or two younger than myself. He had been at Magdalen just after the first war. He had been employed for a time with the Anglo-Iranian Oil Company, with which I had many links; among his clubs he numbered M.C.C. I did not feel that it was necessary for me to do more than sign his book on my arrival. It was unlikely that we should not find we had a good deal in common.

My presentiments were fulfilled. A great many of the good times I had in Denmark were due to his generous and helpful hospitality.

Within two days of my arrival I received an invitation to lunch at the British Embassy. Before I had sipped the red wine that was set before me I had realized from its color and smell that my host kept a good cellar. Before the meal was half-finished I had realized that he was as much an amateur of wine as of cricket. The Danes, he told me, had many points of resemblance with the English. They could grow the same kind of apple—the Cox Pippin—and they loved good claret. There was something in the air of Copenhagen, something in its dampness, that accentuated the quality of red Bordeaux wines. He said that claret which had been shipped in wood and bottled in Copenhagen often tasted better than wine that had been "Château-bottled."

"It is of course cheaper too that way," I said.

"No doubt, but that was not my point," he said, and smiled. It was an endearing smile, and I could understand how his staff, after they had been reprimanded, would leave his presence, in a chastened mood possibly, but none the less gratefully affectionate. At the end of lunch, with fruit, he served Madeira. "You cannot drink port here," he said. He must have been right. And Madeira is a wine that needs to travel, that is improved by travel, whereas vintage port is a particularly English thing. But even so I do not see why tawny port should not be good in Copenhagen. Perhaps it is a question of quick consumption. Tawny should not be kept in a cellar. It should be drunk within a few weeks of being bottled. It is a barrel-to-mouth commodity. Maybe Madeira, with its richness and power and majesty, is a safer dessert wine in Denmark.

At that first lunch, I met the consul, Dr. Grace Thornton; a few days later at her house she instructed me in the routine of toasting when you drink *Aquavit*, and how you never drink without raising your glass to one of the other guests, and saying "Skol." There is quite a drill to it, the looking into the person's eyes over your glass, the sip, and then the second look into the eyes and the salute. I also learned that you must never toast your hostess; the reason being that a lady should not be forced to drink more than she really wants. There was once, I believe, in Scandinavian life, particularly in Sweden, an excess of formality. Douglas Goldring, who married a Swedish lady, wrote entertainingly of it in *Northern Lights and Southern Shade*, but today in Denmark the ritual of flowers and toasting and saying "Thank you" adds a graciousness to everyday existence. The flower shops even in winter are bright with a variety of plants; Danish silver and porcelain are world-renowned and nowhere will you see tables more pleasantly decorated.

Except when I was a guest at the British Embassy I drank little great wine in Copenhagen. Its cost was beyond my means. But I am a wine drinker, and I drank plenty of the casual beverages that were admitted into the country with a Spanish provenance, at a reduced rate of duty. In most of the restaurants there appeared a starred entry on the wine lists at a very reduced rate. It was by no means bad and in the big department stores you could buy a magnum of table wine that was clean and wholesome for two dollars. I would drink it in my room at the hotel.

I look back on that winter, in spite of the sadness of a personal bereavement, as one of the happiest of my life. It might be the Copenhagen season as far as the Danes were concerned, but as regards American and European tourists it was very quiet. I was let at a minimum rate a large one-room apartment at the Codan Hotel that looked upon the Sound, from which I watched the ferryboat leave at midnight for Aalborg and for Aarhus, and the ships with French and American-British flags sailing up the Sound. I would order, from the long sandwich list, three or four canapés, and eat them slowly, sipping at the strong red wine, walking over to the window to watch the red neon lights of the D.F.S. line glow through the snow. There were double windows and the room was warm. I was very cozy during a winter of long nights and of short days when the twilight began to settle as lunch ended.

Beer and schnapps are the chief Danish liquors, but there is another very special one, Cherry Heering, which was the high advantage of being international. Beer and *Aquavit* are specially designed for the Danish climate and for Danish food, but Cherry Heering can be drunk anywhere. I had never tasted it before I went to Denmark, though I had been with English friends who had ordered it on cold winter mornings. I confessed this to Peter Heering— the present owner of the firm—with a little guilt. He laughed. "I am delighted to hear it. I am always glad to meet someone who never has. I know that I have a new customer, that my business is an expanding one."

I met him in circumstances of promising informality. I had arrived in Copenhagen two weeks before Virginia Sorensen. On her first day there I took her to lunch in Krog's, a quayside restaurant on the fish market. I was enjoying the forerunner's privilege of initiating her into Danish customs. I taught her, over an *Aquavit*, how to respond to my toast of "Skol." We ordered a pickled herring, a sole maison, stuffed with shrimps, and Danish pancakes. The traditional blue coffee cups were set upon the table. "We should have a Danish liqueur with this. We'll ask the waiter what he's got," I said.

There were several Danish liqueurs, but Cherry Heering was unquestionably the best, he told us. We accepted his advice. It was deep red in color. We toasted each other in it. It was rich and sweet, but not sickly sweet. It had a flavor of fruit and sunshine. We had a good time with it. "One glass of this won't be enough," I said.

As we toasted ourselves again, I noticed two tables away a tall blond good-looking man in his early forties, watching us with interest and amusement. It was an unseasonably sunny day for mid-December. I had brought only one coat, a leather one lined with sheep's wool, highly unsuitable for such a day. When I lifted it off the peg, the man who had watched me smiled. "I hope you won't catch a chill," he said. We began to gossip, and I found that he was Peter Heering, a cousin of whom I had already met and who had promised to introduce me to him. A friendship started there that added greatly to the enjoyment of my visit to Copenhagen.

A few days later Heering invited me to his factory, and when I left he gave me a copy of the book that describes the history of the firm that was started by his great-grandfather in 1818. It began in the simplest way as a grocer's shop opened by a young man of twenty-six, Peter F. Heering, who had come twelve years earlier to the capital, a fatherless son, from Roskilde, where his father had been a collector of taxes, to be apprenticed to a grocer. He was promised during his apprenticeship "suitable food, clothing of wool and line, with footwear, and lodging" and when "his boyhood years were over a suit of clothes with the necessary linen such as would not be to his master's discredit." He acquired a great deal of instruction during the tutelary period, he was industrious and quick to learn, but he had no means of guessing that the most important item in his training would be the recipe that his master's wife gave him for making her special liqueur out of cherries.

This liqueur was only one of the many commodities with which he stocked his store, but many of his customers were ships' officers and he soon learned that his cherry liqueur did not appeal only to Danish tastes. It was welcomed in foreign countries. Shipmasters and mates who had taken a few bottles for their private use found it so popular that on their next voyage they took a larger consignment to sell when they went ashore or to exchange for fruit and spices. A young naval officer received so many orders in the Danish West Indies that he retired from the Navy and settled as a merchant in the Caribbean.

At the start it was a question of Heering's Cherry liqueur—it was known in those days as Cherry Brandy—selling itself. So extensive were the first Heering's dealings with sailors that within fifteen years of opening his shop, he had built a ship himself—the schooner *Arnold,* named after his first son who died at the age of four. The venture proved so successful that during his lifetime nine other ships were built to carry the Heering house flag—a seven-pointed star on a white background—to the seven seas. He made a by no means negligible contribution to the general national efforts to restore the fortunes of Danish shipping after the catastrophes of the Napoleonic wars.

At the same time he moved from the small cellar shop that was the base of his first transactions to the gracious ocher-colored eighteenth century house by the Christianshavn canal. It is a traditional Danish house, with an impressive gateway, built round an inner courtyard, and it is a traditional Danish life that the Heerings have lived there, each family with its own flat. The firm's offices are there, the distillery and the warehouses; the office wing which was built between the wars is streamlined with modernity in terms of decoration—the white-lacquered clock face with brass numerals is a symbol—but you feel that you have stepped into an earlier century when you cross the neat paved courtyard into the warehouse wings where a faintly aromatic smell hangs upon the air, and the liqueur matures in large oaken casks, black with age, many of them carved with the Heering coat-of-arms.

Today the firm concentrates upon one product, though it also manufactures a few cordials for local consumption; the economic crisis at the end of the 1850's discouraged the original founder from general trading, and the profits on shipping turned into a loss. The firm retrenched, drew back upon its base but at the same time expanded, opening agencies and branches concentrating on Cherry Heering. There is a room in the Heering office decorated with a map showing the towns to which Cherry Heering is exported direct from Copenhagen. It would be hard to mention a name that is not marked there. The British Isles require a special map to themselves. His office also contains a museum of "forgeries," most from the Far East, particularly Japan.

The house on the Christianshavn canal is the center of the firm's activities, but all over Zeeland are cherry orchards which supply the factories, and forty miles south at Dalby, set about by farms, is a new distillery.

Every year in May, as soon as the trees are in blossom, Peter gives there a party for his friends. Owing to the late spring, it fell on my last Sunday in Denmark, at the end of

May. I could not have had a better curtain. It was a bright, sunny, windy day. There is usually a wind in Denmark. There is nothing to stop it. The country is flat, the nearest northern mountain range is on the other side of the North Pole, and one of the most charming features of Danish life in summer is the sight of young women bicycling to work or pleasure with their skirts billowing in the wind.

We met, some two hundred of us, in the courtyard of the Copenhagen offices. Those who had not already seen the plant were taken round it; the others embussed to be driven out to Dalby. It was a lovely drive. In recompense for the long gray winter, the Danish beech trees have a freshness of color that is not found under more equable skies. It is a short-lived brilliance but in May its brightness dazzles you. It did that morning, and afterwards, by contrast, there was the pale pink of the cherry blossom flowering on many thousand trees.

The buildings, on which work was only started after the war, are single-storied, clean and airy, and harmonize agreeably with the surrounding farms. After we had seen the various processes to which the fruit was subjected, there was an ample and typical Danish sandwich luncheon, with the smoked salmon spread on bread so thickly buttered that the bite of the teeth was clearly marked in it; with ice cold *Aquavit* and beer and finally cream cakes and Cherry Heering.

I recognized during that last Sunday how very close to my heart Denmark had come to lie: so close that I doubt if I shall go back there. *Aimez-ce que jamais on ne verra pas deux fois.* There are several places on the map—Tahiti and the Seychelles are two of them—which are too nostalgic for me. But in Denmark's case I have amulets against forgetfulness: there is the excellent Danish restaurant in New York where the walls are decorated with life-size photographs of

Danish scenes. Peter Heering gave me as a Christmas present a charming flagon in Copenhagen porcelain which holds
an exact bottle of Cherry Heering; it stands on the sideboard at Edrington and is kept replenished. Candles play a
large part in table decoration. In the restaurants whenever
you take your seat at table, a candle is promptly lighted. I
carry with me a small Jensen silver candlestick, and a small
blue liqueur glass. I am opposed to colored glass, it spoils
the color of the wine, but I was given this one in Copenhagen. It has a sentimental value, and on solitary evenings
in New York I light the candle, read poetry by it and sip
Cherry Heering.

As I SAID in an earlier chapter, I was self-educated in a taste for wine. I went to my first large dinner party in December, 1918. I was twenty and a half. I had recently returned from a German prisoner-of-war camp. My public school novel *The Loom of Youth* was still selling briskly and the editor of the *Sunday Times*, Leonard Rees, asked me to write him an article on the effects of the war on public schools. The article reopened a controversy.

It was Rees' agreeable habit to entertain his contributors every three or four months at dinner at the Savile Club. He invited me to his next dinner. There were fourteen other guests. I do not suppose one of them is alive today. It is many years since I have seen any of their names at the head of a column. I was the youngest person there by quarter of a century. For someone of my age this might have seemed an awe-inspiring occasion, but shyness is an emotion with which I have the good fortune to be unfamiliar. I do remember, however, being disconcerted at the start of the meal when the man on my left turned to his left and the man on my right turned to his right, and I was left stranded, staring across the table to the other guest who found himself in a similar quandary. But that is not my salient memory of the evening.

By the time we left the table, I was beginning to feel increasingly unwell. I wanted to be sick, but could not. I rested my forehead against the cool porcelain of the Savile Club's lavatory, praying for deliverance, but none came. I was afraid to go upstairs, lest I should vomit. I did not know how long I could stay away without causing offense. I wanted to make a good impression on my seniors. I wanted to be a good guest. I also wanted to enjoy myself. It was a very bad quarter of an hour, but eventually the nausea passed.

Next morning I recounted my experience to my father. He asked me what I had had to drink. A glass of sherry, I told him, champagne, port and brandy. It was in fact exactly what Thackeray's Mr. Foker had recommended—"a bottle of sherry, a bottle of sham, a bottle of port and shass caffy." My father shook his head. "Champagne and port. A fatal mixture, my dear boy."

From then on I followed his advice—avoiding champagne when I was to be offered vintage port, accepting champagne when I was uncertain of my host's cellar. In the course of those years, five or six times I was taken violently ill, a couple of hours after dinner, when I had done nothing to deserve such retribution. It was as late as 1925, when I had my own flat and housekeeper, that I discovered the cause. "Mrs. Dickenson," I said, "I was sick last night. What could have disagreed with me?" We went over the menu. It all seemed blameless, till we reached the savory. Bacon wrapped around an oyster. Ah, that might be it! I thought back over the other occasions when I had been sick. Each time there had been oysters. Clearly I had an allergy to oysters. I reflected, resentfully, on the number of occasions over seven years, when I had refrained from mixing champagne and port.

This incident exemplifies one of the greatest fallacies about wine, namely that you should not mix wines. I have been assured that it is fatal to drink red wine after white. A brother novelist, dead these many years, who undeniably drank much too much, had a termagant of a wife who was always embarrassing their friends by trying to control his drinking. I remember a Ladies' Night dinner at the Odd Volumes when she leaned across a table and from two places down, removed his glass of claret. "Frankie mustn't mix red and white." She could not have been more wrong, unless he had an allergy against mixing wines and if he had, he would have been very foolish to have mixed them, for no one wants to make himself feel ill. There was indeed every reason why he should have taken a red after a white, since the whole sequence of wines at table is designed to prepare the palate for a big wine. A big wine has to be led up to.

The first advice that most of us receive about the serving of wines is as unsound as could be. "Every man at the beginning doth set forth good wine, and when men have well drunk, then that which is worse, but thou hast kept the good wine till now." The incident casts a somber reflection on the drinking habits of the Gallileans. It suggests that by the time the meal was three-quarters over, the company was so drunk that it did not care what it drank. For many centuries, the discriminating have followed an entirely opposite procedure that has this corollary—a big wine must be sipped. It cannot be quaffed. At the beginning of a meal a man is thirsty and hungry. He needs a light wine and substantial nourishment; at the end of a meal when thirst and appetite are allayed, he wants to trifle with food and wine that are both delicate and rich. For those who contend that they cannot afford to buy big wines, there is this counter-argument, that they and their guests will consume half as much in volume of a big wine as of a light one. One Chambertin does the work of two Beaujolais.

Anyone who drinks alcohol must now and again suffer from a heavy head next day; and a number of cautionary admonitions have been delivered for the guidance of the inexperienced—particularly in connection with spirits. "Never mix grain and grape"; that as a phrase is so effective that it is hard not to give it credence, but it is of dubious veracity. I have once or twice drunk Scotch whisky through a meal with vintage port afterwards and had a headache later. I would not think a couple of Scotch and sodas would be a good preparative to a dinner at which wine is to be served, but many New Yorkers do. On the other hand, I have never felt anything but the better for a Bourbon Old-fashioned directly before a meal. If one comes in from golf at six o'clock, there is nothing better than a Scotch and soda before one goes upstairs to change; and last thing at night, it is an admirable nightcap, no matter what one has drunk before, provided that it was within reason.

There is another warning.

*"Whisky on beer, never fear.*
*Beer on whisky, makes you frisky."*

This may be true for some people. It is not for me. Whereas things that are true for me, are not for others. Thirty years ago, I was forced to recognize that cognac made me not only bad-tempered but mean-tempered. Reluctantly I abandoned it, for I love the taste of it. We each have our individual allergies. Sooner or later we discover what they are and if we are sensible we obey their dictates. It is impossible to lay down rules, each man makes his own rules for himself. The general principle holds good that you work up, in terms of food as of wine, from lesser to greater, preparing the palate and digestion for a supreme experience.

The idea that you should not mix white wine and red is one of the first and most obvious fallacies in connection with wine, but there are others, several others, which may be enumerated under the following headings.

1. All wines improve with age.
2. Alcoholic strength increases with age.
3. Good red wines should be served from a basket.
4. Red wines should be decanted through muslin.
5. Hot water brings out the bouquet of wine.
6. White wine should be iced.
7. Only red wine can be served with red meat.
8. Napoleon brandy.
9. Cut and colored glasses.
10. Spirits spoil the palate.
11. Smoking ruins the palate.

As regards 1. All wines improve up to a point when they are in cask. But only the best improve after they have been bottled. A bourgeois claret improves very little. No little wines improve. Sherry does not, nor does Tawny port. Ruby port, on the other hand, does.

2. Age brings no increase of alcoholic strength.

3. The idea that red wine should be served in a basket derives from the very proper principle that the wine that has lain on its side in a cellar should not be shaken like an Indian club on its way to the table. But the basket does not fulfil this function. Watch an average waiter—French waiters provide no exception—pour wine from a basket. He will pour the wine into your glass, then jerk it back into a vertical

position, at the best an angle of 45 degrees, and proceed to the next guest. Such sediment as there was in the bottle must have been well distributed before the bottle is quarter way round the table. A basket is only useful for one purpose, to convey from the bin to the decanting table the bottle that you propose to drink at the next meal.

I keep two baskets, one for large bottles, the other for half-bottles, because it is easy to draw a cork from a basket. It is difficult otherwise unless you have a special cage in your cellar, and I have only seen one in my life—at the Château Loudenne. If you see a red wine in a basket, watch carefully how the host, butler or wine-waiter pours out the wine. If he jerks back the bottle, as he almost certainly will, you can dismiss him as a connoisseur. If he does not . . . well, there is an argument on his side, but surely it would have been simpler to have decanted the wine.

4. Red wines should be decanted through muslin. Red wine looks better, its color is shown off better, in a decanter. Some red wines throw a sediment, vintage port throws a crust. It is important that the sediment and the crust should not be mixed with the wine; if they are, the taste of the wine will be spoiled. If you pour a bottle of wine through muslin, none of the sediment can pass into the decanter, but there are those who maintain that the passage through muslin affects the taste of the wine. If you have a cellar of your own, you need never use muslin. If the bottle has rested on its side for an adequate length of time, the sediment will be gathered on its side, and if when you decant it, you have a light under the bottle, you can see when the dark stream of sediment reaches the neck of the bottle, and you stop pouring. If you have broken the cork, a glass or silver filter will catch the broken pieces; in the case of vintage port it will catch fragments of the crust.

All red wines need to rest for a little while after purchase; the length of time depends on the type of wine. Old wines need to rest longer than young wines, Bordeaux wines longer than Burgundies because they throw a bigger sediment. This involves a problem for those living in a modern apartment building who have not got a cellar. If you want to serve a fine wine at short notice, there is only one thing to do: ask your wine merchant to decant it for you in his cellars.

My visits to New York usually last six weeks; on my first day I order from my wine merchant a little champagne, some white Burgundy, some claret and red Burgundy. The champagne and white Burgundy are ready for immediate drinking. I stand up the red wines. They should be ready within two weeks. But they are not always. A year or two ago I ordered some 1947 Mouton-Rothschild. I opened the first bottle after a three weeks' rest, on a dark day when I had not examined it carefully. It was magnificent on the nose, but the wine was not clear and its taste was muddy. It was a warning reminder to me that a big wine needs a longer rest than a small one. But I should not have improved it by decanting it through muslin, because the sediment had become integrated with the wine. Sediment must be given time to settle.

5. There is much confusion about the temperature at which red wine should be served. The word *chambré* is deceiving. It means that the wine should have taken on the temperature of the room, but the word *chambré* to an Englishman suggests conflagration, it suggests exposure to heat; putting a bottle of wine before a fire, or plunging it into a bottle of hot water. Thirty years ago—I do not think you would now, so much more widespread is the knowledge about wine —you would hear an Englishman say in a Soho restaurant, "A little *chambré*, please." That means absolutely nothing. A bottle is *chambré* or it is not. What the client meant was, "Warm it up a little."

We tend to laugh at him, but in one way he was completely right; except in private houses most red wines are served too cold. I have found this particularly true when I have dined with gastronomes. The red wines at the Saintsbury Club dinners are always served too cold. They are decanted in the cellar an hour or two before the meal. The dining room is chilly. It only achieves a congenial warmth a minute or two before the guests assemble. One has to warm one's glass for several minutes before it is palatable. It is heretical to suggest that it would have been much wiser to let the decanters warm in a cradle of tepid water; but is there any difference between the warmth of the human hand and the warmth of water provided the temperature is the same? The experts say there is, but is there? At the gala dinner in Beaune served in *les grands celliers des Hospices,* the wines were much too cold, at first—till they were *chambrés,* that is to say. Big red wines must be "off the chill." But at the same time it is untrue that hot water brings out the bouquet in a wine.

6. White wine should be cool, but it should not be frozen—unless it is very poor champagne, and then extreme icing takes away its taste. The flavor of a Montrachet or a big hock is destroyed if it is served very cold. Sauternes should be served very cool, otherwise it is too sickly. *Rosé* wines should be served cold. So should dry sherry. Half an hour in a refrigerator makes all the difference. In the south of Spain they serve Tio Pepe *chambré* and it is not pleasant. There are those who consider that Beaujolais should be chilled. I do not agree with them, but every man is entitled to his own opinion. Certainly it should not be iced.

The serving of red wine in the tropics presents a problem. There are those who would say, "Don't serve it at all," but a French wine salesman recently gave this advice to his clients in Bangkok. "A red Burgundy ages as much in a month during a journey through the tropics as it would in a year if it was left in a cellar in Beaune. You can drink a two-year-old wine as soon as it has rested. Leave it in a cool cellar, or else chill it, very slightly: bring it on the table just before you drink it. You will find that its temperature is satisfactory." It seemed alarming advice to me. But a friend served me with a bottle of claret that he had subjected to this treatment. The first sip was a slight shock, possibly because it was unexpected, but the rest of the bottle was excellent.

7. Only red wine should be served with red meat. This is the obverse side of the statement that white wine can only be made from white grapes and red from red. You can make white wine from red grapes, but you cannot make red from white; since it is the coloring of the skin that gives the color, and if you remove the grape-skins you have white wine. Red wine should not be served with fish, but a big hock or white Burgundy or champagne is an excellent accompaniment of grouse or steak. White wine goes with everything, so does Beaujolais and so does Tavel *Rosé*. But rich food demands rich wine. If you are going to serve white wine with saddle of mutton or wild duck, then it should be a Meursault or Montrachet, champagne or a big Rheingau wine.

8. Napoleon Brandy. There is no such thing, or if there were, it would be valueless. Cognac does not mature in bottle, and a cognac that had been poured into a cask in 1815 would have been by now so replenished with newer wines that little of its residue would remain.

9. Cut and colored glasses. The serving of German wines in green-tinted glasses has nothing to recommend it and is to be deplored. Colored wineglasses were first introduced in the Victorian age to conceal the cloudiness of certain immature white wines. They destroy the charm of appreciating a finely colored hock, Moselle or white Burgundy. They are fine for very dry Martinis as they conceal a

lack of vermouth. There is nothing to be said in favor of
cut glass either. Anything that detracts from a complete appreciation of the color of a wine is to be avoided. On the
other hand, it heightens the attractiveness of water.

10. Spirits spoil the palate. The purists never cease to
inveigh against the cocktail habit, and it cannot be denied
that no one who has been drinking dry Martinis for ninety
minutes is in a temper to appreciate good wine. Nor do I feel
that it is wise to drink a couple of Scotch and sodas immediately before dinner. There should be a pause. The arguments against cocktails are familiar. They deaden the palate, over-excite the gastric juices; but there is a great deal
of difference between one or two Martinis and five or six.
Moreover, we have to take into account the mental peace
that is induced by the sharp shock of frozen spirits. The cocktail has banished *le mauvais quart d'heure*. There are those
who contend that sherry is the perfect *apéritif*. I have not
found it so. Dry sherry is an excellent wine with soup, and
a rich sweet sherry comes well at the end of a meal with
fruit, instead of port or a Sauternes. Any kind of good sherry
is welcome at eleven o'clock in the morning with a dry biscuit, but as a prelude to dinner, no.

In the middle 1930's there was a vogue for sherry parties in London, as an economy. They were very dreary. In
1934 I gave one in New York. It was shortly after repeal
and I thought it might be welcomed as a novelty. My friends
made it quite clear that though they were ready to sample a
European experiment once, this particular one did not travel
well.

We have in terms of wine as of so much else to recognize the demands of the day we live in. Our main contemporary trouble is that life contains so many problems that no
single man can cope with all of them. An impossible load is
laid upon those who guide and guard our destinies. Each of

us in his lesser way is in the same position. We have innumerable problems that we cannot share with those who are closest and dearest to us, which we can share far less with those whom we call our friends, and our acquaintances, whom we meet once a month, once a quarter, once a year.

We come to each new meeting, out of the conflict of our private and our professional life. A hundred and one different issues are beating in on us. We have to silence their voices, in order that we can concentrate on this particular rendezvous. How better can we do it than with a dry Martini? We have to have a common denominator. We arrive at the flat, the house, the restaurant, our nerves jangled. Our problems are most of them different from our guests' or hostess's. We need to be hit upon the head with a heavy mallet, so that we forget those problems and become not two separate individual selves but fellow travelers who have shared one Martini. We can then start in from there and be ourselves. We have not time nowadays to thaw out slowly.

I am prepared to believe that a dry Martini slightly impairs the palate, but think what it does to the soul. Our ancestors may have been able to manage without cocktails, and I will willingly concede that the best preparation for a meal is a glass of dry champagne. I am also ready to argue that champagne is not an expensive wine because you drink less of it than you do of a table wine. But apart from champagne I consider that the best preludes to a good dinner are a Bourbon old-fashioned or a very dry, five-to-one Martini.

11. Cigarettes spoil the palate. I do not smoke and it is very difficult to be tolerant of the indulgences that one does not permit oneself. I find the manners of cigarette-smokers intolerable. They will light a cigarette, then turn in another direction and allow its odor to drift acridly across a table. They will throw the stubs into urinals. They will get up to dance and leave cigarettes smoking on the table. They will

half-stub them out when they have finished them, so that the
smoke still rises. I have been assured that the late Victorian
custom of drinking claret at the end of a meal was abandoned because cigarette-smoking destroyed the fine flavor of
claret. I detest the manners of cigarette smokers, but at the
same time I do not believe that cigarette-smoking ruins the
palate. Some of the best judges of wine I know are cigarette-
smokers.

O WOMAN likes to dine alone. She feels self-conscious. It looks either as though she had been abandoned or there were a less creditable explanation for her solitude. In point of fact she practically never does. After waiting half an hour in the lobby, she goes back home, disconsolate and indignant, to open up a tin.

A man on the other hand rather enjoys dining by himself. He feels free. He is under no obligation either as guest or host. He can order according to his taste. The wine list is unmortgaged territory. He can sit as long or rise as early as he likes. His thoughts are free to travel. No frontiers limit him. He can follow the stream of reverie. He recalls that Worcestershire was then called Fostershire, and on one Saturday he was taken by his father—he was then just fifteen—

to lunch with Mrs. Basil Foster—known to the footlights as
Gwennie Brogden—and how he was torn between his excitement at lunching with a "real live actress" and his anxiety
to get back to Lord's and see who won the cricket match. And
that sets him wondering as to who was the second actress
that he met. . . . So the stream of reverie flows on, aided
by the flow of wine, in a way that it can never do in company, even the most congenial. The charms of such a reverie
are indeed so insidious that solitary dining might become as
much a vice as secret drinking, were not the opportunities of
indulging it so slight.

Usually it is the result of some mistake. I doubt if any
man looking through his next week's engagements decides
that on the following Thursday he will take himself to dinner at the Savoy. The Puritan streak in him would revolt. He
would feel guilty before such premeditated self-indulgence.
He would not have a clear conscience about doing himself
really well, and the whole point of dining alone is that one
should dine expensively. It is only when our plans have been
deranged, a train has been missed or a date broken, when
we have, that is to say, been disappointed that we feel entitled to a recompense, that we feel we owe it to ourselves to
let our eye travel down the wine list.

I have had in my time quite a number of solitary meals
under such conditions and by the time I left the table I have
invariably managed to make myself believe that I am on
the whole relieved that my plans had been disarranged.
There has always been a recompense—of some kind. Sometimes of a quite unlikely kind. I remember for instance a
lunch at the *Jardin des Gourmets* that went awry. It was
quite a long time ago. I had made the date during a dance.
She was a married lady, to whom I could not for reasons of
discretion telephone, and I had a suspicion that colors seen
by candlelight might not look the same by day. I was right:

they didn't. One o'clock became quarter-past. Half-past became quarter-to. I was disappointed, very. So disappointed that I ordered a second Martini and then a third; which was very much too much to take before a Chambertin '04—its date will tell you how long ago this happened. It was a very noble wine. And by the time I had reached the second glass, my thoughts had begun to wander from my own misfortune, to become objective; to catalogue the various reasons for which dates are broken; to dramatize the predicaments of other victims; before my third glass was finished, what I suppose I must call the creative urge was fluttering. A story had taken shape. There it all was: beginning, middle, end; conflict, suspense, reward; the formula fulfilled, a natural for "the slicks." I had only to write it down.

That was my most profitable meal in solitude. But the meal of that kind that I shall, I fancy, remember longest and most gratefully was a quite recent one. I was alone in Cincinnati, I was "on the house," and the concern that was "taking care of me" had charitably checked me at the Terrace Plaza.

I could write an entire essay about that "pub." It was then barely a year old; and only one adjective is adequate, the overworked transatlantic one of "fabulous." The Terrace Plaza is an anthology of gadgets. When you press a button, you are just as likely to operate a T.V. set or to convert your Chesterfield into a bed, as to release illumination. It has a twilit cocktail lounge, separated by a sheet of glass from an open-air skating rink. It has a dining hall with Steinberg murals that presents a table d'hôte menu, and a gourmet's á la carte French cuisine restaurant on the twentieth floor, which is without exception the most poetic restaurant in which I have ever dined. It is round, with a radius of some twenty feet. Two-thirds of it is composed of glass, sloped outwards at an angle of 70 degrees. The roof is studded with electric bulbs, whose lights, reflected in the glass, mingle with the further and fainter lights of the streets and hills. You feel you are on a mountain top, as indeed you are. It is a brownish room with Miro murals and there is muted music.

So poetic is the atmosphere, indeed, that I began to wonder whether I had not made a mistake in coming here alone; it was a kind of sacrilege not to be in romantic company. Had I not better order a single dish and hurry back for highballs to that twilit cocktail lounge? That was what I had almost planned but as I sat there sipping my Old-fashioned, I became aware of something rather curious, namely that though the room was fairly full there were only two women there. I looked to my left and to my right. On the curved banquette that ran round the unglassed section of the room, there were men like myself sitting by themselves alone. In the center were small masculine groups of twos and threes talking quietly over their wine. It was all very subdued. For a moment I wondered if I had stumbled into some *oubliette* of a Proustian paradise. But only for a moment: a more careful scrutiny reassured me. I ordered a second cocktail, and sat back to think.

I was not puzzled for long. I remembered how when I had gone to open-air cinemas in the Middle East I had found it difficult to concentrate upon the film. The drama of the screen had seemed very trivial when set against the dark immensities of a tropic night. In just that way I fancied a man dining in this gourmet's restaurant, feeling himself upon a mountain top, looking upon the night, would have found it hard to concentrate upon romantic company. In such a place he needed masculine philosophic talk or introspection.

I have a suspicion that that restaurant represents one of the most considerable contradictions between intention

and achievement in modern planning. It was designed as a
romantic restaurant, yet it is a place to which men go either alone or in masculine company. It does not fulfil the
intended function. Yet it is a great success. Even in the modern world apparently, men need to go apart, to high places.
and to brood.

There is only one drawback to dining alone and it is a
big one. You have to content yourself with a single wine unless you order a quarter-bottle of champagne to accompany
your fish, and champagne is not at its best in quarter-bottles.
Two half-bottles are too much, and it is a crime to send
away good wine. In your own house it matters less, because
what is left of a bottle of a light white wine can be used in
cooking, but it is more often in a restaurant or in his club
that a man dines alone.

In one of his books of reminiscence, Clifford Bax says
that four is the ideal number for a dinner party. Cyril Connolly contributing to a symposium in the Sunday Express,
on happiness, listed as one of the best things in life the sitting down to a dinner party of six. The ideal figure is a
subject for discussion, not for argument. Myself, I prefer
six. With four the conversation is general nearly all the
time. With six it can be general, but scope is offered for
duologues. There is, too, this advantage for the host, if it is
a mixed party. He can place furthest from himself the lady
in whom he takes most interest so that the meal is for him
flavored with anticipation; when the party moves into the
drawing room, he can sit beside her, saying, "I have been
looking forward to this moment all the evening."

Moreover, six is a better number for wine. You can,
that is to say, have more wines, four bottles at least: a bottle between six gives each one a glass and a half and you
cannot appreciate a big wine till you have drunk half a
glass.

Yet when it occurred to me that it would be a happy idea to finish this book with the description of as good a dinner as can be had without undue extravagance in London in the year 1958, I decided to invite nine guests. Ten would give it the appearance of an occasion, would give scope for the tasting of a greater variety of wines, yet ten was a sufficiently small number to allow me to enjoy a personal talk with everyone.

I decided to make it a masculine evening: the presence of women would inevitably have proved a distraction; not all the women whose company I enjoy the most are specialists in wine, and I wanted to invite only those with whom the years had forged long chains of personal friendship.

The nine men I asked were the Earl of Huntingdon, whom I first met in Tahiti, over thirty years ago; A. D. Peters with whom I have played much cricket—for M.C.C., at Hampstead, for J. C. Squire's Invalids and Clifford Bax's Old Broughtonians and who, as my literary agent, has given me wise and salutary advice since 1925; Desmond Flower, whom I have had the good fortune to have had as my publisher since 1930; David Carver, the secretary of the P.E.N. Club under whose aegis I have traveled as far as Tokyo; Antony Grinling, a sculptor in his spare time, who persuaded his fellow directors at Gilbey House to commission my *Merchants of Wine*; Vyvyan Holland and James Laver, two of the most distinguished members of the Saintsbury Club; my younger son Peter, at that time doing his military service, and finally the doyen of writers about wine, the well-loved André Simon.

With appropriate humility, I put myself unreservedly in André Simon's hands, co-opting Vyvyan Holland as his A.D.C. André should decide on the restaurant and should choose the menu. I made only two stipulations, that the big wine should be a red Burgundy and that we should finish

with a Sauternes other than d'Yquem. At that point André
made a suggestion that was typical of his graciousness and
generosity. "I have in my cellar two bottles of Burgundy
that are as good as any that can be found today. I have
been looking for a suitable occasion on which to open them.
I think that this is it. I will donate them to the dinner." They
were 1928 Château Gris, a small vineyard in Nuits-St.
Georges.

Vyvyan asked me how much I was prepared to spend
upon the dinner. Was twenty dollars a head too much? I set
this figure down for the sake of record. Thirty-five years
ago, in the early twenties, I would usually after a party get
some change back out of six dollars a head. Guy de Maupassant describes in *Bel-Ami* a dinner given in the early
eighteen-eighties in the private room of a good bourgeois
Paris restaurant by a young grass widow Madame de Marelle, for a married couple (the Forrestiers) and Bel-Ami
(Georges Duroy) in whom she took a budding romantic interest. They fared sumptuously, and so much wine was consumed that Forrestier had a choking fit and the hostess on
the way home in a fiacre invited Georges to display enterprise. (The bill for this party was a hundred and twenty
francs. The rate of exchange was then five francs to the
dollar.) Madame de Marelle handed Georges her purse.
How much, he asked, should he give the waiter? "What you
like." He put down five francs. I have always wondered
whether the size of this tip was an indication of Georges'
meanness or his ignorance of the ways of the big world, or
whether de Maupassant considered four per cent an adequate remuneration. In those days a service charge was not
added to accounts. A hundred and twenty francs for such a
dinner!

How quickly money loses its value, and I am sure that
fifty years from now the oenophil who turns the pages of

this book, in the casual way that I in the London Library have recently been looking at old books about Madeira, will be astonished that a meal such as the one I am shortly to describe could have been obtained for twenty dollars a head. Oh, to have lived in the nineteen-fifties! He will forget that it took me as much effort to earn fifty dollars in 1958 as it now takes him in 2010 to earn two hundred, just as I forget that de Maupassant at the height of his fame was glad to get a hundred dollars for a short story.

The gourmet of 2010 will no doubt be paying five hundred dollars when he entertains nine of his friends gastronomically, but I hope he will not grudge the cost. In Arnold Bennett's *Journals* there were a good many entries that the editor, Sir Newman Flower, had reluctantly to omit. One of them concerned a self-made millionnaire. "I spend," he told Bennett, "sixty thousand dollars a year on women."

"Isn't it worth it?" Bennett asked.

"Of course it is," the answer came.

Of wine as of women. A man is ungrateful to life if he grudges the seconds and the pennies that he devotes to the two things that make it most worth living.

Max Beerbohm noted in his essay *Guests and Hosts* that whereas when you dine at a Ritz-class hotel your bill is always less than you expected, it is always more when you dine in a Soho-Greenwich Village restaurant.

It was decided to hold this dinner at the Belfry, a lunch and dining club in West Halkin Street, architecturally one of the most quaint in London, having been designed originally as a chapel, for the furtherance of an eccentric spiritualist cult, the "Society of Progressive Souls."

The upper room which we reserved had been fashioned out of the organ loft, and the roof was curved into a point. It was very ornate, reminding me of the anterooms in that hospitable pre-1946 establishment in the Rue Chabanais.

The table at which we were to dine was narrow, so that it would be possible to talk across it. On a small serving table were set out the wines that we were to drink.

I was in some doubt as to how I should inscribe the menu. Vyvyan and I discussed it with André Simon. I suggested "A dinner offered by Alec Waugh to nine . . ." but there I broke down. How should I describe my guests? "Wine-conscious friends," said André. It was a happy phrasing. Yet one of my guests was Peter Waugh. "Can one call one's son a friend?" I asked. Merlin Holland, Vyvyan's twelve-year-old son was with us, patiently waiting for his mother. Vyvyan turned to him. "Am I your friend?" he asked. Merlin at the question registered a broad grin and said "Yes." So we let the wording stand.

The dishes read as follows:

Canapés de Foie Gras

Barquettes de caviare

———

Profiteroles de Cervelle Mignonette

Sauce Moutardée

———

Darne de Saumon Lucullus

———

Aiguillettes de Caneton Rôti Duxelles

Pommes Allumettes

———

Soufflé au Fromage

———

Fraises Romanoff

Petits Fours

———

Café

There are two kinds of gourmet's dinner; there is the dinner where a number of big wines are tasted one against the other—I have already referred to those dinners of Vyvyan Holland's in the 1930's, when the glasses were numbered and we would sample three or four different clarets of presumably equal quality—and the dinner where you slowly prepare your palate for the last great wine. This was of the second type and as a result we had, I fancy, rather more general talk. Where the purpose of a dinner is to compare a series of wines it is inevitable that one should talk about wine for the greater part of the meal. In the previous month I had attended in New York, as Charles Rolo's guest, a very interesting dinner that was graced by Alexis Lichine and Alfred Knopf, in which ten Château-bottled Lafites were sampled. The years chosen were 1954, 1953, 1949 1945, 1926, 1918, 1914, 1906, 1900, 1890. The talk concentrated upon the wine; it was a mixed party. The women were highly decorative and I suspected that some of them toward the end had come to feel themselves neglected.

As the purpose of my menu was to appreciate fully André's majestic Burgundy there was not a great deal to be said about the wines preceding it, beyond "This is very pleasant," and "This is really rather good." The following wines were listed on the menu:

KRUG (en magnum)
with the amuse-gueules

---

Kaseler Herrenberg 1953
Estate-bottled, von Kesselstadt

---

Bâtard-Montrachet, 1947
Bottled at the Domaine by Louis Poirier

---

## ✤ *Lucullus in 1958* ✤

Château Canon 1953
Château-bottled

———

Château Gris—Nuits-St. Georges, 1928
Château-bottled

———

Château Coutet, 1953
Château-bottled

———

Hine, 1922

In my opinion, the white wines could have been cooler, but that is a matter of opinion. I have possibly developed a transatlantic palate. A white wine can lose its flavor by being iced, and the refrigerator's function in cheap night-clubs is to conceal the lack of quality of a fourth-grade champagne. Lord Huntingdon said that he felt he got the flavor of the Montrachet more fully because it was no more than chilled, and James Laver was in agreement. But I would still have preferred it cooler.

The Château Canon is a St. Émilion, one of the *premiers crus classés,* that I had never tasted previously or for that matter heard of. I found it a little disappointing; it seemed slightly thin, lacking in body, but that may have been because it accompanied a duck that was as good as anything that I have ever eaten. Its flesh was tender, the sauce was rich, but not so rich that it disguised the flavor of the meat; so often meat is treated as a kind of bread, as something to spread sauce on; but rich though this sauce was you tasted the duck through it. Possibly however it was too strong for the wine. So much food is.

There are certain purists who maintain that great wine can only be appreciated with the simplest food, and some of Cyril Connolly's friends complained after he had inherited

Richard Wyndham's cellar that he entertained them with
nothing more appetizing than cold roast beef and cheddar
cheese, so that they could better appreciate the flavor of
Château-bottled clarets. I think he was ill-advised. Surely
if the pleasures of the table are to be fully enjoyed the food
must match the wine in quality. A cigar may detract from
the full enjoyment of cognac, and cognac may diminish the
enjoyment of a cigar, but the two go very well together. And
certainly the St. Émilion fulfilled its role in preparing the
way for the Château Gris.

The soufflé that accompanied the Burgundy was firm but
feathery, hot and succulent, playing a subsidiary role with
grace and elegance—a bandillero to a matador. And never
have I tasted a Burgundy to match that Château Gris. It
was supreme, full and soft and rich and heavy. I had been
afraid that so old a Burgundy might have begun to tire, but
1928 was a curious year. Several of its red Bordeaux have
not yet reached maturity, and only a few of us will ever
know to what heights they might have risen. They were drunk
too young during the second war and the period of austerity
that followed it. André's Burgundy was a tremendous wine.
I never expect to drink a nobler. It is hard to measure the
gratitude that I feel for André Simon.

The fraises Romanoff and the Sauternes that followed
provided in my opinion the perfect finale. Arnold Bennett
maintained that the climax of a novel should come four-
fifths of the way through its length; the rest being a round-
ing-off. It is an aesthetic principle that holds good for the
arts of the cellar and the kitchen. Not everybody likes sweet
wine and some of my guests would have no doubt preferred
a vintage port, but I felt that I could afford to be selfish,
this one time.

Two days later I received the following letter from
A. D. Peters.

# ✤ *Lucullus in 1958* ✤

Savile Club 69 Brook Street W.1.
April 30th. 1958

My dear Alec,

Just a line to thank you for a most memorable dinner. I do not think I have had better food or better wine anywhere in the world. Some talk of Paris, and some of La Réserve and other great restaurants in provincial France. But they could produce nothing better. The test lies in the fact that though I ate well of each course, which was superb in its kind, there was no feeling of having eaten too much —or drunk too much.

Such occasions are all too rare. Nobody bothers very much, these days. But your care and attention to every detail certainly earned their reward in the stomach and the mind of your devoted friend

Peter

Other guests said much the same, that they felt extremely well next day, although we had drunk twelve bottles of wine between us. That is the point about fine wine and food. You do not feel ill next day.

For myself, it was a most happy evening, with nine such close friends gathered round me. I am particularly happy that my son should have been there. It is important that the young should meet men older than themselves; it gives them in the autumn of their days a sense of distance. Raymond Mortimer recently pointed out that Walter Savage Landor was alive in the lifetime both of Voltaire and Eden Philpotts. Vyvyan brought to that dinner a menu he had attended at Cambridge that was signed by Rupert Brooke. If the fates are kind, Peter Waugh at the centenary of Brooke's death will feel himself linked as a contemporary by that signature upon a menu with the "young Apollo golden-haired" of that halcyon pre-war decade.

As long as I remember anything, I shall remember those two bottles of Château Gris. They will be an amulet against the raucous, self-assertive voices of modernity. Every day life becomes more standardized; more and more do individual idiosyncrasies and eccentricities get ironed out; yet along the slopes that flank the Médoc and the railway line that runs south of Dijon there are these reminders of intrinsic quality, of treasures that have not been casually bestowed; of how in His infinite mercy the great Architect of the universe has set His seal on certain folds of soil. It is a knowledge that restores one's faith in the eternal verities. Whenever the *Mistral* carries me north to Paris and I see those sacred slopes softened by the amber radiance of a Burgundian sunset, I shall remember those two bottles which could have been produced at no other time and in no other place, and I shall see the whole process of living enriched by the miracle that is in wine.

# APPENDIXES

*Appendix 1*

## THE CLASSIFIED GROWTHS OF THE MÉDOC

### *First Growths*

| CHATEAU | COMMUNE |
|---|---|
| Lafite-Rothschild | Pauillac |
| Margaux | Margaux |
| Latour | Pauillac |
| Haut-Brion | Pessac (*Graves*) |

## Second Growths

| CHATEAU | COMMUNE |
| --- | --- |
| Mouton-Rothschild | Pauillac |
| Rausan-Ségla | Margaux |
| Rauzan-Gassies | Margaux |
| Léoville-Las Cases | St.-Julien |
| Léoville-Poyferré | St.-Julien |
| Léoville-Barton | St.-Julien |
| Durfort-Vivens | Margaux |
| Gruaud-Larose | St.-Julien |
| Lascombes | Margaux |
| Brane-Cantenac | Cantenac |
| Pichon-Longueville-Baron | St.-Julien |
| Pichon-Longueville-Lalande | St.-Julien |
| Ducru-Beaucaillou | St.-Julien |
| Cos-d'Estournel | St.-Estèphe |
| Montrose | St.-Estèphe |

## Third Growths

| CHATEAU | COMMUNE |
| --- | --- |
| Kirwan | Cantenac |
| Issan | Cantenac |
| Lagrange | St.-Julien |
| Langoa | St.-Julien |
| Giscours | Labarde |
| Malescot-St.-Exupéry | Margaux |
| Cantenac-Brown | Cantenac |
| Boyd-Cantenac | Margaux |
| Palmer | Cantenac |
| La Lagune | Ludon |
| Desmirail | Margaux |

| | |
|---|---|
| Calon-Ségur | St.-Estèphe |
| Ferrière | Margaux |
| Marquis d'Alesme-Becker | Margaux |

## Fourth Growths

| CHATEAU | COMMUNE |
|---|---|
| St.-Pierre-Sevaistre | St.-Julien |
| St.-Pierre-Bontemps | St.-Julien |
| Talbot | St.-Julien |
| Branaire-Ducru | St.-Julien |
| Duhart-Milon | Pauillac |
| Pouget | Cantenac |
| La Tour-Carnet | St.-Laurent |
| Rochet | St.-Estèphe |
| Beychevelle | St.-Julien |
| Le Prieuré-Lichine | Cantenac |
| Marquis-de-Terme | Margaux |

## Fifth Growths

| CHATEAU | COMMUNE |
|---|---|
| Pontet-Canet | Pauillac |
| Batailley | Pauillac |
| Haut-Batailley | Pauillac |
| Grand-Puy-Lacoste | Pauillac |
| Grand-Puy-Ducasse | Pauillac |
| Lynch-Bages | Pauillac |
| Lynch-Moussas | Pauillac |
| Dauzac | Labarde |
| Mouton-d'Armailhacq | Pauillac |
| Du Tertre | Arsac |
| Haut-Bages-Libéral | Pauillac |

| | |
|---|---|
| Pédesclaux | Pauillac |
| Belgrave | St.-Laurent |
| Camensac | St.-Laurent |
| Cos-Labory | St.-Estèphe |
| Clerc-Milon-Mondon | Pauillac |
| Croizet-Bages | Pauillac |
| Cantemerle | Macau |

## SAUTERNES

### Grand First Growth

| CHATEAU | COMMUNE |
|---|---|
| d'Yquem | Sauternes |

### First Growths

| | |
|---|---|
| La Tour-Blanche | Bommes |
| Lafaurie-Peyraguey | Bommes |
| Rayne-Vigneau | Bommes |
| Clos Haut-Peyraguey | Bommes |

### First Growths

| CHATEAU | COMMUNE |
|---|---|
| Suduiraut | Preignac |
| Coutet | Barsac |
| Climens | Barsac |
| Guiraud | Sauternes |
| Rieussec | Fargues |
| Rabaud-Sigalas | Bommes |
| Rabaud-Promis | Bommes |

*Second Growths* (selected)

| CHATEAU | COMMUNE |
|---------|---------|
| Filhot | Sauternes |
| Doisy-Daëne Dubroca | Barsac |
| Doisy-Dubroca | Barsac |
| Broustet | Barsac |

## *Appendix 2*

### THE RED WINES OF GRAVES

| COMMUNE | CHATEAU |
|---------|---------|
| Pessac | Haut-Brion |
|  | La Mission Haut-Brion |
|  | Pape-Clément |
| Léognan | Domaine de Chevalier |
|  | Carbonnieux |
|  | Olivier |
|  | Haut-Bailly |
| Martillac | Smith-Haut-Lafitte |

### THE WHITE WINES OF GRAVES

| COMMUNE | CHATEAU |
|---------|---------|
| Pessac | Haut-Brion |
| Léognan | Carbonnieux |
|  | Olivier |
| Martillac | Smith-Haut-Lafitte |

### THE BEST KNOWN RED WINES OF ST. ÉMILION

| | |
|---|---|
| Château Ausone | Château Figeac |
| Château Cheval-Blanc | Château Tertre-Daugay |
| Château Pavie | Château Troplong-Mondot |
| Château Canon | Château La Gaffelière-Nandes |
| Clos Fourtet | Château Soutard |
| | Clos de L'Anglelus |

### THE BEST KNOWN RED WINES OF POMEROL

Château Pétrus
Château Évangile
Château La Conseillante
Château Gazin

*Appendix 3*

### THE BETTER KNOWN OF THE GREAT WINES OF BURGUNDY

*RED*

*Côte de Nuits*

| COMMUNES | VINEYARD |
|---|---|
| Gevrey-Chambertin | Chambertin |
| | Chambertin Clos de Beze |
| Morey St. Denis | Clos de Tart |
| | Clos St. Denis |
| | Bonnes Mares |
| Chambolle Musigny | Musigny |

|                       | Part of Bonnes Mares    |
| Vougeot               | Clos de Vougeot         |
| Flagey-Echézeaux      | Grands Echézeaux        |
|                       | Echézeaux               |
| Vosne Romanée         | Richebourg              |
|                       | La Romanée              |
|                       | Romanée Conti           |
|                       | Romanée-St. Vivant      |
|                       | La Tache                |
| Nuits-St. Georges     | Les St. Georges         |

### Côte de Beaune

| Clos-Corton          | Corton            |
|                      | Clos du Roi       |
|                      | Bressandes        |
| Savigny Les Beaune   |                   |
| Beaune               | Clos des Mouches  |
|                      | Grèves            |
| Pommard              |                   |
| Volnay               |                   |
| Santenay             | Santenots         |

## WHITE

### Côte de Nuits

| COMMUNE             | VINEYARD       |
|---------------------|----------------|
| Chambolle-Musigny   | Musigny Blanc  |

### Côte de Beaune

| Aloxe Corton | Corton-Charlemagne |
| Meursault    | Les Charmes        |

|                      | La Goutte d'Or (second growth) |
| Chassagne & Puligny  | Le Montrachet                  |
|                      | Bâtard-Montrachet              |
| Puligny              | Chevalier Montrachet           |

## Appendix 4

### AMERICAN WINES

The American wine industry has made immense progress during the quarter of a century since repeal. I cannot say that I have really ever enjoyed any of the dessert wines of the port and sherry type; the sparkling wines are in my opinion too expensive to justify their cost; if you are going to be that expansive, why not spend a little more and buy French champagne? But the table wines are excellent, as good as any except the great French and German wines, the equal certainly of anything that Switzerland, Italy, South Africa or Australia can produce.

Because of the cost of production and transportation, American wines are unlikely to become popular outside America; the vintners have in the past aimed at a high general standard rather than at special high quality vintages. It is not yet known whether California contains vineyards that will challenge the great growths of Burgundy and Bordeaux, of the Rhine and the Moselle. It may very well be that it does. In the meantime there can be no doubt of the quality of the best Californian and New York State wines.

New York State wines come from the Finger Lake region, Californian wines from five main areas around San Francisco Bay—Sonoma, Napa, Almeda, Santa Clara, San

Benito. Most American wines are dated, and labeled in terms of European nomenclature as Sauterne, Burgundy or Chablis, but the date means little on a bottle of Californian wine because, owing to the steadiness of the climate, there is not a great climatic difference between one year's grapes and those of the next. The word "Chablis" or "Sauterne" is only intended as a rough guide as to the dryness or sweetness of the wine, as to how it will taste. The important points on an American label are the names of the vintner and of the grape from which the wine has been made.

The word "varietal" is used in the nomenclature of American wines. The vines have been imported from Europe, the *Cabarnet Sauvignon* from Bordeaux, the *Pinot Noir* and *Gamay* from Burgundy for red wines: For white wines the *Pinot Chardonnay* and *Pinot Blanc* from Burgundy; the *Johannisberger Riesling* from the Rhine; the *Sylvaner*, the *Framiner*, the *Grey Riesling* from Alsace; the *Sémillon* and *Sauvignon Blanc* from Bordeaux. A varietal wine is one that states the kind of grape from which it has been made; from a trusted vintner such a designation is a guarantee of authenticity. The quality depends upon the grape—for red wines the *Cabarnet Sauvignon* is the best, for white wines the *Pinot Chardonnay* and *Johannisberger Riesling*. In California as in Burgundy the *Pinot* is superior to the *Gamay* grape.

Whereas the student of French wines memorizes the five growths of the Médoc and the years of the great vintages, the student of American wines memorizes the distinctive qualities of the different grapes and the names of the vintners whom he has learned to trust. Myself I greatly enjoy Almadén, Beaulieu, Cresta Blanca and Inglenook wines, red and white, the red wines of the Italian-Swiss colony and Widmer's white wines from New York State.

## Appendix 5

### SIZES OF BOTTLES

Vyvyan Holland writes:

A question that is often asked is what are the names of all the fancy bottles into which wine, particularly champagne, is frequently presented. For some reason, which no one seems able to explain, the larger bottles have all been given the names of Biblical characters. It has been suggested that all these characters had some outstanding quality of size or appearance. Even the actual contents of the bottles seems to be in dispute, the names being often used indiscriminately to describe any outsize bottle. However, the generally accepted names for all sizes are as follows; the figures after the names give their contents in bottles, the bottle being the champagne bottle, which contains $1\frac{2}{5}$ pints:

Baby—$\frac{1}{8}$

Nip—$\frac{1}{4}$

Pint—$\frac{1}{2}$

Imperial Pint—$\frac{3}{4}$

Bottle—1

Magnum—2

Jeroboam or Double Tregnum
  or Tappitt Hen. Magnum—4

Rehoboam—6

Methuselah—8

Salmanezar—12

Balthazar—16

Nebuchadnezzar—20

Vyvyan Holland comments:

I only once saw a *full* Nebuchadnezzar. By the way, I prefer the Roman Catholic liturgical spelling and pronunciation Nebuchodonozor, with the accent on the second "o." It was at Dorothy Warren's wedding, and had been presented as a wedding gift by Stulick, of the Eiffel Tower Restaurant. There were sixteen guests, including the happy pair, and only the one bottle between them. I was deputed to draw the cork. It was a very solemn moment, because the thoughts running through the minds of all of us were (1) would it be corked? and (2) would it be flat? However, the cork came out with a gentle "pop" and a kind of sigh of relief, echoed by all those present and, held by three stalwarts, with myself at the operating end, it poured out beautifully.

In claret:   Jeroboam = 5 bottles

Impériale = 8 bottles

#### MEASURES OF WINE

Port:   A pipe equals 672 bottles

Bordeaux:   A tonneau equals 4 barriques

A barrique contains 24 cases of 12 bottles each

A feuillette contains half a barrique

Burgundy:   A pièce contains 288-300 bottles

A queue equals two pièces

A feuillette contains half a pièce

Wines are sold by the tonneau and queue although such barrels do not exist.

Other areas have different measures.

# BIBLIOGRAPHY

ALLEN, H. WARNER. *A Contemplation of Wine*. Florida: Transatlantic Arts, 1953.

BUNYARD, EDWARD. *The Epicure's Companion*. New York: E. P. Dutton & Co., 1938.

CAMPBELL, IAN M. *Wayward Tendrils of the Vine*. London: Chapman-Hall, 1947.

CONSTABLE'S WINE LIBRARY

CRAIG, ELIZABETH. *Wine in the Kitchen*. London: Constable & Co., 1934.

DRUITT, ROBERT. *Report on Cheap Wines*. London: Henry Renshaw, 1865.

HALLGARTEN, S. F. *Alsace and its Wine Gardens*. New York: British Book Centre, 1957.

HEALY, MAURICE. *Stay Me with Flagons*. London: Michael Joseph, 1940.

HUGGEN, H. E. *Vaux Rhenish*. London: Privately printed, 1929.

*La Fleur de la Cuisine Française.* Paris: Editions de la Sirène, 1920-21.

LAVER, JAMES. *Victorian Vista.* New York: Houghton Mifflin Co., 1955.

LICHINE, ALEXIS. *Wines of France.* New York: Alfred A. Knopf Inc., 1951.

MARRISON, L. W. *Wines and Spirits.* London: Penguin Books, 1957.

*A New System of Domestic Cookery* by A LADY. London, 1817.

PANZER, N. M. *The Book of the Wine-Label.* London: Home & van Thal, 1947.

REDDING, C. *French Wines and Vineyards.* London, 1860.

SCHOONMAKER, FRANK AND MARVEL, TOM. *The Complete Wine Book.* New York: Simon and Schuster, 1934.

SHAND, P. MORTON. *A Book of Wine.* New York: Brentano's, 1926.

SIMON, ANDRÉ L. *Bibliotheca Gastronomica, A Catalogue of Books and Documents on Gastronomy.* London: The Wine & Food Society, 1953.

———. *Bottlescrew Days.* London: Gerald Duckworth & Co., 1906.

———. *A Dictionary of Wine.* New York: Longmans, Green & Co., 1936.

———. (comp.) *The Gourmet's Week-end Book.* London: Seeley Service & Co., 1952.

———. *Vintagewise.* New York: British Book Centre, 1945.

———. *Wine and the Wine Trade in England.* London: Privately printed, 1932.

———. *Wine in Shakespeare's Days and Shakespeare's Plays.* London: Privately printed, 1931.

TENNENT, SIR JAMES EMERSON, K.C.S., Ll.D. *Wine, Its Use and Taxation.* London: James Madden, 1855.

WILSON, REV. A. M. *The Wines of the Bible.* London: Hamilton, Adams & Co., 1877.

# INDEX